Spiritual caregiving in the hospital

To Jes,

It has been a privilege to spend the summer with you in spiritual caregiving. Blessings to you as you minister with your many gifts.

Leah Daw

8/16/07

Spiritual caregiving in the hospital

Windows to chaplaincy ministry

Leah Dawn Bueckert
and Daniel S. Schipani, editors

Published by Pandora Press,
Kitchener, Ontario

In collaboration with
Institute of Mennonite Studies,
Elkhart, Indiana

Library and Archives Canada Cataloguing in Publication

Spiritual caregiving in the hospital : windows to chaplaincy ministry /
Leah Dawn Bueckert and Daniel S. Schipani, editors.

Includes bibliographical references.

ISBN 1-894710-65-7

1. Chaplains, Hospital. 2. Church work with the sick. I. Bueckert,Leah
Dawn II. Schipani, Daniel S., 1943- III. Title.

BV4335.S64 2006   259'.411   C2006-902507-X

Spiritual caregiving in the hospital
Windows to chaplaincy ministry

Copyright © 2006 by Pandora Press
33 Kent Avenue
Kitchener, Ontario N2G 3R2
All rights reserved
ISBN 1-894710-65-7

Book design by Mary E. Klassen. Cover photograph—"Tiger swallowtail on
purple flowers"—by J. Tyler Klassen, used by permission; all rights reserved.
The editors chose the image of the butterfly as a fitting symbol for spiritual
caregivers as ministers of hope, healing, and transformation.

All Pandora Press books are printed on Eco-Logo certified paper.

Unless otherwise indicated, the scripture quotations in this book are from
the New Revised Standard Version of the Bible, copyright © 1989 by the
Division of Christian Education of the National Council of Churches of
Christ in the USA, and are used by permission.

Contents

Gratitudes

This book is the result of a research and writing project undertaken at Associated Mennonite Biblical Seminary. It reflects the commitment of the school to contribute to the formation of hospital chaplains via its Master of Divinity with concentration in Pastoral Care and Counseling program. Our efforts were made easier by the academic encouragement and financial support we received from AMBS in the course of our work. We wish to acknowledge President J. Nelson Kraybill and Dean Loren Johns for their affirmation of our vision.

Grants from the Mennonite Foundation of Canada and Mennonite Mutual Aid, plus several gifts from individual donors, ensured that the binational research and publication project culminating in this book would be realized in a timely fashion. We are grateful for such unqualified assistance.

Special thanks go to our colleagues Muriel Bechtel (Mennonite Church Canada), Clair Hochstetler (Goshen General Hospital), and David Hudson (Elkhart General Hospital), who readily endorsed our project, gave us opportune counsel, and facilitated contacts with our writing partners. We are indebted to the fifteen Canadian and U.S. chaplains who joined us in creating a book on spiritual caregiving in the hospital setting.

We are also grateful to several people who supplied much needed help in the final phases of the writing process: Christine Guth and Barbara Nelson Gingerich generously provided editorial expertise, Mary Ellen Klassen designed the book, including the cover, James Nelson Gingerich did the page layout and gave overall technical support with grace and competence, and Rosalie Grove served as efficient secretary and proofreader. Mary Schertz, Institute of Mennonite Studies director, wholeheartedly supported our research and writing. Finally, we thank C. Arnold Snyder and the Pandora Press staff for their excellent publishing work and for making sure that the book would be ready for distribution by late spring 2006.

Finally, we are thankful that our collaboration in this project has been a joyful endeavor for both of us and a source of personal and vocational enrichment. It is our hope and prayer that the fruit of our labor may also bless the readers.

Leah Dawn Bueckert and Daniel S. Schipani
June 2006
Associated Mennonite Biblical Seminary
Elkhart, Indiana

Introduction

Daniel S. Schipani and Leah Dawn Bueckert

The paradoxes confronted within a hospital are the paradoxes of life: suffering people's infinite aspirations running smack up against their finite boundaries. It's an ageless struggle, true for all peoples, for all generations, and no less true for us, in and out of the hospital. Hospitals do not create paradoxes and mysteries; they merely focus them. Suffering dispels the illusion that we are infinite, without limits. In that regard, suffering can be a great moment of truth for the sufferer. It is the hospital chaplain's privilege and responsibility to share in that rich moment of truth. ...

If the hospital is a place of paradox for its patients, it is not less so for its chaplains....That paradox or tension is most dynamically experienced in the dual identity of the chaplain....The hospital chaplain walks between two worlds: religion and medicine. The tension can be painful, confusing, exciting, creative.... It is never fully resolved and perhaps never will or should be. ...

To effect and maintain a balance in pastoral functions ... is the compelling challenge that confronts today's hospital chaplain....When this freedom and balance are maintained, a chaplain can remain faithful to a basic pastoral role (to help others experience as fully as possible the reality of God's presence and love) and yet fulfill that role in a variety of creative and relevant ways. For indeed, a hospital chaplain has one primary role, which can be carried out through many functions.[1]

Daniel S. Schipani is professor of pastoral care and counseling, Associated Mennonite Biblical Seminary, Elkhart, Indiana. Leah Dawn Bueckert is a chaplain resident at Lutheran Hospital, Fort Wayne, Indiana; the publication of this book coincided with her completion of an M.Div. degree at AMBS.

[1] Lawrence E. Holst, *Hospital Ministry: The Role of the Chaplain Today* (New York: Crossroad, 1985), 11, 12, 52.

In these paragraphs from *Hospital Ministry: The Role of the Chaplain Today*, Lawrence Holst succinctly describes the context, nature, and purpose of the ministry of spiritual caregivers in health care institutions. We are honored to continue the work of this important volume in examining hospital chaplaincy in the contemporary context. Participation in this ministry involves the sacred privilege of being available and present to people—patients, their relatives, and staff. The spiritual caregiver embodies and communicates good news in word and deed or in silence. Competent hospital chaplaincy includes a commitment to provide holistic care for the sake of healing and wholeness.

With Holst's vision of the ministry of spiritual caregiving in mind, we crafted this volume centered on the following three goals:

- To acknowledge and celebrate the unique, essential contribution of hospital chaplains as spiritual and pastoral caregivers.
- To foster understanding and encourage support for the work of hospital chaplains.
- To elicit interest in the ministry of spiritual and pastoral caregiving in hospital settings.

As we began to develop the design for writing and publication, we chose to make the project bi-national, involving chaplains from Canada and the United States, in part because Associated Mennonite Biblical Seminary, where Daniel Schipani teaches, is jointly sponsored by Mennonite Church Canada and Mennonite Church USA. Further, we sought contributions from a wide spectrum of perspectives within the Anabaptist-Mennonite Christian faith tradition. On the one hand, the essays reflect this tradition's shared vision of spirituality and healing expressed through a polyphony of voices; on the other hand, these essays are meant to be a resource for the wider Christian community and beyond.

This publication addresses a perceived need for a collection of real-life experiences and stories, accompanied by brief reflective analyses. We offer the book as a complement to existing texts in the field. We believe that chaplains, pastors, health care professionals, and other caregivers, whether in training or already practicing, will find it valuable. We hope that professors, supervisors, and students of Clinical Pastoral Education and pastoral care and counseling will also read this work. Chaplains in various healthcare settings, some of whom experience a measure of professional alienation and isolation because of their unique role, will find it a helpful resource as they engage in caregiving ministry. We wish to provide support to chaplains who are already practicing and motivate others who are considering this type of ministry.

The book contains three parts. Part 1—"The place of spiritual care in the hospital"—explores the unique function of spiritual care in the hospital as one discipline among others (medicine, nursing, social work, and so on). The essays focus on the chaplain's role in promoting integration of these disciplines for the sake of healing. Part 2—"The chaplain as caregiver in specific settings"—explores particular contributions of chaplains with patients, families, and staff, in contexts of crisis, death, grief, and illness. Part 3—"Special concerns in chaplaincy ministry"—consists of four essays that reflect systematically on foundations and guiding principles for the practice of hospital chaplaincy.

We introduce here our understanding of certain key terms that we use within this book. When we use the term *holistic* to describe care, we imply a commitment to the ethic of care we have outlined in chapter 18. Holistic care further implies the comprehensive nature of professional hospital chaplaincy, involving functions such as supporting and comforting, officiating in administration of sacraments and worship services, counsel and guidance or ethical discernment, consulting and resourcing with medical and other staff, and witnessing and confronting for the sake of justice.

We wish to distinguish between the *pastoral* nature of many instances of caregiving with patients, relatives, and staff, on the one hand, and the *spiritual* significance of chaplaincy ministry in its many forms, on the other hand. *Pastoral care* is the dimension of the ministry of the church that has concern for the well-being of individuals, families, institutions, and communities. It may include various functions—guiding, nurturing, sustaining, comforting, reconciling, and healing—in diverse settings, including hospital chaplaincy.[2] Christian chaplains may view their ministry as an expression of pastoral care; however, care-receivers do not necessarily share this perspective. Increasingly, patients, their relatives, and staff represent a variety of faith traditions, backgrounds, and frameworks. We adopt the understanding of *faith* as a human universal that may or may not find expression in terms of a specific religious tradition and content (beliefs or rituals).[3] Because such traditions include both religious and nonreligious faith, we find the term *spiritual* to be more inclusive of the diversity of understandings chaplains encounter. Further, many care-receivers nowadays prefer to identify themselves as spiritual but not religious. We understand that every person is spiritual by virtue of being human. By *spiritual*, we mean the fundamental capacity to have faith, to make meaning, to create community and culture, to long for and practice love, peace, and justice, and to be oriented toward wholeness. We recognize that understandings of the sources and nature of human spirituality are diverse. According to our Judeo-Christian tradition, human beings are spiritual in the sense of bearing the image and likeness of God (Gen. 1:26).

---

[2] Alastair V. Campbell, "Pastoral Care," *The New Dictionary of Pastoral Studies*, ed. Wesley Carr (Grand Rapids, MI: Eerdmans, 2002), 252–53.

[3] This is the understanding articulated in the faith development theory and writings of James W. Fowler: *Stages of Faith: The Psychology of Human Development and the Quest for Meaning* (San Francisco: Harper & Row, 1981); *Weaving the New Creation: Stages of Faith and the Public Church* (San Francisco: Harper, 1991); *Faithful Change: The Personal and Public Challenges of Postmodern Life* (Nashville: Abingdon Press, 1996); *Becoming Adult, Becoming Christian: Adult Development and Christian Faith*, rev. ed. (San Francisco: Jossey-Bass, 2000).

Finally, we offer a word about the title and subtitle of this book. Growing out of the understanding of spirituality just described, we chose *Spiritual caregiving* as an inclusive way to state the purpose of hospital chaplaincy. The subtitle—*Windows to chaplaincy ministry*—refers to the promise within this book and to its limitations. Through the windows that our authors open into hospital chaplaincy, readers will see portraits of spiritual caregiving, shared from a variety of viewpoints. Firsthand accounts in each chapter lead into interpretive reflections on the nature of spiritual caregiving in health care institutions. We hope that readers will be inspired to open other windows, describe what they see, and join us in the conversation.

Part 1
The place of spiritual care in the hospital

A chaplain's vocational journey

Jan K. Kraus

"Did you make that up all by yourself?" a churchgoer asked me, following my sermon in a Mennonite church one Sunday morning.

After confiding with me that talking about her physical, emotional, and spiritual pain had been helpful, a woman inquired, "When will you be assigned to a real job in a church?"

"You mean you have to go to school to become a chaplain?" the new public relations staff person asked me incredulously in an interview for a newsletter article.

"Yeah, they have lots of women priests now. I see them here all the time," I overheard a Jewish hospital patient inform his Greek Orthodox roommate.

"You constantly surprise me. You don't act like a priest at all!" declared a nurse practitioner, whose commentary on life in the intensive care unit (ICU) always makes me laugh.

At the end of a Sunday morning service, one worshiper offered feedback hesitantly, for fear it would not come across in positive way. "I really like it when you lead worship, because I forget that you're leading. You're more like a window than a leader. You seem to get out of the way so that I can really focus on God during worship."

As a chaplain, comments from the people I encounter make me laugh, make me wonder, and warm my heart. They remind me of what I love about being a chaplain, especially on days when the bureaucracy, human tragedy, and/or lack of sleep are getting me down. Chaplaincy, like any other job, has its highs and lows. All too often, I find myself saying, "It's not healthy to be working in healthcare these days." Or, "There's got to be an easier way to make a living." A typical day for a chaplain includes accompanying staff, patients, and family members who are making life-and-death decisions. It involves exposure to contagious and deadly diseases. It consists of preparing and leading worship services, memorial services, baptisms, and prayers. It involves balancing budgets and allocating resources. It may also entail teaching, mopping a floor, mediating a conflict, crowd control, fund raising, networking, counseling, sending and receiving e-mail, attending a seminar,

Jan K. Kraus is a chaplain, Spiritual Care Department manager and teaching supervisor, Clinical Pastoral Eduction, St. Michael's Hospital, Toronto, Ontario.

or raising an ethical question. The day may bring celebration of the wonder of daily life or rejoicing at good news. It calls for remembering, identifying, and naming the healing, even when there is no cure. Chaplaincy is listening, managing, leading, supporting, being, and doing—and trying to get the balance right.

My personal entry into chaplaincy was a long and sometimes painful journey. My first career was nursing. After earning a Bachelor of Science in Nursing from Goshen College (Goshen, Indiana), I set out to save the world, beginning with a voluntary service (VS) assignment on an Indian reservation in Mississippi. There I first began to sense a calling into ministry. After returning from VS, when the church I attended began exploring ways to incorporate a holistic health program into congregational life, I heard about Granger Westberg's concept of the parish nurse program.[1] I found the possibilities exciting, so I enrolled for a semester at Associated Mennonite Biblical Seminary (AMBS), anticipating a Master's degree in Nursing. During that first semester, I got sidetracked. My first year at seminary was one of the best in my life. The ideas, the people, the potential, and the possibilities so energized me that I signed up for a second year. I immersed myself in church life by taking a yearlong internship, including two units of Clinical Pastoral Education (CPE) in the congregational setting. This year was one of the most difficult in my life, because I needed to do intense personal work, including vocational discernment. I came through the year deeply shaken and broken, although stronger and wiser. I decided to complete a Master of Divinity degree with the goal of becoming a congregational pastor, believing that was God's calling in my life.

On graduation day at AMBS, my female peers and I were painfully aware that only our male peers had obtained paid pastoral positions in the Mennonite Church. I interviewed for several jobs (none as congregational pastor) and tried to be content with a job in community services. I was grateful for the opportunity to meet and learn from truly dedicated and gifted people, but I was not educated or well skilled as a community services worker. I sought counseling. In the process of exploring my gifts and the opportunities available to women, I decided to immerse myself in further discernment and education by taking a yearlong residency program in CPE. Within the first two weeks of the chaplain residency program, I felt as if I had come home. The combination of my life experience, my personal gifts, skills, and talents, and my nursing and theological education came together in the role and duties of chaplain.

---

[1] For an overview of parish nursing (including Granger Westberg's history) especially as it intersects with chaplains, clergy, hospitals, and congregations, visit the following sites: http://ipnrc.parishnurses.org/aboutrev.phtml; the International Parish Nurse Resource Center, http://ipnrc.parishnurses.org/index.phtml; The Canadian Association for Parish Nursing Ministry, http://www.capnm.ca/. See also the classic by Granger Westberg, *Good Grief: A Constructive Approach to the Problem of Loss* (Philadelphia: Fortress Press, 1962).

Even with residency experience, my quest for a paid position did not easily find fulfillment. Despite my academic credentials and clinical experience, institutions were looking for ordained ministers. In the mid-1980s, in almost all faith groups, that still meant male. I did finally receive my first job offer as a chaplain; I was blessed to work with a well-seasoned, experienced senior chaplain who helped me along the way. For several years, I was better known in Anglican and United Church circles than in my own denomination, because these traditions were open to women in ministry. In these denominations, I found female and male colleagues who were supportive, encouraging, and challenging of me, personally and professionally. They were also willing to challenge my own faith group leaders in ways that I could not.

I often asked God to send me a registered letter because I wanted to be 100 percent sure that I was on the right track. I did not want to waste my time, and I certainly did not want to make a mistake. I have never yet received a registered letter signed by God. As I age, I am learning to enjoy wasting time. I think it is a sign of growth that my recent journey into painting classes is teaching me the delight of happy accidents (mistakes). Yet I continue to ask for registered letters.

I have now been a full-time paid chaplain for twenty years. The reasons I went into chaplaincy are not the reasons that keep me in chaplaincy. Yes, the bureaucracy of the healthcare system drives me crazy. Yet all I need to do to get some perspective is attend a church business meeting and I leave saying, "Thank God I'm a chaplain!" Recently at the close of a particularly trying staff meeting, another chaplain persuaded us to stay and listen while she read these words from a sermon by the late Archbishop Oscar Romero as an inspiration to maintain a hopeful yet modest vocational perspective:

> It helps now and then, to step back and take a long view. The kingdom is not only beyond our efforts, it is even beyond our vision. We accomplish in our lifetime only a fraction of the magnificent enterprise that is God's work. Nothing we do is complete; which is another way of saying that the kingdom always lies beyond us. No statement says all that could be said. No prayer fully expresses our faith. No confession brings perfection. No pastoral visit brings wholeness. No program accomplishes the Church's mission. No set goals and objectives include everything.

> That is what we are about. We plant seeds that one day will grow. We water seeds already planted, knowing that they hold future promise. We lay foundations that will need further development. We provide yeast that produces effects far beyond our capabilities.

> We cannot do everything, and there is a sense of liberation
> in realizing that. This enables us to do something and do
> it very well. It may be incomplete but it is a beginning,
> a step along the way, an opportunity for God's grace to
> enter and do the rest. We may never see the end results,
> but that is the difference between the master builder and
> the worker.
>
> We are the workers, not master builders; ministers, not
> messiahs. We are prophets of a future not our own.[2]

As a Christian who is thoroughly Mennonite, I frequently turn to the Bible
for inspiration, wisdom, challenge, and comfort. As a chaplain and teaching
supervisor for the Canadian Association for Pastoral Practice and Education
(CAPPE), I look to the Bible for images and role models that offer insight
for my pastoral work. The biblical narrative and all of salvation history are
rich with such images that represent the story of God calling people into
community in new and surprising ways. I also closely observe "the living
human document"[3] for glimpses of the presence of God.

For me, pastoral images that contain meaning, comfort, hope, and challenge include midwife, weaver, potter, doorstop, skycap, tree, Jonah, Judith,
Zacchaeus, Abraham, Mary, and Martha. Each of these images has been fully
fleshed out—incarnate today—for CPE students I have supervised. Most of
all, Ruth and her companions continually resurface for me with new and
fresh insight and inspiration. The characters in the biblical story of Ruth,
Naomi, and Boaz have long served as pastoral portraits for me. Therefore I
will share in more detail who, what, how, and why Ruth is the pastoral image
that guides my life and work as a staff chaplain, specialist in institutional
ministry, teaching supervisor in CPE, and department manager.

Remembering Ruth's story

The story of Ruth is one of the most exciting and beautiful dramas in the
Bible. I recommend that you read the entire story for yourself. You are likely
to find at least one character with whom you identify closely. It is a story that
is still very alive for me. It continues to reveal deeper layers as the years go

---

[2] Oscar Romero, source unknown.

[3] This phrase "the living human document" is part of the language often used by professional
pastoral caregivers. It alludes to the narrative quality of human experience and the importance of knowing how to "read" (that is, interpret) personal life stories and situations as the
starting point for fruitful caregiving. The image of the living human document comes from
Anton Boisen, who is considered the founder of the clinical pastoral education (CPE) movement in North America. For a thorough discussion of this question and its application to the
field of pastoral counseling, see Charles V. Gerkin, *The Living Human Document: Re-Visioning
Pastoral Counseling in a Hermeneutical Mode* (Nashville: Abingdon Press, 1984), especially
chapter 2, "The Living Human Document: Boisen's Image as Paradigm" (37–54).

by. After summarizing the story of Ruth, I will offer my interpretation and application in light of my vocational journey and chaplaincy experience.

The book of Ruth begins with sickness and death. Naomi's husband and two sons have died. Naomi is bereaved, bereft, alone, full of grief, sadness, pain, and fear. A widow in the days of ancient Israel was lumped together with aliens, slaves, children, and domestic animals—a piece of property with no owner. She was not eligible for welfare, old age pension, or any government assistance. To make matters even worse for Naomi, she is in the wrong country. She has no family, no faith community to fall back on. In the midst of her despair, she hears that God is at work in her homeland. In Judah, her home country, the famine is over and there is food. So she decides to return to Judah.

As Naomi sets off to leave Moab for Judah, she tells her recently widowed daughters-in-law, Orpha and Ruth, to return to their mothers. Orpha kisses Naomi, weeps and returns home, but Ruth cries and clings to Naomi. Naomi protests emphatically: "God has dealt bitterly with me. There is no future for me in Moab. Be reasonable Ruth—go home!" Ruth replies,

> Do not beg me to abandon you,
> to return from following you,
> for where you go, I will go,
> and where you stay, I will stay.
> Your people are my people,
> and your God my God.
> Where you die, I will die,
> and there I will be buried.
> Thus may Yahweh do to me [throat-cutting gesture],
> and thus may he add,
> if death separates me from you.[4]

Ruth makes a solemn promise to Naomi. She promises loyalty to death and even to the grave. With these words—no church membership classes, no baptism, no particular fanfare—Ruth joins the people of God.

Together Naomi and Ruth begin the long walk back to Judah. What a stir they make as they walk in. The neighbor women remember Naomi and enthusiastically greet her. However, Naomi is in no mood to celebrate. She says, "Stop calling me Naomi because that name means pleasant, and there is nothing pleasant about my life. Call me Mara, which means bitter. I am bitter and God has dealt bitterly with me. God has made me empty and afflicted me and brought calamity to me." This is how Naomi returns home.

Ruth, the young widow and foreigner, takes responsibility for both of them. She goes out into the fields to harvest the leftovers. People around Ruth

---

[4] Ruth 1:16-17; my paraphrase.

notice her hard work. When the owner, Boaz, comes to see how things are going, he sees Ruth, too. Boaz asks his servants about her. They tell Boaz all about this foreigner, the hard times she has been through, her commitment to Naomi, and her commitment to God. The story touches Boaz. He invites Ruth to join his servants for the noon meal and even gives her something to eat and drink.

That evening when Ruth returns to Naomi, Ruth shows her the huge amount of grain from her day's work. Ruth even gives Naomi some of the lunch that she has saved from work. Naomi is more than a little surprised. She is worried about this big pile of grain. She wonders what Ruth has been up to. Ruth is a foreigner and she had better watch her step here in Judah.

As Ruth tells about her day, Naomi begins to perk up. A light is ever so slowly beginning to shine through the dark depression and bitterness that has settled into Naomi's life. Naomi asks God's blessing on Boaz, exclaiming that God has not forsaken the living or the dead. Naomi remembers that Boaz is their relative. She explains to Ruth the Israelite custom whereby a relative marries a childless widow to keep the family line going. Naomi tells Ruth how to go about seeking the protection of Boaz.

Ruth follows Naomi's orders. She washes, gets dressed up, and goes to meet Boaz secretly at the threshing floor. This part of the story is full of puns, intrigue, mystery, and suspense. Ruth does exactly what Naomi says to do—up to a certain point. However, Ruth does not gently hint; she comes straight out and says to Boaz, "I am Ruth, your maidservant; spread your wings over your maidservant, for you are next of kin."

Ruth's action and words put Boaz on the spot! Here we hold our breath, because there is a catch. Boaz knows another man is a closer relative. Boaz could answer Ruth's request by arranging her marriage to the other man. Boaz assures Ruth that one way or another he will settle this matter the next day.

In the morning, Boaz finds the other relative. Boaz publicly tells the other man that Naomi is offering to sell the plot of land that belonged to her late husband. The relative immediately decides to buy the land. Then Boaz mentions the responsibility to Naomi and Ruth included with the ownership of this land. Now the relative pauses, reconsiders, and decides it is not in his best interest to buy the land, given the accompanying responsibility for Naomi and for Ruth, the foreigner.

Boaz proclaims his own desire to purchase the land, to care for Naomi, and to marry Ruth. The elders and people who witness this event approve the union of Ruth and Boaz. They ask God to bless the couple and give them many children. To these two childless people a son is born.

The neighbor women rejoice with Naomi and proclaim, "Blessed be Yahweh who this day has not let there cease to be a redeemer for you; there-fore may his name be celebrated in Israel. He will be a life-restorer and one to sustain you in your old age. For your daughter-in-law, who loves you, has borne him and she means more to you than seven sons." Here the neighbor women, as witnesses, declare that Ruth, the foreigner, has been and continues to be of greater value to Naomi than the ideal seven sons. The women name the child born to Ruth. They call him Obed, Naomi's son.

Reflecting on Ruth's story

The story of Ruth has strong significance for my own pastoral identity and role. Like Ruth, I have not followed the expected route in life. My work is sometimes frightening, sometimes painful, and often exhausting. It is also an exciting challenge to enter new territory. I am becoming more accepting of my own way of being in relationship with God, others, and myself. It is important to me to try to walk with others (patients, their families, staff, students, and colleagues) in their own life situations. In the story of Ruth, I see a variety of people with a variety of gifts and experiences working together for the good of individuals and the larger community. As a chaplain, I try to help others see God in today's situation, in today's culture, in today's ordinary routines. Helping others see God's involvement in undesired events is even more challenging. My methods vary with the needs and wishes of the other—whether patient, patient's family, staff, student, or colleague. The story of Ruth reminds me that no one person carries all the responsibility. Like Ruth, I need to combine the old and the new in creative ways. I keep in mind that we are on this journey together, and we are not alone. The Lone Ranger need not apply for a position as chaplain. The Lone Ranger serves as a symbol of those who remain separate and disconnected, who stand apart from the people they are trying to help—the very antithesis of a chaplain.

As a professional chaplain, I need to be aware of my weaknesses and limitations and rely on others for support in a number of ways. For example, I make referrals to other professionals: I help people connect with others personally and professionally. For my own personal and professional health, I participate in personal therapy and peer consultation, I am an active member of my local congregation, and I maintain friendships outside the hospital-CAPPE-CPE circle.

In my work as a chaplain, I, like Ruth, sometimes hear a cry of pain, of fear, of anger, of deep anguish: "Why? Where is God now?" In Ruth's story, God does not break into history with a supernatural voice from heaven or a miraculous event for Naomi, Ruth, or Boaz. In this story, we imagine that God is present in the pain and the suffering as well as in the growth and the rejoicing. God was and is in the midst of events that seem insignificant or even wrong, such as death and despair; illness and injury; program cuts and financial crises; and the trauma of industrial, natural, or environmental disasters.

A challenge for the chaplain is to help people experience divine caring in their current situation—in society and culture, and in the present institutional setting of hospital, acute care, trauma center, mental health facility, prison, long-term care, group home, hostel, shelter, safe house, or other facility.

Hospitals and other institutions are places of crisis that accentuate lone-liness, pain, isolation, alienation, despair, anger, and rejection for patients, families, staff, and chaplains. In the face of a crisis, people often feel helpless and at the mercy of circumstances beyond their control. When in physical, emotional, or spiritual pain, people find it hard to see any way out of the chaos, let alone brainstorm a variety of options. Yet crisis demands change.

Facing change is difficult. It involves taking risks. The biblical story of Ruth and Naomi shows us people who had chaos forced on them through no fault or wrongdoing of their own. Some, such as Orpha and the near kinsman, chose the reasonable and the safe option, while we remember Naomi, Ruth, and Boaz for the risks they took in going the unexpected way. Each of them is a good role model or pastoral image for a chaplain. They give us examples, encouragement, incentive, and hope. They show us that relationships and situations can change for the good of all. One person's triumph does not have to mean the defeat of another. One program or one institution's success does not have to result in the failure of another. The whole community benefits by the combined actions of Naomi, Ruth, and Boaz.

Embodying the story in chaplaincy ministry

The chaplain, like the biblical narrator of Ruth, first arrives on the scene in the midst of illness, death, grief, and famine. Today's hospital is a place of figurative famine for many people. It is the place of crisis, illness, death, and suffering. In famine, there is a shortage of everything good and a plethora of suffering, chaos, frustration, anger, and pain. The hospital chaplain is frequently in the midst of famine. The shortage of resources may include food, water, finances, staff, time, or bed space.

God was with the people in the biblical story of Ruth in their life situ-ation, in their culture, and in their daily routines. God was present and at work even in the parts of the story that are devoid of "God talk." God was and is continually present, whether or not we acknowledge God's presence. Divine will and human action go hand in hand. When we look for God at work in ordinary events, we can imagine divine caring for people through people. Like Ruth and everyone else in the biblical story, the chaplain is on the move, changing and growing through the experience. The chaplain is called to assess the situation and to name the spiritual reality as well as to develop a plan of action. This demands the strength and the will to be pres-ent and engaged in the events of the day, to become part of the story, not a detached observer, not a knight on a white charger, not a Lone Ranger, but a fully present human being.

Naomi as patient referred to the chaplain

"Chaplain, could you visit Naomi today? She's not coping with the death of her husband and sons very well. Says she's going to sell the house and move out immediately. Both the social worker and I told her that would be a big mistake. See what you can do, will you?"

At the beginning of the story, Naomi is hurt, angry, and in pain. She makes her lament known! Not only does God hear and welcome her lament, we too recognize her voice as that of one who takes God seriously.

By today's wisdom, Naomi would be encouraged to stay in Moab where she has lived for many years, where she knows the town and is known and loved by others. In spite of Naomi's grieving protests, the story shows that her daughters-in-law love her well. Healthcare professionals advise against making major changes in living situation, especially in the early stages of grief and bereavement. Moving out of the family home is risky. Today, Naomi would be advised to make no major decisions and would definitely be discouraged from moving to another country, even if it was the country of her birth. Naomi's choice to leave Moab would be counterintuitive in today's culture. Her choice and the assumption of God's action within that choice become more meaningful toward the end of the story.

Naomi declares herself empty and alone, even as Ruth stands beside her and makes a profound commitment to her. Naomi knows intimately the struggle between life and death. As the story unfolds, we see Naomi's bitterness slowly transformed. No miraculous instant cures here. She experiences the strong pull toward despair. Yet Naomi is touched by the fullness of love and care through another woman and later through a grandchild. It is challenging to be the chaplain for Naomi, when she is making choices that the chaplain's education and experience indicate are inappropriate under the circumstances. It is not easy to be the chaplain for Naomi, especially if the chaplain is called to walk all the way from Moab to Judah with a grieving, complaining, despairing woman. Naomi reminds me to be gentle with myself and others who lament bitterly. (In fact, Naomi wanted to be called *Mara*, which means "bitter"!) Naomi reminds me that bereavement is a process that is as hard on companions as it is on the primary mourner. She reminds me that God is just as present in the moments of pain and grief as in the happy resolutions.

Naomi as pastoral image for the chaplain

In this day and age, the chaplain must know her own strengths and weaknesses, her own growing edges, her own places of death and suffering. She must grieve and say goodbye to the familiar places. She must make the long, difficult, and sometimes dangerous journey home under changed circumstances. She must return repeatedly to the homeland, where God is at work. She must continue to engage in serious conversations with God, her supporters, her neighbor women, and her community. She must look for the new life, the baby Obed, and let the unexpected foreigner be of more value to her than seven sons.

Ruth as pastoral image for the chaplain

We can visualize God caring for people through people in the person of Ruth. Ruth is not a superhero; she is no stranger to the human condition. She is as affected by famine, scarce resources, illness, and death as everyone around her. She is bound to the laws of nature, of the land, of time, of culture, of the nation. Ruth also has lost her husband. She too is childless. She too has lost her means of support. Yet in the midst of all this personal, familial, and national pain and suffering, Ruth makes an unheard-of commitment to another woman. Ruth hears her loved one's despair and seems even to be ignored by that loved one. She works hard to make a living for two people under very difficult conditions. She needs Naomi to help her find her way in the land. At one point, Ruth acts boldly and goes to Boaz rather than waiting for him to come to her. Later, she has to wait patiently to see how things will turn out.

The chaplain, like Ruth, needs to rely on others—on colleagues, on mentors, on "the elders" who know the lay of the land, who can explain the political, cultural, and social expectations of this particular institution, as well as the local, regional, and national norms. She needs to read the signs of the times, work hard, assess the advice given to her, make plans, and act. I believe it is important to listen attentively and patiently for divine wisdom in order to know when to act and when to wait.

Ruth, the chaplain, is a foreigner. She is the Moabite. She is in the minority. She may be the only "Moabite" in the whole hospital. The chaplain lives and works within the hospital, but her education, her heritage, her point of reference, her mandate, her identity, are from outside the institution. She is the minority voice. According to the laws of her day, Ruth was not afforded the same rights or privileges as the insiders, the Israelites. She was not even allowed to worship in the temple. The chaplain's focus and area of expertise is spiritual assessment and spiritual care, with special attention to the interconnectedness of body, mind, and spirit. However, in our current day and age, physical cure is the goal and therefore the focus in an institution. Chaplains are the minority presence and voice in the institution, even in religiously based hospitals, mental health centers, or homes for the aged. We chaplains are foreigners, like Ruth, in the institution that employs us, because our focus is spiritual and religious care, which is often the least valued and least understood aspect of the "product" the institution seeks to provide.

Because chaplains move back and forth between "Moab" and "Judah" so frequently, we often feel like foreigners in both lands. Chaplains often feel like Ruth, the foreigner, as we stand at the fringes of the established church or congregation. Chaplains are visionaries, prophets, and pioneers; rarely are chaplains settlers. We are foreigners in the institutions that employ us, and we often feel like foreigners in the churches that have ordained or commissioned us. We are foreigners in the church, because others may view us as too removed from orthodoxy to be trustworthy. Our experience and training help us be attentive to the Spirit of God in unique and unusual circumstances, in multifaith encounters, in life-and-death circumstances, in suffering, as well as in the small events of life. We may be too open to "the other," too outspoken at church meetings, too quick to try something new, and too irregular in attendance on Sunday morning to be considered core members of the church.

Ruth, the foreigner, is a good pastoral image or role model for the chaplain. She reminds us that the true Israelite, or Mennonite, or Christian, or chaplain is the one who genuinely embodies such identity. The real Christian is the one who extends God's lovingkindness and faithfulness to all those around. We have much to learn from Ruth, the refugee and foreigner, about God's love and action in the world.

Boaz as pastoral image for the chaplain

We see God caring for people through people in the person of Boaz, the good administrator. We know Boaz, the solid, responsible citizen. He has an established, profitable business. He cares well for his employees. We also notice that he sometimes needs to be reminded about his responsibilities. We see Boaz attending to legal matters, knowing that they may not work out in his favor. Boaz risks his own reputation and inheritance by accepting responsibility for a widow and marrying a foreigner.

Boaz is a part of the system. Boaz, the chaplain, does indeed have a place on the organizational chart, even if he sometimes feels that it is nearly off the page. Boaz, the chaplain, can go to the head nurse, the hospital CEO, the managers, and plead his case for better spiritual and religious care. Boaz knows that he may or may not find the situation working out in his favor. Chaplain Boaz may find himself risking his reputation and job by accepting responsibility for the voiceless ones—the refugees, the foreigners, people of other faith groups.

The near kinsman does not even have a name in this story. I believe his name is forgotten because he did the safe and sensible thing. Like Orpha, the sensible daughter-in-law, Mr. Near Kinsman acted in a respectable and responsible manner. He did nothing wrong or malicious. He apparently balanced the books, followed all the appropriate policies and procedures, and even negotiated a fair deal with Boaz. Sometime I would like to hear how things worked out for Orpha and for him, because I suspect that much of the time my actions are more like those of Orpha and Mr. Near Kinsman than like those of Boaz. Yet I believe that Boaz is a better pastoral image for the chaplain than Mr. Near Kinsman.

In our day, the chaplain needs to have the skills, energy, and chutzpah of Boaz, the good administrator. The chaplain must know the policies and procedures, as well as where and when to take his case to court. He must listen to the counsel of his elders and directors and at the same time listen to his employees and staff. He must know the official power structures as well as all of the informal and unofficial power systems. He must be willing to take a risk and become intimately involved. It is important for Boaz, the chaplain, to remember that the health and prosperity of the whole community is dependent on the health and prosperity of the foreigner or the powerless ones.

I encourage local clergy and parishioners to work with the chaplain in caring for people who are in the hospital or any other institution. In some situations, the chaplain can be the Boaz, the go-between, for the patient/client and those in power—the doctor, the superintendent, the nurse, the staff. The chaplain often has access to resources and information that can help outsiders/non-staff care for the patient/client, such as hospital/institutional policies and procedures, best times to visit, ways to coordinate care, and ways to facilitate religious rites. The chaplain can remind hospital/institutional staff that the local church community is visiting and caring for a patient. If the patient wants clergy to attend a family and multidisciplinary care meeting, the chaplain can assist in making arrangements.

Neighbor women as pastoral image for the chaplain

The neighbor women serve a prophetic role. The neighbor women are witnesses. They identify, name, accept, support, welcome, and challenge. They comment on events as they see them. This role is prophetic, in that the women raise to awareness both good and bad, light and dark, joy and despair. Awareness enables informed choices, growth, and movement toward wholeness. This is a shared journey. These women welcome home the traveler. They accept the foreigner. They remind Naomi of Ruth's value to her. The neighbor women remind us that community is inclusive; it includes young and old, rich and poor, the insider and the outsider, men and women, administrators and staff, and people of different faith groups, among others. They invite us to speak up, break out of the safety of our silence, and remind Naomi, or another, that God is caring for her through family, friends, staff, or church. They remind us to invite the outsider to join us for dinner or at the communion table. They remind us that we need one another. God cares for us through others, and God cares for others through us.

Conclusion: In step with the divine journey

God is continually being revealed in new and unexpected ways in our life journey. Just as we catch glimpses of the divine in Naomi, Ruth, Boaz, and others in their community, so too do we see glimpses of God in our colleagues. God is revealed in our companions on this journey. As chaplains, we are called to pay attention. We need to be active participants on this journey. Sometimes we need to sit still and wait, to reflect on God's action in our lives. Other times we need to stand up, speak out, and make bold new commitments. Sometimes we need to give, and sometimes we need to receive. We participate in divine love by sharing it. I am certain that God is at work within each of us as we accept and share responsibility for one another within the ordinary events of our time and our culture.

Leroy Joesten writes:

> Chaplains are not responsible for other people's beliefs. They are responsible for their own. As persons of faith, chaplains are often called to be witnesses to that personal faith. But a chaplain's personal faith is only a foundation through which others are helped to summon their own faith, to make choices about their own beliefs, about their own dying or grieving. Though we all feel helpless in the face of death, or at the mercy of circumstances beyond our control, there are nevertheless choices to be made. In such ministry the chaplain's task is to help others find those areas where individual choices can be made, while at the same time helping them to accept those larger, universal truths over which they have no control.[5]

The work of the chaplain is different from the work of the nurse, the medical doctor, the social worker, the administrator, the physiotherapist, the family member, and the local clergy. Each one is an integral part of the total community that lives and works together to promote a life of wholeness. Such wholeness takes seriously both the good and the bad, the joy and the sorrow, the health and the illness, of the people who live and work in the institution as well as of the community and world that surrounds us.

Many of us who are writing or reading this book serve on multidisciplinary teams in the hospital, or on the church council, or on community committees. These are places where we need to share our expertise, our ability to reflect theologically, our ability to see and to name the spiritual and religious issues. When others around us are responding to the identified problem by saying that the government, senior management, or the executive committee should do something about the problem, perhaps that is the time for the chaplain to name the spiritual and religious issues that are present, to call for a personal response, to set the pace. As chaplains, we must weigh the risk of maintaining the status quo and the risk of a different response. Maintaining the status quo is often the safe response. It is the response of the sensible Orpha and Mr. Near Kinsman. The risk management department of any institution carries the responsibility to ensure that everything is "under

---

[5] Leroy Joesten, "The Voices of the Dying and the Bereaved: A Bridge between Loss and Growth," in *Hospital Ministry: The Role of the Chaplain Today*, ed. Lawrence E. Holst (New York: Crossroads, 1987), 150.

control." It does not encourage employees to emulate the risky choices of Naomi, Ruth, or Boaz. A chaplain who makes a new or different response is often seen as countercultural. The alternative response may pose a real risk to the institution, a subject that deserves attention elsewhere. The biblical story of Naomi, Ruth, and Boaz is the story of real people who make risky decisions that become transformative for themselves, their community, and their descendents.

The people in the story of Ruth, Naomi, and Boaz challenge us to speak up, to act, to follow new paths, to keep going even in the midst of pain and suffering, to break out of the safety of our silence. They show us God caring for people through people. Chaplains and other people of faith are like the One who goes beyond the sane, the sensible, and the expected. People of faith participate in God's love by sharing it. Let us support, encourage, challenge, and nurture each other as we remember the neighbor women's words: "Blessed be God who has not forsaken the living or the dead."

Becoming a competent chaplain

Character and training

Marvin Shank

Chaplains come to their work with energies of vocation, compassion, and commitment. They also live with healthy questions about effectiveness, about how others experience their contribution, and about how they might develop themselves and their abilities for ministry. As in any vocation, competency starts with positive intention that is nurtured through training and lifelong learning. In chaplaincy, a primary process of ministry is the art and practice of relationship with cared-for persons and groups and professional health-care colleagues. Chaplains' investment of themselves becomes essential to the discipline. Developing competency in an ongoing way necessitates integrating vocation with self-awareness, personal functioning, and skills. Along with positive purposes for ministry, chaplains need to cultivate abilities and personal capacities for effectiveness, by supervision and training that engages the whole person of the caregiver.

Supervision of chaplain interns has much in common with biblical images of Christian discipleship, through which people are supported to integrate the teaching and grace of Christ into their living. Supervision parallels discipling—the process of sponsoring growth in discipleship—in its purpose to support trainees to grow in abilities and in personal integration of vocation with practice. This process gives opportunity to reflect on pastoral identity, to consider ministry experience, and to contemplate how the chaplain might further integrate theological and professional values into the art and skill of spiritual caregiving.

Supervision is a highly personalized adult education process, pursued in experiences of ministry and supported by a teaching mentor and a group of peers. In this chapter, I discuss supervision in the context of healthcare chaplaincy training, in processes that are guided by standards of Clinical Pastoral Education (CPE) and accredited by the Canadian Association for Pastoral Practice and Education. In the United States, the parallel accrediting body is

Marvin Shank is a chaplain and spiritual care educator (Clinical Pastoral Education), St. Joseph's Health Care, London, Ontario.

the Association for Clinical Pastoral Education.[1] Though based in healthcare, competencies and training for chaplaincy have application to congregational church ministry. In my experience, a majority of people pursuing CPE do so as training for congregational church ministry. Many pastors and churches choose CPE as part of preparation for pastoral challenges, both in churches and in healthcare. CPE is training in the midst of ministry, where chaplains grow and learn as much as the people in their care do.

In the following section, I consider some of the fundamentals of the formation process, visualized in the framework of clinical pastoral education, in light of my experience and practice. Then I reflect on challenges and themes in chaplaincy through which trainees receive support to find opportunities for spiritual care and to build viable competencies for ministry.

Highlights of the formation process in the framework of CPE

The education process begins when people inquire about the training program, gather information, and discern how this will contribute to their vocational directions. In their application documents, they reflect on their vocational journeys and identify learning goals. An application interview engages further reflection on vocational strengths, areas of growth, and personal learning goals.

CPE units of training typically involve 400 hours, in which chaplain interns spend half of the time engaged in spiritual caregiving ministry and half in various aspects of education and supervision. Interns prepare documentation of their work as one way to examine what they have experienced and to learn from it. In verbatim reports, the intern describes preparation and intentions for the visit and then writes a script of the visit, so the relational process can be examined. In the last part of the report, the intern does self-evaluation and reflects on the encounter with the persons visited, using theological, psychological, and sociological perspectives. Interns also write learning journals, which they share with the supervisor for feedback and discussion. To support learning, ten to twelve individual supervisory sessions are provided over the duration of the course. Interns meet regularly together with the supervisor for peer group supervision. In group sessions, interns take turns presenting ministry situations. Learning happens through discussion and role-playing pastoral visits to examine relationships and to explore additional approaches in spiritual care giving. Another kind of group supervision engages interns in learning about group dynamics and interpersonal relationships. Here they give and receive feedback as they interact in care for one another and themselves, exploring ways to grow in relationships. Interns support one another to grow in self-awareness and to increase the range of viable options

---

[1] For a list of accredited training centers and extensive additional information, see the web pages of these two professional associations: www.cappe.org for Canada and www.acpe.edu for the U.S.

for caregiving. Training is guided by standard objectives for CPE as well as personal learning goals in processes of adult education. Teaching sessions on various aspects of chaplaincy ministry contribute theoretical support for experiential learning.

Healthcare institutions expect that professionals in any discipline will have certification with recognized professional associations. Typically, this is the situation for chaplaincy. People seeking certification in chaplaincy with a professional association need to familiarize themselves with standards. Preparation requires two sequential units of CPE at the basic level, followed by application for admission to advanced training and two CPE units at that level. This is followed by work experience, writing a set of papers about self and ministry, and engaging in a certification process. In addition to all the CPE work, a person seeking certification must have academic theological training and endorsement for ministry within a faith community. A chaplain with certification is expected to be an active member of the certifying association and to honor standards for practice and ongoing certification.

CPE at any level is guided by objectives for that particular level of training. The standard objectives for basic CPE identify competencies in which trainees are evaluated. These also represent the competencies that chaplains seek to demonstrate throughout their work in ongoing ways. The following are objectives for basic CPE:

1. To become aware of one's personhood in ministry and of the ways one's ministry affects other persons, including sensitivity to ecumenical, multifaith, and multicultural issues.
2. To become aware of how one's attitudes, values, and assumptions affect one's ministry.
3. To become aware of one's pastoral presence in interdisciplinary relationships.
4. To develop the ability to use the experiential method of learning.
5. To develop the ability to use the peer group for support, dialogue, and feedback in a way that integrates personal characteristics with pastoral functioning.
6. To use individual and group supervision for personal and professional growth and for developing the capacity to evaluate one's ministry.
7. To integrate the learnings of theology and the social and human sciences in understanding the human experience.

This training engages the soul of the learner. The person traveling deeply along these paths of learning usually experiences personal and professional transformations. One chaplain intern said, "This course does not have a learning curve. It went straight up. I need to continue for another twelve weeks." To understand this dynamic, we will explore major themes of training and competence.

Key themes of training and competence

Diversity: Spiritual care in the midst of challenging differences

In social conversations, talking about religion can be so problematic as to suggest the proverbial etiquette principle: Do not discuss religion in polite company. Yet pastors are frequently called to talk about this volatile aspect of life. Commitments to God, values, culture, community, and oneself can converge to fuel passionate clashes about religion. Pastors of congregations often struggle with how to provide ministry to diverse interests in a congregation, that is, to people within their own group who have conflicting theological and religious views. Healthcare chaplains constantly work with people who have diverse religious backgrounds. Their interdenominational and interfaith context parallels the challenge of diversity in congregational ministry, while making it more immediately obvious and intense. Others have asked me how it is possible to provide nondenominational pastoral ministry. Chaplain interns are invited and supported to engage this issue frequently (objective 1). In supervision, interns reflect on their assumptions and beliefs about religion and spirituality, both in their own lives and in the lives of the people for whom they care (objective 2).

Often people experience spirituality and religion simultaneously, without making a distinction. However, for purposes of providing pastoral care and leadership in the midst of religious diversity, the chaplain supports effectiveness by seeing and engaging spirituality and religion as distinct phenomena that overlap significantly. Spirituality can be described as a universal human disposition and a fundamental capacity for making meaning, and for hope, faith, love, and vocation. Religion can be described primarily as tradition that gives tangible expression to making meaning, and to hope, faith, love, and vocation. Of course, specific religions embody their tradition through rituals, beliefs, prayers, and so on. The essential distinction is between spirituality as capacity and religion as tradition. Both are human phenomena, in which people may be especially blessed and guided by God.

People will tend to guard their beliefs and practices from the questions that arise when meeting diversity. Religious diversity can feel threatening within a specific congregation as well as among different denominations and among world religions. This tension is an ancient issue. For example, the apostle Paul grappled with ways to embrace religious differences within the church in Rome (Romans 14). Important religious commitments (for example, normative views of salvation) that define spiritual capacity can divide people from one another. Yet people with religious differences can have similar spiritual needs, strengths, and aspirations.

The chaplain's discernment and appeal to spiritual capacity must focus on lived experience and journey. With this focus, the chaplain develops flexibility to engage people about issues of life, faith, and hope, in ways that are less tied to religious differences. At the same time, the chaplain is able to affirm religious traditions of belief and practice that contribute to faith, hope, and the moral life. This affirmation of tradition supports engaging diverse participants in processes that elicit hope in the midst of personal experience. For example, one chaplain intern expected that religious differences between herself and a patient with Jehovah's Witnesses affiliation would prevent conversation. However, the patient readily revealed emotional struggles with her health concern and received support in talking about her experience. In another situation, a patient told the chaplain that he disliked religious people because they tend to give ready-made answers. The chaplain thanked him for his honesty and affirmed his spirited commitment to his own emotional and spiritual process. This led to a more open discussion about values for self-care and a specific hope that supported wellness. In yet another example, a teenage patient attended a hospital worship service with a few other patients. In the informal worship of this small group, the teenager reported having a Christian background and a present connection with Wiccan religion. The chaplain affirmed her courage to explore, her value for diversity of religion, and her desire for the sacred. To facilitate ministry across diversity, the chaplain can derive flexibility and possibility while distinguishing and integrating religion and spirituality.

Soul listening:
Skills and art of engaging spiritual energy in personal story

A chaplain intern reported having spent an hour listening to the stories of a long-term care resident. He observed that the content of the visit seemed to be social and wondered how he might have engaged the person's spirituality. Another chaplain intern, reflecting on her visit, described it as a ministry of listening presence. Asked what this meant, she explained that she just sat and let the person talk. In both of these situations, we could claim the visits provided beneficial companionship. However, in both, we explored whether the intern might have neglected spiritual focus and engagement. In supervision, interns consider what they are listening for, and by what processes they listen.

Spiritual care listening becomes more effective with intentionality and active participation in the conversation in ways that clarify personal spirituality. In supervision, chaplain intern visits, as represented by verbatim reports, are examined with a view for spiritual issues expressed or implied by the person visited. Examples include what the person cares about or values, what meaning the person attaches to particular experiences, where the person has demonstrated faith and how that faith is focused, how and when the person's hope has been sustained, and in what ways the person has fostered spiritual strengths. Such issues inform a spiritual, religious, and theological assessment of the person in the midst of lived experience. Attention to this aspect in turn leads the chaplain to evoke, along with the patient, the faith, hope and other spiritual strengths available to the person in the midst of the difficult situation.

Active spiritual listening is an art of supporting self-revelation with feedback that validates what people express. By contrast, a chaplain's questions can be experienced as controlling, with the result that the chaplain risks less vulnerability. In one visit, the chaplain intern worked hard to know the patient and to discern spiritual issues. When the patient became tired and ended the visit, the intern concluded that the patient was not interested in talking. The verbatim report of the visit revealed that, of the twenty occasions when the intern spoke, fifteen were questions for more information, in a process that neglected to focus on available information. The supervisor challenged the intern to pursue a future visit using feedback and no more than two questions. Interns discover how questions for information usually reduce effectiveness. In practicing the art of meaningful feedback, interns become attentive to their own interpretive processes. These processes in turn rely on the beliefs, assumptions, language, and perceptions with which the intern filters the speaker's message (objective 2). Using feedback, a listener attempts to inform the speaker about what has been understood so far and to discern if this understanding sufficiently matches the intended message. The assumptions that are naturally part of listening become a barrier or an asset for effectiveness depending on what the intern does with them. In effective communication, assumptions should lead the listener to curiosity and not to certainty about what the speaker means. Interns practice eliciting clarity, using feedback to enter the world of the cared-for person.

Often chaplain interns need multiple visits to engage a patient's spirituality. Though quantity of time with a person can add depth of conversation, interns are supported to become more efficient in soul listening. What a person says in any given moment of the visit can offer a variety of options about how to give feedback. The listener can improve efficiency by feeding back content that holds the most personal energy for the speaker. A typical process involves inviting an initial personal story, listening for spiritual issues and intensity of energy; using feedback to clarify questions, passion, or strengths; then listening for additional story and again clarifying questions, passion, or strengths. In this way, spiritual listening becomes a process of descending a stairway into the soul of another person, from social conversation to pastoral conversation, to spiritual intimacy that makes possible the exploration of spiritual questions and strengths.

Listeners can be distracted from effective spiritual care by personal desires, such as a wish to provide advice and solutions for problems, to provide guidance, to teach, or to build the chaplain's self-esteem. Although a pastoral care visit might result in any of these outcomes, the chaplain's purpose is to evoke spiritual capacity, competence, and possibility in the patient. This intention can guide the chaplain to discern spiritual capacity in the midst of story and to engage or amplify this capacity, evoking increased spiritual strength.[2] The soul listener enters the world of the cared-for person by means of the person's story, interpretation, values, and concerns, to evoke spiritual strength. Soul listening is an art to be learned, a competency to be nurtured in supervision.

Intense feelings:
Anger, resistance, and grief as opportunity for pastoral care

Hospitalization and illness often elicit particularly intense emotions. Under these circumstances, people may express resistance as well as deep feelings of anger and grief. For many reasons, a chaplain might be uncomfortable with intense feelings. For example, previous experiences of anger might have led to abandonment or to physical harm. Alternately, the chaplain might respond from the belief that intense feelings should be suppressed as evil or problematic. Some caregivers assume they are responsible for fixing causes of intense feelings. In supervision, chaplain interns are encouraged to notice their responses to intense feelings, to distinguish their feelings and story from those of the cared-for person, and to explore how expression of these feelings is part of the personal spiritual journey. Intense feelings reveal soul experience in the midst of difficulty, through which chaplains might support people to wrestle theologically with the deepest questions of the human condition (objective 7). Intense feelings become windows into the soul and opportunity for pastoral care by the competent chaplain. Training cultivates this competency.

Anger, a disorienting feeling, is often a response to the experience of a value having been violated. While hearing the feeling, the active listener discerns behind the anger a person's passion for particular values. Anger can be the spiritual breathing of personal values. While receiving validation of both the anger and the values, the cared-for person can clarify values and explore additional options for response.

A person might also express values through resistance. When a patient resisted having a visit, the chaplain intern simply acknowledged this resistance with feedback. The patient proceeded to explain how tired she was of staff people prodding her with endless questions. The chaplain acknowledged how tiring this must be, promised not to ask any questions, and clarified that he just wanted to offer support. Bit by bit, the patient shared more feelings and story, supported each step of the way by the intern's carefully focused feedback. Through discerning and acknowledging the function of resistance as an act of self-care, the chaplain facilitated an effective pastoral encounter.

---

[2] The story of Jesus healing blind Bartimaeus (Mark 10:46-52) provides an inspiring example of how we might look for, evoke, identify, and validate spiritual energy.

In a patient's expressions of grief are many opportunities for pastoral care. Through grieving, a person might need to review and explore difficult feelings such as guilt or disappointments in a relationship. Grief might raise questions about life, death, and faith. Alternately, the person might need support to celebrate a loved one with rituals that express attachment and letting go. In many ways, grief is a spiritual journey and a sacred opportunity for pastoral care.

Chaplains need competence for genuine presence with many kinds of intense feelings and for finding ways to engage and support people in their predicament at the hospital. During the training process, one intern discovered that he avoided his own feelings. In discovering the possibility and benefit of embracing more of his own feelings, he found greater flexibility to be with the feelings of patients and to provide spiritual care through feelings they expressed.

Boundaries: Spiritual care that facilitates effectiveness

Chaplains and pastors everywhere work with boundaries, whether they do so consciously and intentionally or by default. On a daily basis, they respond to ethical questions about workload priorities and limits in relationships. Boundaries in pastoral care can appear to diminish compassion and the care that people need. However, closer examination of this issue in the experience of ministry reveals that conscious choices about boundaries are essential for sustaining effectiveness. Chaplains need competence in setting boundaries that facilitate spiritual caregiving.

The workload of chaplains is fed by seemingly endless opportunities for service. Motivated by vision and passion for ministry, some chaplains tend to go beyond what is appropriate as they serve those needing care. Thus, chaplains can soon become overwhelmed. They need to set limits to take care of themselves and sustain their well-being for continued service. They also need to set boundaries to define purposes and processes for effectiveness. Through the many questions of what work to do, how much to do, and in which contexts, the chaplain makes choices that are based on values, principles, assumptions, and relationships. Making such choices requires ethical thinking. A chaplain is an everyday ethicist, choosing which needs to assess and whether and how to respond. For example, a patient asked for more and more attention from a chaplain intern. In giving increased time and energy to this one person, the intern neglected the care of others and neglected self-care. In supervision, the intern clarified her pastoral role and evaluated whether she was functioning beyond her role, doing work that other caregivers might do. She also considered whether her increased support might foster dependence and diminish the self-reliance of the patient (objective 1). The intern planned to set specific boundaries of time and purpose in a way that emphasized the support she was offering more than the service she would not do. When the patient subsequently asked for more, the intern reviewed her positive commitment and effective results. Boundaries strengthen both the quality of care provided as well as the chaplain's professional competence and care of self.

In the surprising turns of pastoral relationships, the chaplain needs to exercise flexibility, imagination, and resourcefulness. When a male psychiatric patient expressed sexual interest in a female chaplain intern, she wrestled with challenging questions that led her to new clarity and confidence about options in managing boundaries. Supported by supervision, she planned to end the relationship and to refer his care to someone else. She facilitated ongoing spiritual care while ending the inappropriate dynamic and maximizing her safety. She also consulted with treatment team members to benefit from collective wisdom and to build mutual support for personal safety. She planned to tell the patient about the consultation, demonstrating for him her partnership with and accountability to the broader healthcare team. This incident led the peer group of interns to consider additional options for boundaries. For example, so that the person sees the relationship as professional and not as a personal friendship, the chaplain should negotiate specific times and places for visits. Further, the chaplain should focus on the patient's story, referring to the chaplain's own story minimally, and only when doing so enhances the pastoral purpose. Active listening that selectively engages spiritual content enhances purpose. Such boundaries strengthen spiritual care effectiveness.

In spiritual care, the chaplain seeks to enter the world of cared-for persons by way of their stories, perspectives, values, needs, and strengths. Caregiving rarely involves providing advice and direction based on the chaplain's story and strength. Doing so tends to jeopardize empowerment of the cared-for person. Empowerment is not about the chaplain transferring or giving power to the person. It is about evoking spiritual power from within the person. Effective pastoral care elicits capacities of the cared-for person to experience more hope, resilience, spiritual strength, and options for self-care.

Chaplains need training and ongoing consultation to support competence in interpersonal distinctions around personal story, feelings, needs, and perspectives. In the midst of the intimate spiritual and emotional encounters of pastoral care, chaplains risk blending their feelings and perspectives with those of the cared-for person in ways that compromise effectiveness. For example, the chaplain might feel so much sympathy with the patient's experience that she loses capacity to support the patient's reflection and choices for additional responses. Alternately, the chaplain might react strongly against an attitude in the patient and lose capacity for empathy and support of spiritual growth. To be effective, chaplains need to remind themselves that a patient's feelings, needs, and responses are just that. Strong personal responses around what a patient says or does should prompt chaplains to remind themselves that the patient's personal agenda is not about the chaplain. In training, chaplain interns examine their own feelings in relationships. The competent chaplain is attentive to interpersonal dynamics in ongoing ways, including self-reflection and consultation with colleagues.

The intimate encounters of pastoral care can awaken in the chaplain personal needs for intimacy. The chaplain might be tempted to enjoy the closeness of the pastoral relationship to satisfy such personal longing. However, this relationship is not for the benefit of the chaplain. Chaplains must be attentive to their own needs for intimacy, pursuing these in various ways outside of ministry. Chaplains need to make time for intimacy with family and friends, to pursue recreation, and to nurture personal development through reading, prayer, spiritual direction, and consultations.

Ethical reflection further enlivens hospital ministry. Chaplains seek support and clarity for ethical practice by consulting with colleagues in various healthcare disciplines, as well as spiritual care colleagues. As members of a professional association, chaplains are committed to honoring the code of ethics of their association. Interns are introduced to this code of conduct as part of their training. Chaplaincy training also includes input about the practice of ethics in healthcare. Chaplains often have responsibility for supporting ethics committees within hospitals, where they participate in the decision-making processes of medical ethics. Ethics is an aspect of theological reflection that chaplains continually need to integrate in their practice of ministry (objective 7).

Collaboration in community: Ministry with valued partners

The experience of healthcare chaplaincy gives particular meaning to the statement that no person is an island. A new chaplain intern walked into a busy intensive care unit and stood bewildered, wondering about where to begin and how to discern his role and contribution. All the staff moved with intense focus on the specific and important life-saving work they had to do. Everywhere he looked, the novelty, stimulus, and life-or-death importance of this place overwhelmed him. Eventually he focused his attention on one person, to whom he introduced himself. She was the unit secretary, who introduced him to a nurse who was walking quickly past. When he asked if she was aware of any spiritual care need, the nurse told him of a patient who had come out of surgery, was very anxious, and had been heard praying. She brought the intern into a large room with multiple beds where patients had no privacy. She led him to the bedside of a patient hooked up with a heart monitor, intravenous tubes, and a catheter. He tried to look past all of this to the face of a man. The nurse made a brief introduction and left. The intern initiated conversation and then prayed with the patient. Suddenly an alarm sounding from the patient's medical machine interrupted the visit. In panic, the intern stopped. A nurse quickly appeared, adjusted something, reset a switch, and just as quickly disappeared. The intern continued prayer with thanksgiving for the nurse. In this visit, he was discovering and developing two particularly important competencies of chaplaincy. The first was to keep learning from experience (objective 4). The other was to enter and trust collaborative approaches to ministry (objective 3).

Chaplain interns are trained and evaluated on their pastoral role in interdisciplinary relationships. In healthcare contexts, ministry must always be provided within relationships of collaboration to discern when and how to engage in spiritual caregiving and how to communicate with other healthcare providers the meaning of the ministry. A competent chaplain is a skillful team player. A chaplain learns about the roles of other healthcare disciplines, learns about illness and health difficulties, increases awareness of the patient's needs, strengths, and support systems, and discerns contributions of spiritual care to healing and wellness. In some contexts, the chaplain's very safety can depend on collaboration, such as when working with a potentially violent psychiatric patient. Collaboration is a daily practice.

Chaplains work interdependently in many ways. When an intern proposed a spiritual support group for nursing home residents, she worked interdependently with the residents to discern their needs and devise a group process. Interns are interdependent whenever they invite feedback from patients about ministry, such as to a worship service. When they engage in peer supervision or with the teaching supervisor, they also exercise interdependence (objectives 5 and 6). Chaplains and supervisors are interdependent with one another in a professional association to develop and implement standards for chaplaincy practice and education.

To strengthen their ministry, chaplains reflect theologically and theoretically about their work, including their collaborative processes (objective 7). Collaboration is well supported by Christian tradition. For example, the apostle Paul taught that in the body of Christ, diverse participants need one another in an interdependent way that is similar to the way parts of a human body function together as an organism. Informed by such theological perspectives, chaplains look for opportunities to initiate, animate, and otherwise support options of collaboration. A smoothly functioning, collaborative healthcare team that welcomes spiritual care does not develop automatically. Hospital staff might neglect to make referrals to the chaplain, potentially indicating a lack of appreciation for spiritual care as an integral part of well being. This neglect might prompt the chaplain to intentionally build relationships with staff and patients that demonstrate the value of spiritual care. Chaplains can support their sensitivity and ability to collaborate by reflecting on philosophy of practice. For example, insights of postmodern philosophy deepen understanding of personal, interpersonal, and social experience. A postmodern approach to a situation calls for assessing a problem through many perspectives, including various contributions of many participants, and seeking evaluation from multiple sources. In practice and theory, interdependent collaboration is essential to chaplaincy.

Theological education as experiential learning and faith journey

After a visit, a chaplain intern reported that the conversation had been devoid of any theological or spiritual content. Using his verbatim script to examine the visit in supervision, the intern reconsidered several statements in which the person implied spiritual values that were worth validating and exploring. Chaplain interns practice theological reflection that does not necessarily depend on theological language or religion as such but rather starts with personal stories and perspectives that are rich with beliefs, attitudes, and values that imply personal theology and spirituality. Providing feedback that acknowledges and validates such content, the chaplain supports further reflection and clarification.

Spiritual care starts with an assumption that God is everywhere and that people are spiritual beings created in the divine image. CPE is a form of theological education designed to engage theology and spirituality in relationship to personal narratives and life experience. It is training to support people in reflecting theologically on their experiences, making use of their theological understanding, and learning to enhance spiritual strength. Explicit and traditional theological language in conversations might in fact neglect the faith journey, particularly for those who do not usually express their experience in such traditional language.

Chaplain interns also reflect theologically about themselves, about their pastoral identities, and about the processes and content of their ministry. For example, in leading a worship service with patients, an intern wanted to proclaim the inclusive and welcoming love of God. He received feedback that he had so completely managed every detail of the worship process and content that participants were excluded from contributing. The theology implied in his worship process spoke of exclusion, diminishing the strength of the theology of inclusion that he tried to proclaim. Interns seek congruence between the explicit theology of their message and the implicit theology of their processes in ministry. Congruence contributes to ethical qualities in pastoral care. Teaching supervisors also attend to such ethical qualities. For example, in the mentoring process they seek to honor learning contracts with interns and to work with interns' personal learning styles and backgrounds.

In engaging the story of a cared-for person and in considering any aspect of ministry, chaplain interns may engage in theological reflection. Insights from the social sciences complement such reflection. Training is guided by the seventh objective of CPE, to integrate theology and social science in understanding the human experience.

The experiential learning process nurtures the chaplain in self-care and growth in the practice of spiritual caregiving. We are never done learning in ministry; we continually enter new relationships and new situations. If we approach ministry entirely on the basis of competence and knowledge from the past, we overlook fresh insight available in the present. Chaplains continue to learn from new situations and relationships about needs and options for care. Effectiveness involves openness to novelty and to learning from care-receivers as well (objective 4). Experiential learning is supported by reflecting on and evaluating ministry through written reflection, consultation with a mentor, and peer supervision (objectives 5 and 6). Beyond CPE, chaplains find ways to continue experiential learning, for instance, by participating in continuing education, professional workshops, peer-group supervision, and so on.

Healthcare chaplaincy is a challenging journey of faith and vocation. Travelers on this journey nurture themselves through connecting with the Source of their vocation, trusting a partnership with the divine. In the midst of ministry, chaplains need to trust that they are influenced by, and channels of, a divine energy of guidance, love, and healing, a Source that is more than their best efforts. They inform their learning and work with a sense of grace, an attitude of trust and acceptance of self and others. To support lifelong learning, chaplains need a spirituality of humility—an attitude that embraces being a finite human and approaches all of life with curiosity and love, discovery and wonder. Humility supports the competent chaplain in considering many perspectives by which to evaluate and inform ministry. With grace and humility, competent chaplains flourish as partners in interdependent, collaborative relationships with God, professional colleagues, and with the people in their care.

Interdisciplinary teamwork
The role of the chaplain

Jerry Nussbaum

A seventeen-month-old child arrives at the emergency room (ER) in respiratory distress. His mother, who has been following close behind the ambulance, enters the waiting room. As chaplain, you meet her as she arrives. Her son, born prematurely, has frequent complications because of respiratory disease. You know Jane and her son Derrick, because he has been here frequently with asthma and other respiratory distress.

Jane asks to be with her son. She says, "I know Derrick is fragile. I need to be with him. I want to be there. If Derrick dies, I want to be there."

The ER staff is intubating the child. You speak with the ER doctor, a new resident who does not know the family. He replies, "Now is not a good time. This child is very stressed and we are trying the best we can to get him stabilized." You acknowledge their work and note that the mother has accompanied her son through previous crises, including intubations in the emergency department, and that she specifically said, "I want to be there if he dies." You offer to stay with her while she is in the room. One of the ER nurses remembers Jane. After some discussion with the nurse, the physician agrees that the mother may come in, as long as someone remains with her.

Jane enters the room. You bring a chair near the bed, between the respiratory therapist and the nurse. Jane holds Derrick's hand, talking to him, saying, "Mommy is here. Mommy is with you." You sense the staff's anxiety at having family there, but they also emanate calm and focus as they work with Derrick.

The team is successful. Derrick stabilizes. He spends a week in the pediatrics unit, where you follow up with him and Jane. Jane expresses gratitude that Derrick is okay again. She was glad she could be in the emergency department with him to help calm him. You affirm the experience and reflect with her on what it meant to be there. "I'm his mother, and I want to be there for my children," she affirms.

Jerry Nussbaum is a chaplain and perinatal grief coordinator at Mount Carmel Health System, Columbus, Ohio.

The hospital chaplain as part of interdisciplinary care

"Whole-person care requires a caregiver who is whole … [but] until [such a person] comes along, use a team,"[1] recommends Balfour Mount, a physician and advocate for palliative care. Current literature strongly affirms the notion that we as humans are multidimensional and that our physical, emotional, spiritual, and mental capacities are connected and interrelated. Leading medical journals and authors from many disciplines—including physicians, chaplains, nurses, psychologists, social workers, psychiatrists, and other professionals—are taking part in efforts to understand, evaluate, and integrate the spiritual into the physical, emotional, mental, social, and cultural aspects of our lives. While scientific researchers may dispute among themselves about methods of measuring the spiritual, most agree that spiritual care is significant and that it belongs in a healthcare institution's plan of care.

Spiritual care involves much more than attention to one's relationship with God or belief in God. Spirituality encompasses one's sense of meaning and purpose and one's relationship and connection with self, others, creation, and the transcendent. It includes how one finds hope and meaning in difficult events and one's understandings of death and mortality. Spirituality affects one's values and choices in life. In today's healthcare context, many affirm that the relationship between spirituality and health is significant and relevant. Disagreement is common, however, about how these two are interrelated. It is also unclear how hospitals should respond to this acknowledged interrelationship.

In the United States, the Joint Commission on the Accreditation of Healthcare Organizations (JCAHO) mandates that healthcare institutions, at a minimum, assess and accommodate patients' spiritual beliefs and practices into patient care plans.[2] Spiritual care departments are now routinely reviewed as a part of the hospital accreditation process. I have taken part in several reviews from JCAHO that included direct questions about how chaplains function as part of the healthcare team. On interdisciplinary teams, chaplains have the unique function of viewing the person as an integrated whole. As a professional caregiver among other professionals, the chaplain[3] provides

---

[1] Balfour Mount, "Suffering and Healing in Life Threatening Illness" (address to Joint Conference of Association of Professional Chaplains, Canadian Association for Pastoral Practice and Education, National Association of Catholic Chaplains, and National Association of Jewish Chaplains, Toronto, ON, February 25, 2003).

[2] 2003 Comprehensive Accreditation Manual for Healthcare Organizations: The Official Handbook (Chicago: Joint Commission on the Accreditation of Healthcare Organizations, 2003).

[3] Throughout this essay, the simple term chaplain refers to the professional or trained hospital chaplain. I differentiate this role from that of local clergy who may at times function as hospital chaplains (usually on a part-time, crisis, or referral care basis). Those who on occasion serve as chaplains may or may not have advanced training (Clinical Pastoral Education and a theological degree) that would qualify them to deal more readily with the variety of spiritual care needs in contexts of medical, social, emotional, and mental health care.

needed language and expertise to communicate the spiritual perspectives of the patient to the healthcare team. I view the hospital chaplain as the primary resource person for spiritual care issues in the hospital.

With the rising awareness of the interconnectedness of spiritual care with other aspects of healthcare, institutions and healthcare teams worldwide are asking not *whether* spiritual care is important or valid, but *who* assesses the spiritual needs and *who* is the best person to provide spiritual care. Do physicians, nurses, social workers, counselors, chaplains, clergy, religious community visitors, and hospital housekeepers have an equal part in the spiritual care of patients? Is it enough that a hospital admission screening asks if a person has a personal religious preference? If we describe spiritual care as a natural dimension and basic need of every human being,[4] then how does a hospital provide spiritual care for the patient who is not "religious" or the person who does not have a local church, synagogue, mosque, or other place of religious connection? What happens when the patient has no local clergy person? Who then provides for spiritual needs? Among the disciplines that provide medical care to the hospitalized patient, which of them pay attention to the spiritual concerns of the hospitalized person? These are the kinds of questions that one might ask in the hospital setting when addressing the need and development of interdisciplinary care to include the spiritual dimension.

Hospitals are increasingly hiring physicians who specialize in hospital medicine. These physicians, called hospitalists, are "usually internists, who are hospital-based and whose primary focus is managing the general medical care of inpatients."[5] The hospitalist focuses on care of patients within the hospital from admission to discharge, in contrast to the primary care physician who manages comprehensive care from an office outside the hospital. The hospitalist is better prepared to manage multiple medical needs that arise while a patient is hospitalized. Such care indeed has advantages, because hospitalists provide coverage twenty-four hours a day, seven days a week in the hospital; thus they are available for emergent care and consultations at all times. In addition, the hospitalist provides leadership and education to staff, working as part of the hospital staff to manage many hospital-specific medical conditions.

Chaplain Mark LaRocca-Pitts uses the hospitalist as an analogy for describing the role of a hospital chaplain. "As a metaphor, the hospitalist compares to PCP (primary care physician) as the chaplain compares to local clergy," LaRocca-Pitts suggests. The hospital chaplain receives specific

---

[4] See Larry VandeCreek and Laurel Burton, eds., *Professional Chaplaincy: Its Role and Importance in Healthcare* (Chicago: Joint Commission on the Accreditation of Healthcare Organization, 2001), 2.

[5] R. M. Wachter and L. Goldman, "The emerging role of 'hospitalists' in the American Health Care System," *New England Journal of Medicine* 335 (1996): 514–17.

training for interventions in the hospital setting, so that "among clergy, the chaplain is the 'hospitalist.'"[6]

It may be helpful at this point to consider who is responsible for spiritual care, especially in the context of interdisciplinary teams. Is it the chaplain? the physician? the entire team? Chaplain George Handzo and physician Harold Koenig recognize that the question of who provides spiritual care can be a delicate one, because every major profession involved in health-care—medicine, nursing, social work, psychiatry, psychology, and pastoral care—claims at least a part of this task.[7] Although Handzo and Koenig agree that each of these professionals is important and each contributes to spiritual care, they assert, "The specific roles of various professionals are not the same, and are, in fact, definably distinct." "Spiritual care is everyone's job," the authors continue. "As a caring human being to another human being who needs help, we are giving spiritual care. We firmly believe, along with many others, that this care is a powerful contributor to healing."[8]

In differentiating the roles of chaplain and physician, Handzo and Koenig argue that the physician should attend to a patient's spiritual well-being, in addition to the physical and psychological domains. "The [physician's] assess-ment should be brief but cover the necessary areas relevant to the intersection of the patient's beliefs and issues of health and illness, and how the patient wants those beliefs and practices incorporated into their healthcare."[9] Handzo and Koenig designate the physician's and chaplain's tasks as *spiritual screening* and *spiritual assessment*, respectively. The chaplain, as "spiritual care special-ist," has the appropriate training and expertise for the latter.[10]

The document, *Common Standards for Professional Chaplaincy*, adopted in 2004 by the six primary spiritual care groups in the United States and Canada, provides standards for board certified chaplains and summarizes the required education, clinical training, and expectations for professionally trained spiritual care providers:

> While many health professionals and community religious leaders provide cultural, spiritual, and religious care to patients and families, professionally trained and certified chaplains who work within a department overseen and held accountable by the hospital leadership bring the highest standards of care. Spiritual assessments, and outcome-based

---

[6] Mark LaRocca-Pitts, "The Chaplain as Hospitalist," *Plainviews* 2, no. 3 (March 3, 2005), 1.

[7] These claims would seem to recognize and validate an understood integrating energy to the spiritual dimension of the whole person.

[8] George Handzo and Harold G. Koenig, "Spiritual Care: Whose Job Is It Anyway?" *Southern Medical Journal* 9, no. 12 (December 2004), 1242–43.

[9] Ibid., 1243.

[10] Ibid.

spiritual plan of care, interventions based on professional spiritual care standards of practice, the ability to work effectively within an interdisciplinary team and provide leadership all significantly contribute to the organization's ability to uphold JCAHO's standards and elements of performance. Professional spiritual care departments work with community religious and cultural leaders to facilitate their care to their members while also serving as a liaison and educator for the organization.[11]

Koenig and Handzo expand on the standards to suggest that the general practitioner is responsible "to perform a thorough assessment of all systems that could possibly have a bearing on the cause of the presenting symptoms."[12] The general practitioner focuses on the physical symptoms primarily but keeps an eye on the psychological, social, or spiritual factors that may contribute to or exacerbate a physical symptom. If there are signs that the patient is dealing with issues of hopelessness or loss of meaning in life, the physician can decide whether a referral is necessary, and if so, what kind of specialist to contact. If spiritual factors seem to be contributing a positive or negative effect, then the chaplain is incorporated into the plan of care to assess and explore these issues more completely.

Addressing spiritual issues continues to gain acceptance; it is becoming a regular part of assessments done by nursing staff and physicians.[13] Koenig advises physicians to take a brief spiritual history and include it in the medical record. He suggests that a physician address the following questions:

- Are religious beliefs a source of comfort or a cause of stress?
- Are religious beliefs in conflict with medical care?
- Are there religious beliefs that might influence medical decisions (and how)?
- Is there a supportive faith community likely to check on and monitor the patient's recovery?
- Are there any other spiritual needs that should be addressed?[14]

According to Koenig, if a patient experiences significant stress in any of these areas, or experiences religious conflict with treatment, then a referral to a chaplain or pastoral care professional is appropriate. He explains, "Offering spiritual advice or trying to solve the patient's spiritual struggles is beyond the range of most physicians' experience unless they have received special

---

[11] Adapted from the Association of Professional Chaplains Website 2005, www.professional-chaplains.org.

[12] Hanzo and Koenig, "Spiritual Care," 1243.

[13] Harold Koenig, "Religion, Spirituality, and Medicine: Research Findings and Implications for Clinical Practice," *Southern Medical Journal* 97, no. 12 (December 2004): 1194–99; Melanie McEwen, "Spiritual Nursing Care," *Holistic Nursing Practice* (July/Aug 2005), 161–67.

[14] Koenig, "Religion, Spirituality, and Medicine," 1197.

training to do so."[15] Chaplains with an interdisciplinary mindset would not view such interaction with physicians or nurses as crossing boundaries; on the contrary, they would welcome it as enhancing interdisciplinary care.

Requests that physicians give more attention to spiritual issues sometimes elicit controversy. Stephen Kliewer names possible barriers to physician involvement with spiritual issues, including lack of training, time constraints, imposing one's own beliefs, and trivializing complex issues. Those opposed to the addressing of spiritual issues by physicians suggest that the practice may cause more harm than good, by linking health status to spirituality, thus potentially inflicting further suffering. [16] These boundary-related issues are relevant and deserve continued study and dialogue.

The chaplain, as identified spiritual care specialist, works with the interdisciplinary team that focuses on treating the person as a whole. Identifying the chaplain's specialized role helps lessen boundary and training concerns and provides a model of holistic care. Having a spiritual care specialist reminds the team to maintain awareness of spirituality and to begin with the patient, not the caregivers. Any member of the team—nurse, doctor, social worker, or therapist—may keep an eye out for spiritual connections or contribute to the team's addressing of identified spiritual needs. The interdisciplinary team also benefits the spiritual caregiver by contributing their perceptions of and responses to common concerns about meaning, hope, suffering, or other spiritual issues related to the patient's illness.

Recognizing the importance of the spiritual dimension and integrating this dimension into healthcare is not new; for decades, this has been the work of Clinical Pastoral Education (CPE) in training clergy and chaplains. The competencies of a board certified chaplain include the ability to "integrate disciplines of psychology, sociology, and theology into spiritual care" and to "establish and maintain professional and interdisciplinary relationships."[17] These competencies, among other team- and system-oriented skills, outline

---

[15] Ibid.

[16] Stephen Kliewer, "Allowing Spirituality into the Healing Process," *Journal of Family Practice* 53 no. 3 (August 2004): 616–24.

[17] Association of Professional Chaplains, *Board Certified Chaplain Competencies* (Schaumburg, IL: Association of Professional Chaplains, 2005). The standards were adopted in 2004 and affirmed by the six primary professional spiritual care groups in the United States and Canada. These groups represent over 10,000 members who serve as chaplains, pastoral counselors, and clinical practice educators in specialized healthcare settings. In summary, board certified chaplains are required to possess: (a) an undergraduate degree and a graduate-level theological degree from a college, university, or theological school accredited by a member of the Council for Higher Education Accreditation; (b) a minimum of 4 units (one year) of Clinical Pastoral Education, which is nationally recognized clinical training in the provision of professional spiritual care; (c) board certification by a national professional care cognate group through which the chaplain demonstrates competencies in pastoral theology and care, professional and personal identity and conduct, and commitment to a code of professional ethics; (d) continued professional development by active membership in a professional association

a distinctive role for the chaplain in the hospital setting; they are essential to working as a fully functioning member of the interdisciplinary team.

How chaplains function on the interdisciplinary team

When people from various professions work with one another on a daily basis in the hospital, they may think of themselves as an interdisciplinary team. However, interdisciplinary teams also function in more intentional ways. For example, a group of individuals from multiple disciplines might meet periodically to discuss particular cases or review critical incidents. Such a group is an interdisciplinary team even though the members may not work together every day. Likewise, an ethics committee typically consists of individuals from various disciplines; it may even include members from the community external to the organization in order to assure representation of diverse views.

Palliative care teams, rehabilitation units, and psychiatric and other specialty care units are examples of teams that work together on a daily basis, with regular meetings to review and update goals. In these settings, representatives of multiple disciplines discuss the needs of particular patients and progress toward goals of care developed in collaboration with the patient. Chaplaincy departments in some settings are taking seriously the practice of working on interdisciplinary teams, focusing intentionally on "outcomes-based" goals and care.[18] Such work is an example of chaplains taking ownership and leadership in developing care strategies that collaborate with medical models.

Members of an interdisciplinary team have distinct roles but share responsibilities for spiritual care at the basic level of spiritual screening and support (for example, identifying religious affiliation, if any). In situations of spiritual crisis or distress, when issues are more complex, the chaplain, as specialist, takes primary responsibility. When a hospital team works with an interdisciplinary focus, the team as a whole is responsible to identify and meet particular patient needs through a multidimensional approach that includes attention to medical, social, spiritual, psychological, and emotional needs. An interdisciplinary team's effectiveness depends on collaborative leadership and attention to group dynamics.[19] Chaplains who have received training

---

including professional continuing education and peer review. For a complete list of common standards for professional chaplaincy, see the appendix at the end of this chapter.

[18] Rev. Art Lucas and Barnes-Jewish Hospital chaplains, St. Louis, MO, have developed a framework to integrate spiritual care in healthcare teams. They presented these concepts in a workshop, "Fundamentals of outcomes-oriented spiritual care," at the Association of Professional Chaplains/ National Association of Catholic Chaplains joint conference, February 2000, Charlotte, NC.

[19] Questions pertinent to group dynamics include how interdisciplinary teams are formed, who is in charge, what the legal and ethical obligations of team members are with respect to patient care, and how conflicts and differences of opinion are addressed. Often the physician is in charge and bears the responsibility for the patient.

in basic CPE, and who meet current standards of professional competence, have ample training to collaborate effectively as team members. Members of interdisciplinary teams who have similar training in group leadership and dynamics include social workers, psychiatrists, and counselors.

Identifying the chaplain as a spiritual care specialist who works in collaboration with the healthcare team provides a basic framework for integrating spiritual and physical care. The trained hospital chaplain has an important voice on the interdisciplinary team. Without the unique voice of the chaplain, the treatment and care of patients as whole people suffers and fails to reach its full potential. Ideally, such care includes helping patients heal, adjust, recover, cope, and live effectively with disease, illness, and unexpected life changes.

Pastors' knowledge of their parishioners' history, family and wider context, can make a significant contribution to care. But many patients do not have connections with a clergy person or membership in a faith community. Even for those patients who do have such connections, their local clergy may lack the network within an institution that could enable them to address spiritual issues in relation to holistic patient care with the effectiveness and expertise the chaplain can bring to the situation. Local clergy, as spiritual generalists, are often limited in the spiritual care they are able to provide in the hospital setting.

Chaplains as advocates for families and support to staff

A family whose child had suffered many setbacks in the Newborn Intensive Care Unit felt that everything possible had been done for their son, and it was time to allow his unresponsive body to die peacefully. The chaplain, with access to the institution's processes for dealing with end-of-life issues, worked with the family, the physician, and the ethics committee to ascertain the appropriate response in such circumstances. The physician disagreed with the ethics committee regarding the futility of care. The chaplain suggested to the family that they could, therefore, work with a physician who affirmed their understandings, beliefs, and ethical values. The child was transferred to the care of another physician and died soon after the removal of artificial life support. These arrangements honored the values and beliefs of both the family and the physician. The chaplain was able to assist the process, along with the physician, nurses, social workers, and ethics committee, to make this transition as compassionate and respectful as possible.

Especially during CPE, I learned to appreciate the chaplain's unique and strategic position for dealing with families in crisis or conflict situations. Such situations intermingle with the complexities of institutions, modern medical practice, and patients' religious and spiritual landscapes. In family systems work within CPE, chaplains learn subtleties in the dynamics of anxiety, fused relationships, and identified patients.[20] Chaplains, ministering with a "nonanxious presence," can navigate the worlds of medicine and religion, institution and person, patient and family. Moving freely between these worlds requires an identity that is primarily grounded in the chaplain´s faith community. From such a strategic position, the well-trained chaplain can identify relationship triangles, conflicts, dysfunctional spirituality, and much more.

As a spiritual care specialist, I am separated from the field of medicine, the institution, the family, and the spiritual realities, but I am connected enough that I can address displaced anxiety and issues hidden beneath the surface. I know enough about medicine, disease, and diagnosis to avoid misinforming a family or playing into a family's denial defenses. I know enough about unhealthy religious functioning to avoid playing into a patient's overextended church and religious involvements that have contributed to neglect of the body and basic familial relationships. I may not come from a particular patient's church or religious tradition, but as a spiritually aware and educated person, I am competent to listen, learn, and respond appropriately without imposing my own answers. I am able to establish the way of relating with another that Martin Buber calls "I-thou."[21] The unique position of chaplain allows me to walk intentionally with patients and assist them in identifying their spiritual needs and wants, along with any resources that might bear on the disease process and their ability to cope. This professional versatility is an asset that hospital chaplains may offer to interdisciplinary teams.

The pediatric intensive care unit staff had worked together over many months to provide care for a family whose chronically ill child came in with frequent medical crises. Now the child was dying. The care team adjusted their efforts as the family's needs changed from medical interventions (such as the right kind of home care services, pharmaceuticals, physical therapies, social and financial services) to needs of a more spiritual nature. The care team elicited discussion on what kind of care would be meaningful and consistent with the patient's and the family's values. Some staff wanted a spiritual or religious awakening so that the family would be "saved"; others wanted a priest to visit and administer last rites. Some wanted me to baptize the child and make sure the family had "right beliefs." Other staff thought we were giving up too soon.

The parents of the child started to show signs of anxiety. They wondered why caregivers disagreed about the right thing to do. As chaplain, I was in a position to listen to the staff, the physician, and the family on equal ground and foster communication and clarification of beliefs, hopes, and resources. This listening clarified that the parents wanted to hold their child, have family

---

[20] Edwin Friedman, *Generation to Generation: Family Process in Church and Synagogue* (New York: Guilford, 1985), 11–64.

[21] Martin Buber, *I and Thou*, 2nd ed. (New York: Scribner, 1958).

and friends present, and say their goodbyes. With this clarity, the team was able to support the family in their choices.

As chaplain, I provide for spiritual needs by meeting with the family and communicating their requests and needs to the staff. This frequently involves conflict. Staff members may be vocal about their own religious and spiritual beliefs. In such circumstances, an advocate for the family may be necessary, to represent the primary responsibility of the hospital staff to care for the family's needs. The chaplain as a spiritual care specialist has the tools and ability to advocate for the family. With a variety of resources and training, the chaplain can also help staff debrief after particularly difficult, traumatic, or emotional situations with families.

The chaplain in the hospital is aware of the ways illness and loss affect hospital staff and physicians who care for patients. The staff most directly involved may not be the ones who most feel the significance of the loss. A housekeeper who cleans rooms recently told me how hard it is to go into the room of patients who are dealing with miscarriage or infant loss. She said it reminds her of losses she is dealing with in her family. We talked specifically about how she feels in these work situations and how to manage her feelings.

The chaplain works with teams to help them better understand the spiritual dimensions of particular families. The chaplain also helps team members understand and verbalize their own spiritual definitions and boundaries and explore their own spiritual identity. As spiritual specialists, chaplains can provide staff members dealing with end-of-life situations with the language and tools to talk with families. The aim is to begin to shift from doing, or trying to fix things, to being with people through the journey. Silence, listening, attending to physical needs, and waiting all become aspects of caring for the patient and family, not only by the chaplain, but also by the team. As chaplain, I find the support of the interdisciplinary team an important resource for understanding the dynamics of patient care and, in turn, making an informed contribution.

Hospital care teams often underutilize chaplains. Part of this underuse may be the result of a chaplain's limited self-understanding and assertiveness on the healthcare team. Another factor may be staff misconceptions of the professional training and expertise that present-day chaplaincy requires. Board certified chaplains are required to have graduate level theological education and significant supervised clinical training (CPE). Staff may not be aware that professionally trained, board certified chaplains, although belonging to particular faith groups, do not impose their own faith traditions on the patient. Rather, they receive special training to assess and help a patient maximize spiritual resources, regardless of whether the patient has a particular religious or faith frame of reference.

Chaplains as mediators and interpreters

The chaplain, as "spiritual and religious specialist on the treatment team,"[22] brings at least four additional contributions to the interdisciplinary hospital team:

- sensitivity to multicultural and multifaith issues;
- broad understanding of the impact of illness, trauma and crisis on faith, belief, and the spiritual search for meaning experienced by patients and staff;
- adequate knowledge of medical terminology and spiritual language to effectively assess and communicate the patient's expressed needs and concerns to the interdisciplinary team; and
- accountability to care for the patient's spiritual needs.

Chaplains contribute sensitivity to multicultural and multifaith dynamics. They may assist the patient to use current cultural resources more fully, explore solutions that respect the person's cultural and religious heritage, and bring sensitivity to differences in communication styles. For example, the chaplain may know, when asking questions of a native Pueblo person, to allow longer silences in conversation than do most Western Caucasians. Important answers may be missed if the chaplain cuts short pauses that would allow the person to respond. Pausing at least twice as long as Western Caucasians are used to is a Pueblo custom that communicates politeness and listening. To speak too quickly reflects rudeness and not wanting an answer. In another culture, simple things such as the location of one's heart or stomach can be understood differently. Knowing the person's cultural, spiritual, and religious framework allows one to provide care that is more complete.

A Muslim family who had moved to the United States from Ghana experienced a fetal demise. In Ghana, parents would not usually know where a deceased infant is buried. Not knowing is part of how families deal with the death of an infant. Western European approaches that emphasize mementos and burial rituals would not have respected these practices. The chaplain worked collaboratively with the team, the hospital, and the faith community, assuring that the family's customs were honored. General knowledge of cultural patterns is necessary; however, the unique needs of a family may run counter to expectations. In a situation with similar cultural dynamics, the mother of a deceased child declared to her husband, "We're not in Ghana; we're in America. I want to do it this way." We need to honor and respect the spiritual and emotional needs of each person, regardless of what we expect. In the latter situation, the family asked the chaplain to do a graveside burial service.

An Amish family had a premature infant whose discharge would require specialized medical equipment at home for oxygen and feedings. A

---

[22] Hanzo and Koenig, "Spiritual Care," 1244.

superficial awareness of the Amish community's rejection of electric and telephone service would have suggested limited options for bringing this child home, because of requirements for electricity and communications related to emergent medical care. Yet insistence on institutional care would have contradicted the core value of community involvement among the Amish. As leaders of this family's religious community, bishops participated in the interdisciplinary planning, which included a chaplain, social services, a physician, respiratory therapists, and speech and physical therapists. This meeting allowed the team to explain treatment needs in detail with the family and their community representatives. The bishops responded by affirming the installation of electricity and phone service in the home, in order to care for the child. This action honored the family and Amish community by allowing them to affirm their faith and cultural values in giving care. In this meeting, the chaplain represented the hospital as its spiritual care practitioner and the clergy represented the family's specific faith community. Drawing in the patient's faith community is one way a chaplain can honor the obligation not to impose religious beliefs on the patient.

A compelling book by Anne Fadiman, *The Spirit Catches You and You Fall Down*, illustrates the difficulty of dealing with multiple cultural and religious realities. Fadiman tells the true story of Lia Lee. The Lee family, originally from Laos, of the Hmong culture, migrated to the United States. Lia was brought to a California hospital when she was three months old, following a grand mal seizure that occurred shortly after her older sister, Yer Lee, slammed the front door of their apartment. The Lees believed that "the noise of the door had been so profoundly frightening that her soul had fled her body and became lost."[23] According to the Lees, the seizing symptoms were "*quag dab peg*," a term for epilepsy commonly used by the Hmong, which means, "the spirit catches you and you fall down." Epilepsy is regarded as serious but also distinctive among the Hmong people. According to their view, a person with epilepsy enters a spiritually altered state that allows her access to realms denied to others. The fact that they suffer from an illness gives epileptic persons special empathy. A person with seizures therefore may be given the religious role of shaman or healer. Lia's parents were both concerned and proud.

A series of cultural and religious misunderstandings resulted in Lia's being taken away from her "unfit" parents because of "medical noncompliance." Medical professionals struggled to understand the family's refusal of conventional Western medical treatment, especially because her parents' quiet care was compassionate in every other aspect. After the initial administration of medications, the family appeared to believe, when the symptoms disappeared, that she was cured. In November of 1986, after Lia had come home again, she

---

[23] Anne Fadiman, *The Spirit Catches You and You Fall Down* (New York: Farrar, Straus and Giroux, 1997), 20.

experienced a seizure that lasted a couple hours, putting her in a coma. Doctors told the parents that Lia's life would soon end. The Lee family wanted to take her home and care for her there. In the Hmong culture, it is taboo to foretell death. In fact, to do so essentially indicates that the one who predicts it is the *cause* of death. Her family took Lia home, cared for her, and kept her alive, to the surprise of medical personnel. In cross-cultural situations, chaplains, social workers, physicians, nurses, interpreters, and other hospital personnel must work together to provide the expertise and accountability needed for integrating spiritual and cultural dimensions in the plan of care.

An emergency room physician tells this story about an effective inter-disciplinary approach taken with a Hmong woman who needed to make a decision about her medical care status. In this case, an interpreter was able to use his medical knowledge and knowledge of the woman's culture to com-municate effectively.

> I was an intern or a junior resident at University of Califor-nia Davis Medical Center in Sacramento, California. The Hmong have settled in central California, and there is a large community in the Merced and Sacramento regions. I was on an internal medicine rotation, and we had just admitted an elderly Hmong woman. I don't recall exactly what her diagnosis was, but it might have been community acquired pneumonia or mild congestive heart failure. She was sick enough to be in the hospital but would probably be discharged in a few days.
>
> We had the services of a professional interpreter. We tried to ask her about her code status. The interpreter was well known to our team and he dutifully exchanged our words, but it was obvious that we weren't communicating, because her expression and body language indicated more confu-sion than anything else. After about ten minutes of this, the interpreter asked us if he could speak directly with the patient for a few minutes.
>
> We agreed, and a rapid discussion took place between our patient and the interpreter. After a few minutes, the patient clearly indicated "no" (I can't remember the Hmong word, but I did recognize it at the time). The interpreter then clarified to the staff present that the patient wished to be a No-Code (that is, she wanted no medical interventions used in the case of cardiac arrest). We gratefully checked the box and proceeded with the rest of the details regard-ing admission. Later, we asked the interpreter how he had gotten our question across to the patient in such a quick

and definitive manner without any obvious teaching or explanation about the procedures.

He replied with words to this effect, "I explained that here in the West, there is a religious ritual that is performed as someone dies. The doctors squeeze the heart to make it pretend to beat and push wind into the lungs to make them pretend to breathe. Sometimes when they do this, the spirit gets confused and comes back to the body and stays. Do you want this ritual performed on your body?"

The patient had responded that she didn't believe in that religion and declined the ritual. Of course, my comment is that there was absolutely nothing wrong with that translation, and we respected her wishes completely.[24]

As part of the team, the chaplain knows both the medical and the spiritual terminology that facilitate assessment and communication. The responsibility of a care team to address needs effectively requires each member to be aware of the medical, spiritual, and emotional dimensions of a person's life. A chaplain who does not understand the process of dying and the medical terms associated with that process will have difficulty understanding whether a patient is being hopeless or realistic. Chaplains need to be able to differentiate normal grief reactions from suicidal ideation and communicate appropriate responses to the team, using commonly understood language. Physicians or nurses who are unaware of the person's religious or cultural beliefs and family customs, and how they may affect healthcare decisions, likely will have difficulty communicating treatment plans and options. Because chaplains are familiar with hospital terminology, they can use their understanding to provide effective, appropriate care.

A thirty-three-year-old man was admitted to oncology after coming through the emergency department with chest pain. He had a large mass in his chest. He was diagnosed with metastasized, stage four cancer. His prognosis was bleak, ranging from a few weeks to months. The oncologist was recommending radiation for palliative care. The man's few family members had never dealt with this kind of illness. They seemed oblivious to the physician's diagnosis, saying, "He will be all right. Don't tell him all this. Any negative information would only make it worse." Without an understanding of the serious nature of his disease, and without an adequate understanding, psychosocially, of the dynamics of crisis and grief, a chaplain might have reinforced the family's understandable desire to protect and remain in denial. Such a response would have eliminated the family's opportunity to deal with end-of-life issues and to seek closure with their loved one. The chaplain on

---

[24] Story recounted by permission of David Hill, M.D., Columbus, Ohio.

the team had the expertise to deal with the realities of dying and grief, to provide opportunity for clarification, and to address spiritual needs, treating the person as a whole. The patient, with honest communication and helpful information, was able to make important decisions about the extensiveness of treatment. He was able to have family and close friends nearby in the last weeks of his life. The family's anxiety about his reaction to the truth subsided, as they were able to hear their son and brother come to terms with what he had already suspected.

Where chaplains serve on interdisciplinary teams

Chaplains make significant contributions to interdisciplinary teams that provide care throughout the hospital. Chaplains respond along with other medical professionals to crises and trauma. When a death occurs, chaplains provide resources and assistance with decedent care that may include follow-up through community professionals or clergy. Chaplains may serve on ethics committees and Critical Incident Stress Management (CISM)[25] teams or work with education departments to teach physicians, nurses, and other hospital staff about issues surrounding death, cultural diversity, faith, stress, or spiritual assessment.

Specialized care teams may use the interdisciplinary model in the structure of their programs. For example, palliative care has been using the interdisciplinary team model for healthcare extensively. The CAPC (Center to Advance Palliative Care) Manual describes the contribution of the chaplain to palliative care:

> Severe life-threatening illness challenges the spiritual dimension of every patient and family. The response to the challenge can lead either to intense distress or growth.[26] The chaplain is the team member with training and expertise in meeting spiritual needs. The role of a trained chaplain should not be confused with the role of spiritual leaders of various denominations. Although the latter may play an important role, it should not be assumed that they have any more training or expertise in palliative care than anyone else.
>
> The chaplain:
> • Assesses spiritual distress
> • Provides support and counseling to the patient and
>   family

---

[25] CISM teams are often used in hospitals and in emergency medicine to initiate interdisciplinary debriefings in response to crises. These teams may work together with community organizations such as fire, police, and other emergency management response teams.

[26] I find it interesting that the manual lists only these two options!

- Leads or promotes supporting rituals, as appropriate
- Promotes linkages to the community[27]

Becoming integrated as a hospital team requires personal and professional effort on the part of everyone involved. For teams to be effective, all members should be free to initiate interdisciplinary relationships, speak out about the spiritual dimension, and hold the team accountable for addressing these needs. If the chaplain is to be integrated into the rounds and conferences on various units, he or she will need to make an effort to be visible and available when the team meets, or to take proactive leadership in joining patient care conferences. Physicians who are accustomed to being in charge may find that the interdisciplinary model encroaches on their turf.

A cardiac rehab team I worked with met twice a week to review the care of specific patients. In team meetings, the cardiac nurse specialist, social workers, chaplain, pharmacist, dietician, and staff from the rehabilitation unit each had the opportunity to report on the progress of patients. The team worked together to plan for a patient's discharge. Patients recovering from heart surgery often have problems with eating, so the dietician worked with the patient on dietary changes. The surgical nurse taught the patient about incision care, the rehab specialist put together plans for physical therapies, the psychologist was available for anyone struggling with depression, and so on.

Hank, a sixty-eight-year-old man recovering from cardiac surgery, was progressing very slowly. He was sleeping constantly, eating little, and showing little motivation to get up and move. Discussion with the chaplain revealed that his fiftieth wedding anniversary would have been the following week; however, his wife had died of cancer two years earlier. After exploring Hank's issues of grief and loss and their relationship to his recovery, the chaplain helped the team understand his situation and made additional recommendations for supportive follow-up. As a result, the team was able to address treatment of Hank's needs more fully. The follow-up included paying attention to his depression by conferring with the psychiatrist, discussing support resources with the chaplain, planning for medical care at home, making further connections to resources with the help of social workers, and working toward physical recovery with nurses and wound care specialists.

A hospital's ethics committee is an interdisciplinary team that may include not only physicians, medical services, and chaplains, but also administrators and community representatives. A typical ethics committee includes physicians, nurses, chaplains, social workers, administrators (risk management, legal, and regulatory), community members, and often a health system ethicist. Hospital chaplains are often at the forefront of dealing with end-of-life

---

[27] C. F. von Gunten, F. D. Ferris, R. K. Portenoy, and M. Glajchen, eds., *CAPC Manual: How to Establish A Palliative Care Program* (New York: Center to Advance Palliative Care, 2001).

care and decision making with family members. Having a chaplain on the ethics committee is essential for committees that want to maintain a multi-dimensional approach to holistic care. Frequently, discussions in our ethics committee about "ethics consults" turn out to be communications rather than ethics issues. The interdisciplinary meeting helps the team identify and resolve issues related to communication and misunderstandings between staff members and families, as well as between staff members themselves.

Many kinds of interdisciplinary teams provide varied opportunities for medical professionals to work collaboratively. When developing strategies for holistic care, today's healthcare systems cannot afford to overlook interdisciplinary teams. The chaplain as a trained spiritual care specialist can make a valuable contribution to the care of the whole person. All members on the healthcare team may contribute significantly to the spiritual well-being of the patient. Chaplains, as specialists, take spiritual care to deeper levels for understanding and meeting patients' spiritual needs.

Appendix
Board certified chaplain competencies[28]

The Association of Professional Chaplains
1701 E. Woodfield Road, Suite 760
Schaumburg, IL 60173
Phone: 847-240-1014
Fax: 847-240-1015
Email: info@professionalchaplains.org
Website: www.professionalchaplains.org

TPC1: Articulate a theology of spiritual care that is integrated with a theory of pastoral practice.

TPC2: Incorporate a working knowledge of psychological and sociological disciplines and religious beliefs and practices in the provision of pastoral care.

TPC3: Incorporate the spiritual and emotional dimensions of human development into the practice of pastoral care.

TPC4: Incorporate a working knowledge of ethics appropriate to the pastoral context.

TPC5: Articulate a conceptual understanding of group dynamics and organizational behavior.

IDC1: Function pastorally in a manner that respects the physical, emotional, and spiritual boundaries of others.

IDC2: Use pastoral authority appropriately.

IDC3: Identify one's professional strengths and limitations in the provision of pastoral care.

IDC4: Articulate ways in which one's feelings, attitudes, values, and assumptions affect one's pastoral care.

IDC5: Advocate for the persons in one's care.

IDC6: Function within the Common Code of Ethics for Chaplains.

IDC7: Attend to one's own physical, emotional, and spiritual well-being.

PAS1: Establish, deepen and end pastoral relationships with sensitivity, openness, and respect.

PAS2: Provide effective pastoral support that contributes to well-being of patients, their families, and staff.

PAS3: Provide pastoral care that respects diversity and differences including, but not limited to culture, gender, sexual orientation and spiritual/religious practices.

---

[28] Association of Professional Chaplains, *Board Certified Chaplain Competencies* (Schaumburg, IL: Association of Professional Chaplains, 2005). See also footnote 17.

PAS4: Triage and manage crises in the practice of pastoral care.

PAS5: Provide pastoral care to persons experiencing loss and grief.

PAS6: Formulate and utilize spiritual assessments in order to contribute to plans of care.

PAS7: Provide religious/spiritual resources appropriate to the care of patients, families and staff.

PAS8: Develop, coordinate and facilitate public worship/spiritual practices appropriate to diverse settings and needs.

PAS9: Facilitate theological reflection in the practice of pastoral care.

PRO1: Promote the integration of pastoral/spiritual care into the life and service of the institution in which it resides.

PRO2: Establish and maintain professional and interdisciplinary relationships.

PRO3: Articulate an understanding of institutional culture and systems, and systemic relationships.

PRO4: Support, promote, and encourage ethical decision making and care.

PRO5: Document one's contribution of care effectively in the appropriate records.

PRO6: Foster a collaborative relationship with community clergy and faith group leaders.

Pastoral ministers
and volunteers
Qualifications, training, and functions

Clair Hochstetler

A hot topic currently under debate among professional chaplains in health-care ministries is the place of volunteers in chaplaincy ministry. Professional chaplains have fought long and hard for recognition as equal partners on the healthcare team; it seems essential to protect the profession from anything that would denigrate the status professional chaplains have earned. Consequently, some want nothing to do with volunteer chaplains, because they believe using volunteers compromises the integrity of the profession. Other equally competent professionals train and deploy volunteers at various levels and are willing to risk criticism from peers because of what volunteers have to contribute. In the first section of this essay, I attempt to recognize both perspectives on the issue. By providing examples of high standards and quality of care, maintained within a well-designed volunteer chaplain program, I propose ways of resolving the dilemma. Further, I offer a reminder that professionals themselves may serve as volunteers.

In subsequent sections, I trace the context, history, and development of the spiritual care program integrated into Goshen Health System, offering illustrations of the roles, qualifications, training elements, and policies upheld by chaplain volunteers. I also highlight opportunities to strengthen relationships between local congregational leaders and hospital-based spiritual care training initiatives. I conclude with reflections and real-life stories illustrating some of the functions and tools available for effective volunteer chaplaincy.

The great debate

On several occasions, I have had the opportunity to attend the annual conference of the Association of Professional Chaplains (APC). At each of these meetings, I have made a point to attend the special interest session for those from one-professional-chaplain departments, a gathering that brings together those of us working in small and medium-sized hospitals and other special clinical settings.

Clair Hochstetler is chaplain, Goshen Health System, Goshen, Indiana.

At the most recent gathering, our moderator's opening remark had us splitting our sides with laughter while simultaneously sharing knowing glances. Teasing us about our motivations for working as solo chaplains, he declared, "Well, I guess we're all *here* ... because we're not all there!" Those of us who have sustained our involvement in solo settings beyond a few years have often noted that it takes a certain kind of person to handle such varied expectations gracefully. Solo chaplaincy seems to require a unique combination of pastoral care and crisis management gifts, along with well-honed administrative, time management, and self-renewal skills. It often takes little time for those starting out fresh in the role of solo clinical chaplain to start wondering just what it is they have gotten themselves into—especially if the requisite skills do not come naturally.

At this recent gathering, it took only a few minutes before I observed another phenomenon that manifests itself virtually every time we begin to introduce ourselves and describe our situations. Approximately half of us will describe ourselves as solo clinical chaplains in departments augmented by a corps of trained volunteer chaplains of various designations—clergy volunteers, pastoral care volunteers, pastoral associates, volunteer assistant chaplains, or spiritual care visitors. The remainder of the group, who wrinkle their foreheads at the notion of volunteer chaplains, introduce themselves as solo chaplains for their facilities. They emphasize that, as professionals, they are reluctant to use or even philosophically opposed to using volunteers or laypersons to enhance their ministry. They fear such a program may lower the professional chaplain's standards or the quality of care delivered. The total group will then inevitably engage in reflection around this conundrum. This great, unending, yet healthy debate is a classic tension among professional chaplains, no matter the size of our institutions.

During the recent discussion, I found myself reflecting again on a formative experience I had six or seven years ago, one that still carries a bit of a sting for me. It began when I welcomed the volunteer services of a competent, professionally trained chaplain, while she was in transition and seeking a permanent assignment. Alice (not her real name) spent several months assisting me one day a week, doing rounds, initial visits, and spiritual care assessments, and attending monthly team meetings, much as our other spiritual care visitors have been trained to do. She left our department when she had the opportunity to take a temporary paid position as director of our hospital's volunteer department. After this assignment was complete, she did not return to our spiritual care team.

While we were working together, Alice and I had (I thought) developed a good, open style of communication as she interacted with the diverse personalities on our spiritual care team. She did not seem reticent to give me her careful feedback, which I valued. Soon after she left us—on good terms, or so I believed—an unexpected jolt came in the form of a letter sent to me and copied to our now-returned director of volunteers. Her words set me back on my haunches.

First, Alice expressed anger that by maintaining a volunteer chaplaincy program (which I, of course, felt proud to have had up and running within six months of my arrival at Goshen Health System), I was actually preventing professionally qualified, board certified chaplains such as herself from getting a job. The hospital administration would naturally be glad to continue making do with only one paid chaplain, while expanding programs, services, and unrealistic expectations of the chaplain's role and piling commendations on me for using well the volunteers from the community. Administrators might even assume that volunteer chaplains could do it all, an assumption that could jeopardize my own job in the long run. Second, she argued that using volunteers could compromise chaplaincy standards, because of the many things a professional chaplain is called on to do in subtle and unseen ways, functions that volunteers are unable to perform. Charting is one example. No one is the wiser, she continued, when someone as efficient as I am works so hard that I risk burning myself out in covering all the gaps in the short run. I should seriously consider downsizing the volunteer program and demand professionally trained assistance. Third, Alice planned to propose to the APC that they lead a workshop at annual conference the following year on the dangers and pitfalls of volunteer chaplain programs.

I was stunned. I see through all this, I told myself, attempting to put Alice's words into perspective. I categorized her vociferous letter as a passive-aggressive attempt to resolve her personal agenda while she struggled to find a chaplain position. I tried not to take it personally, but the effort was a challenge.

Later, I began to comprehend the truth in some of Alice's insights. Yet I still needed to take into account the reality of my situation. I was an energetic chaplain with expertise in running volunteer programs (as a former Mennonite Voluntary Service administrator) and experience under my belt in youth ministry and in rural and urban pastorates. I was serving a one-hundred-bed, community-based hospital with a rural and highly churched constituency. My supervisor, the Vice President for Nursing Administration, emphasized that in a hospital of this size, we were "lucky to have a full-time paid chaplain at all." The place she had come from in the southwestern United States had not been so fortunate.

The searing confrontation via letter paid off; it has served to keep me aware of both sides of the volunteer debate. From that point on, I determined to strengthen our volunteer program, intentionally building in high standards with a clear focus on quality of care. In addition, I have continued to educate and model for my colleagues and for key members of the administration what professional chaplains can and should be, with an emphasis on results—thus laying foundations for the future addition of a professionally trained, paid chaplain colleague. It has not been an easy task, to say the least. How I have worked to create a valued and effective spiritual care team with real integrity is the focus of the rest of this essay.

At times in our profession, professional chaplains must demonstrate positive results in order to justify new developments. At Goshen Health System our efforts in spiritual care have contributed to the attainment of consistently high patient satisfaction scores for quality of emotional and spiritual care. We have needed to keep pace with a hospital program that has advanced significantly in the region in terms of market share, and has distinguished itself with a world-class cancer treatment team that shares our concern to integrate spiritual care with the healing of bodies.

At the APC conference, I pulled myself out of my reverie and back to the one-professional-chaplain department meeting. As I listened, I soon felt a need to exercise my sense of self. (Aren't good chaplains supposed to be like that?) I knew that what I wanted to share might startle a few, but it was important nonetheless. One of the "lone-ranger" professionals in our midst had just been eloquently insisting that we do not expect to see volunteer doctors or volunteer nurses in our midst. We do not have nurses bending over patients, saying, "I notice that you aren't able to breathe very well! Would it be OK with you if I called a respiratory therapist to pay you a visit?"

I responded, "Hold on just a holy moment. I accept the last illustration. But surely you recognize that in many rural areas—and even in some of the largest hospitals and health systems in our nation—we can find affiliated health clinics, which specialize in ensuring healthcare access for the uninsured and underinsured. Some of these organizations absolutely depend on the volunteer labor of doctors, nurses, social workers, interpreters, managers, counselors, and the like. As a matter of fact, I happen to chair the board of one such clinic. At this point in its history and under its unique circumstances, it could not get along without volunteers. Yes, prior training, good orientation, accountability, and a whole bunch of other things are vital to the success of such an organization. But I do not doubt the quality of the care those trained volunteers provide at the Center for Healing and Hope in Goshen simply because they happen to be volunteers."

Developing a spiritual care team to fit the context

It was probably just as well that I quit speaking, for we had other important issues to deal with in our meeting. If I had had the luxury of more time to reflect before I spoke, I would have included aspects from a strategic plan I shared later in the regularly offered workshop for those interested in the formation and care of a vital volunteer chaplain program. Why use trained volunteers from the community? Churches and their members and ministers offer a wealth of resources. Volunteers know the community. Using volunteers helps integrate the community with the healthcare institution. It is good stewardship. Hospital patients, especially at a small hospital, benefit from a variety of spiritual support resources and personalities.

My conviction, based on experiences with volunteer program administration, is that when circumstances prevent hiring paid staff, volunteers will respond effectively if the mission is compelling, standards are kept high, and accountability is assured through the guidance of a well-trained supervisor. With regard to spiritual care programs in clinical settings, my distinct bias is that the supervisor should be a board certified or provisionally certified chaplain.

Originally, the small community hospital I serve had an all-volunteer chaplain program, initiated by the Goshen Ministerial Association (GMA) approximately twenty-two years prior to my coming on the scene. GMA members each took a turn as the on-call chaplain of the week, doing rounds each weekday morning. After ten years, GMA initiated a successful campaign to employ a professional full-time chaplain, initially raising funds from the community. A few key volunteers from the earlier era took turns covering for her during vacations and occasional seminars away from the hospital. Although they supplemented her efforts, she was on call all the time, mostly by her choice, because she preferred to function alone. She proved the worth of the professional chaplaincy role early on, to the extent that within a couple years, the hospital budgeted to cover her salary and benefits. Her tenure spanned almost twelve years until she retired, whereupon I succeeded her.

Thus, in early 1998, I became the second solo professional chaplain to serve Goshen Health System. I had shared my vision with the search committee during interviews, and the need to develop a new strategic plan, but I knew I would first need to focus on establishing vital relationships. I began to work with a key group that had been functioning for many years, the Pastoral Care Advisory Committee. Its members were diverse. They included four or five pastors representing at least three denominations in the local community. All had experience in clinical settings, and a few had been involved with chaplaincy in Goshen from the beginning.

This committee also included nurse managers or directors from different departments within the hospital, plus a couple physicians who had a heart for pastoral care. My supervisor at that time, the Director of Patient Services, was part of the committee. Because of internal restructuring, the supervisory role switched after a couple of years to the Vice President of Nursing Administration. In retrospect, this was an important and strategic move.

Having been trained to assess and identify needs, I was working hard. I could hardly wait to develop my vision and get more help in the department, but I learned the value of pacing myself. Because such a plan was not mine to develop alone, after several months I began to work with the Pastoral Care Advisory Committee to sharpen our collective vision for the future and to begin sketching a workable strategic plan to fit our context. First, we reflected together on the types of people needed to fulfill our stated mission. I facilitated this process by clearly defining their volunteer roles and functions. Second, we began networking, working closely with local constituent groups such as the GMA, but also within the wider region, finding the best volunteers within the pool available. I screened the candidates against a clear and compelling set of qualifications. Finally, we never compromised the high standards we set: thorough orientation, ongoing in-service training, and adherence to established policies and procedures, tailored to our own context, yet designed to release people to fulfill a common mission while pursuing a personal sense of call. We have built on this foundation successfully ever since.

I initiated a change of name for the department from Pastoral Care to Spiritual Care, in order to reflect an expansion in the team's composition and mission and in what it has to offer people—patients and colleagues alike—in various settings within the health system. Our ministry no longer confines itself to the hospital, since I was asked to coordinate spiritual care for the Care At Home/Hospice Team. Within a year of beginning my tenure here, our health system began developing the Center for Cancer Care. In addition to my own participation on the center's Integrative Care Team, highly trained and experienced volunteer chaplains visit and offer spiritual care among the outpatients receiving treatment in the infusion room.

Over the past eight years, the Spiritual Care Department team has included an average of fourteen Spiritual Care Visitors, each of whom commit a minimum of two hours per week; most give three or four. These visitors help cover all the basic needs on weekdays, doing initial visits and routine spiritual care assessments, or assisting in following up with patients who do not have regular pastoral care and would like us to provide it as long as they are inpatients. Not all spiritual care visitors have pastoral experience in a congregation or in-depth pastoral counseling skills, although many do. We are currently blessed to have three retired professional chaplains on our team. All of these volunteers have demonstrated gifts of discernment, good judgment, wisdom, and spiritual depth.

Another approximately fourteen on-call volunteer chaplains, all of whom live within a fifteen-minute drive of the hospital, rotate in, as scheduled, to cover weekend shifts and twelve- or twenty-four-hour blocks of time during my vacations and other times away. Until recently our hospital's patient volume had been manageable enough that I could still provide on-call coverage at night during the week, and flex my schedule accordingly. However, as patient volume and acuity of care among the patient population continues to rise (we are undergoing a major facility expansion), changes in this schedule will likely be necessary.

Beyond the basic qualifications, those in the on-call group have come highly recommended by at least two peers. Each carries appropriate credentials confirming ordination or licensing for ministry; each has successfully completed at least one unit of Clinical Pastoral Education or has demonstrated skills from a lifetime of experience in pastoral/crisis care. They are men and women of spiritual depth, community-minded people who continually demonstrate their networking skills and whom I can trust to handle emergencies and crises that may arise when I cannot be present, including code calls and deaths. At times, the pager has gone off two or three times in quick succession, making it expedient for me to call in one of these wonderful people to back me up, in order to ensure quality of care. These people I select carefully and initially screen in interviews that I conduct, often accompanied by at least one other discerning, experienced volunteer. I must add that a Spiritual Care Team coordinator of such volunteers must exercise flexibility, because these gifted individuals, often retired and well traveled, must at times be allowed a great deal of latitude in their schedule, or one could lose them.[1]

The three retired professionals I mentioned earlier double their volunteer efforts by taking on another role. These three serve with me on the Care at Home/Hospice chaplain team within our health system. They undergo both specialized initial training to meet state standards, as well as training in the procedures required for documentation and completion of annual competencies. The team collectively seeks to address the needs of those hospice patients who otherwise would lack adequate spiritual support. Each chaplain takes two or three patients under care at a time, in a sustained relationship for as long as the patient lives.

We initiated the hospice chaplain team in the past year to address the doubling of our census that had occurred in just two years. I am currently heading up efforts to justify and secure appropriate financial commitment to expand these services with an additional part-time professional hospice chaplain, who could then coordinate the spiritual care program with hospice in a more focused manner. I have become stretched too thin, even with the team in place.

Chaplain qualifications and quality of care: Maintaining high standards

The following excerpt from an internal document of Goshen Health System describes the role and qualifications of volunteer chaplains and outlines standards for quality of care:

---

[1] We recently lost one of our most experienced on-call chaplains, who died suddenly on March 31, 2006. Ellis Croyle, who had seemed robust at seventy-five, carried himself with great grace, wit, and wisdom. Much loved by countless colleagues around the health system, he was our first volunteer chaplain in these eight years to die. He had been with the program throughout my administration except for a couple of short-term breaks to take an interim pastorate assignment in the vicinity. Twice he handled both roles simultaneously. I wish to dedicate this chapter in his honor.

Purpose. The effective Spiritual Care Visitor will assist the hospital's professional chaplain by making rounds, as assigned, among patients and their families. He/she will seek to be an expression of God's love by offering a caring prayerful ministry of Christian presence, listening ears, and knowing how to "companion" others in times of suffering or stress. Thus, the volunteer also becomes an additional referral source to alert the hospital chaplain of follow-up needs a patient or family may have. The goal is to create a supportive atmosphere conducive for spiritual, emotional, and physical healing. *The spiritual care visit is not an opportunity to give advice, preach, proselytize, or "fix" problems of the patient.*

The role of a spiritual care volunteer

The volunteer *does*:
- offer—always—empathetic listening and supportive "presence" as an expression of God's love to patients.
- offer prayer and/or appropriate scriptural reading only when mutually agreed upon with the patient and/or family.
- notify the patient's church or pastor of their admission to hospital, if the patient so desires and grants permission.
- document observations, actions taken, and any patient follow-up needs on the (single-sheet) Patient Care Record, always completed between visits and filed in the chaplain's office.
- assist the chaplain in fulfilling requests from patients for information packs on Advanced Directives or Organ/Tissue donation registry.
- communicate to the hospital chaplain any other pertinent observations, particularly with regard to major stressors or life changes, grief issues, or unfavorable diagnoses.

However, the volunteer *does not*:
- give advice (unless specifically requested), preach to patients, or proselytize.
- strive to "fix" the patient's problems.
- become involved in the patient's physical care.
- become involved in the legal or ethical issues of the patient/family.
- promote his/her own religious beliefs or personal church through literature or "sale"

- share one's own personal problems, emotional needs, or
  own health experiences with the patient in order to gain
  their personal support or guidance.[2]

Helpful volunteer qualifications include being a good listener and broad-minded person able to get along with people of diverse cultural and religious backgrounds. Volunteers are personally selected after they respond to specific questions on an application, provide references, and have an interview with the chaplain and another experienced volunteer. We expect our volunteers to be spiritually grounded adults who have a desire to serve others and learn more about themselves and about God's work in healing, pain, and illness. Spiritual care volunteers are men and women who come from a variety of backgrounds and experiences but are actively involved within their own congregations. They are not expected to be biblical theologians or experts in pastoral counseling in order to participate; however, in our context, I expect them to come with some knowledge and training, such as having been a Stephen Minister in their congregation, or having some other congregationally based leadership or spiritual care experience. References and other evaluation from other congregational leaders are crucial. When it comes to the delivery of spiritual care, the quality of a visit must always come before quantity in visitation, so we are not looking for those who measure their success by how much they accomplish. This work focuses on human *being* rather than human *doing*. Flexibility and a keen sense of humor are real plusses.

The best volunteers do not come as a result of pressure or coercion. I believe that the Holy Spirit draws them in. A kindred spirit can help. Our best connections to potential new volunteers are current volunteers, as well as trusted friends within the Goshen Ministerial Association. I have rarely felt the need to recruit. However, I have needed to screen candidates. I have not gone very far down the road with certain zealous types after the interview process began. One case involved a man about thirty years old who felt strongly that he was ordained by God specifically to do hospital ministry. He had credentials from a Bible college I had not heard of, and he had recently switched his attendance from one congregation to another. He wanted practice praying with people. One of his references was the pastor of visitation in the previous congregation. My conversation with the man's former pastor confirmed my worst fears about this candidate. The man must have had a hunch that he would not fit, because he never called back to pursue volunteering. A few people have weeded themselves out after reading the material in the service description or the application form and realizing the level of self-disclosure required and the qualifications desired.

---

[2] Goshen Health System, "Service Description for Spiritual Care Visitors with Goshen General Hospital" (Goshen, IN: Goshen Health System, 2006), 1.

Training

An effective training program is critical, but a variety of models will work. Training needs to fit one's context. Further, I suggest that the training include certain basics, no matter how long or extensive it is, and whether it is given to individuals as needed or to a group at a fixed time each year.

What follows is my list of suggested criteria and elements for training:

- Program overview and expectations
- Orientation to the hospital (including tour)—"Nuts and Bolts" and health screenings
- Checklist of responsibilities and commitments
- Department mission statement, policies, and procedures
- Introduction to personal and pastoral identities—similarities/differences?
- Models for community-oriented chaplaincy and spiritual care
- The art of effective listening—companioning
- Models for prayer and meditation
- Establishing helping relationships
- Making initial visits—spiritual assessment strategies[3]
- Documentation
- Maintaining confidentiality—HIPAA (Health Insurance Portability and Accountability Act)
- Ministering in special settings:
  Crisis/emergency room ministry
  Grief and loss situations
  Among the confused or disoriented
  ICU and vent patients
  Special needs of the elderly in the hospital
  Those with suicidal ideations
  Special needs of children (particularly when a death occurs)
- Self-care strategies
- Basic resources for spiritual care

In our context, I tend to bring new volunteers in sporadically and train them on an individual basis, as needed, incorporating the themes above. We also include the all-important element of shadowing, that is, requiring the potential volunteer to observe my interactions with patients and those of one or two other experienced volunteers. A monthly in-service provides the entire team with ongoing training and teambuilding. I may lead the session on a chosen theme, or I may bring in a resource person, often from another part of the health system or community. Usually I reserve time to discuss a ministry incident or two that has occurred in our context within the previous month. Much can be learned via the careful process of observation, action,

---

[3] See appendix to this chapter, "Enhancing the patient visit by asking good questions."

and reflection. Though many find it challenging at first, from time to time we employ the classic verbatim format in order to capture the richness of an interaction by practicing the art of reflecting on good questions.

Madeleine L'Engle writes, in *Glimpses of Grace*, "Sometimes our very questions are angelic. Questions allow us to grow and develop and change in our understanding of ourselves and of God, so that nothing that happens and nothing that science discovers, is frightening, or disturbs our faith in God."[4] In this spirit, I developed the resource list found in the appendix to this chapter, "Enhancing the patient visit by asking good questions." These questions are a tool many have found helpful in making spiritual assessments. They also provide a good structure for making initial visits, and I encourage all our Spiritual Care Volunteers to draw from them.

Many professional chaplains have concerns about volunteers failing to document their interactions appropriately. Record keeping is vital. Volunteers should be well trained in this aspect, so that the baton can be effectively passed from caregiver to caregiver, as patients with complicated cases receive care over the course of their stay. Some years ago I devised a standard one-page Patient Care Record for all volunteer chaplains, both those doing routine visits on the care units and on-call chaplains summoned for emergencies. Volunteer chaplains use the form to document any visit with a patient, in whatever context. They complete the record right away after the initial visit or add to it immediately after a follow-up visit. The Patient Care Record is ultimately returned to the office for appropriate filing.

Until recently, this form has been the mechanism by which professional staff enter notes into a patient's chart, as warranted. Our hospital began charting electronically almost two years ago. I have recently discovered a way to grant volunteer chaplains access to only the spiritual assessment page of a patient's electronic record, thus creating the possibility for volunteer chaplains to record the results of an initial visit they have made. But some of my veteran volunteers will not go near a computer. A second reason I have been reluctant, thus far, to initiate the new procedure is a concern to control the quality of what is permanently recorded on a patient's chart by a volunteer. Nevertheless, I am developing a list of standard observations, actions, and responses that another specially trained volunteer with computer skills could check off on a patient's assessment on the screen, parallel to the observations checked on the paper Patient Care Record. Such a system would eliminate most of my reservations. I understand that most electronic charting systems would provide a similar capability.

---

[4] Madeleine L'Engle, *Glimpses of Grace: Daily Thoughts and Reflections* (San Francisco: Harper Collins, 1998), 30.

Extending volunteer ministry in the community

One vital aspect in the training of spiritual care volunteers remains to be addressed. I believe it is incumbent on professional chaplains with volunteer programs to make themselves available to community clergy, lending a hand to train and equip their respective deacons and elders (whatever title the churches give them) toward more effective ministry among their parishioners. This training is especially important when the pastor is unavailable and another congregational leader may be expected to minister to a fellow parishioner in the midst of a healthcare crisis. Congregations sometimes place such responsibilities on lay members without providing adequate training, with the result that problems arise in the hospital setting.[5]

Many congregations allocate funds for long-term involvement in Stephen Ministry. This ministry has an excellent training program built in and confidentially links caregivers and care-receivers within a congregation. People with Stephen Ministry training are a welcome sight for professional chaplains who count on volunteers having received the first level of quality training elsewhere before entering the more advanced volunteer spiritual care program associated with their hospital.

Local clergy have called on me several times to serve as a resource to their church deacons or elders groups interested in developing basic chaplaincy skills. In response I have developed a brief curriculum I call Spiritual Care 101. The final section suggests ways one can debrief after personal engagement in an intense ministry opportunity. In it I invite participants to process the dynamics and issues involved by selecting a few of the following questions to reflect on, or to journal about.

- What did I bring into this encounter with the patient?
- What happened, what developed (or did not develop) in this patient relationship?
- Were there any conflicting, hard, or puzzling issues for me?
- Where is this patient likely to be in her/his spiritual journey?
- How do I perceive this person experiencing God? (Feelings, images, problems shared, etc.)
- Where and how did I sense God working among us during this visit?
- What surprises (or questions) does God seem to be posing to me for my own growth?

Myra Raab has developed an excellent model, "The Ministers of Care Training Program," based on her work in the spiritual care program of St. John's Health System in Anderson, Indiana. This is a thirteen-session weekly

---

[5] One excellent resource available for appropriate congregation-based lay visitation training is Richard Kauffman, "Training for Lay Ministry (Elder-Deacon) Visitation" (2001), Mennonite Church USA, OneSource, http://www.mennoniteusa.org/onesource/BP-1-Visitation-Training-for-Elders.doc.

series that begins with a one-and-a-half day introductory retreat. St. John's views this ongoing training program as part of their mission to serve the surrounding community. The guiding statement for the course reads, "Saint John's Center for Spiritual Care will train committed persons to be a spiritual presence in providing care for members of their faith community(ies) and/or serving as volunteers in the health care setting."

Tools for the task: Five smooth stones

In my context, the volunteer chaplains who carry out most of the routine visitation are a tremendous resource for helping me identify the patients that need my attention. As in Jesus' day, most present-day ministry takes place in the context of interruptions. Then come responsibilities a professional chaplain must handle and cannot delegate to spiritual care volunteers. Personal examples include medical ethics consultations; family care conferences; interdisciplinary rounds; response to complicated deaths, grief issues, and certain types of emergency calls; counseling; networking with community clergy and other outside contacts; colleague education; administration and in-service training for the spiritual care team; hospice and cancer team case conferences; referrals for hospice or cancer outpatient follow-up; time to read and refurbish the soul, attendance at any number of meetings that one may be leading or participating in to effect performance improvement initiatives—plus the interminable charting! All this the professional chaplain does in addition to specialized direct patient care, and more.

Yes, the task can be daunting, but together we can and must find ways to slay the giant—the volume and complexity of need in a stressful healthcare environment that constantly threatens to overwhelm. How best to cope with all of it? Like David, the young shepherd facing the formidable Philistine Goliath, we choose five smooth stones.[6] The smooth stones in our work are the tools the whole spiritual care team should keep polished, as we maintain focus on our mission, and then employ as we confront the formidable task!

Compassion is the first smooth stone. Leo Buscaglia said it well: "Too often we underestimate the power of a touch, a smile, a kind word, a listening ear, an honest compliment, or the smallest act of caring, all of which have the potential to turn a life around."[7] Compassion was the source of the bond that drew an Amish family to Ellis Croyle's visitation, prior to the funeral. The father in this family had helped the Croyles build a simple wooden casket that now lay in the fellowship hall of College Mennonite Church where I stood, viewing Ellis's lifeless body. The Croyle family wanted the man to help them build it in his workshop, and he gladly did so because of the special bond he had formed two years earlier with Ellis and his wife, welded in compassion

---

[6] 1 Samuel 17:40.

[7] Leo Buscaglia, in http://en.thinkexist.com/quotation/too_often_we_underestimate_the_ power_of_a_touch-a/213531.html Source otherwise unknown.

and strengthened by exchanging family visits. The relationship had begun one day when Ellis, as on-call chaplain, was summoned to the emergency room to meet the family, who had just learned that their little child lay dead, never to walk or play again. He had listened to their anguish and their questions, holding the two of them in the depths of their grief, deeply touching them with his concern. Now, as I looked on, it was their turn to offer compassion to grieving members of Ellis's family.

Accountability is the second smooth stone. A couple weeks ago, when I was coming back to the hospital late one night to distribute flowers after the memorial service for my mother, I saw a note on my desk from Nancy Kidder, who had been the spiritual care visitor earlier that afternoon. Her note urged whoever was on call, "just in case you happen to see this note yet this evening," to stop in to see a troubled woman who was dying on the medical care unit, and her distraught daughter. Nancy had met with them, but she knew they needed more. Ordinarily I would not have gone there under the circumstance of my own fresh grief, but Nancy's note tugged at my soul. When I arrived, the room was dark. As I was turning to leave, the nurse in charge of the patient said she was glad that she had caught me, because she was sure the daughter would want to be awakened should someone come to pray and counsel with her mother.

When I went in, I listened to their anguish, and then I simply, softly sang. I opened up a subject with the dying mother that her daughter seemed unable to bear, yet the mother seemed to want desperately to talk about: to acknowledge openly that death was near, to ask for forgiveness, and to commend her spirit into the Lord's hands. This daughter had brought her aging mother to our town several years ago, yet neither had made any connections with a pastor or caring congregation, in spite of an avowal that "we still believe." The daughter had no idea whether the former pastor, in another city, was still around. It had been years since they had made any contacts, yet it was obvious that ours was not the town in which to have a funeral, because all the family friends of yesteryear were "down there." Fortuitously, I helped reestablish those pastoral connections yet that night, only a few hours before the woman died. The episode significantly lifted my spirits, clouded as they were by my own grief. I felt light as a feather as I walked home.

A few weeks later the daughter, back in town again, talked with me about her desire to reconnect to her Presbyterian faith roots. She asked if I would help her meet the local Presbyterian pastor, a friend of mine. She mentioned her hope to get her own teenage daughter involved in the youth group. Had Nancy not been accountable to leave that note, had the nurse not been accountable to urge me onward, had I not been accountable to these divine signals, the distress for the daughter and mother that evening would have compounded. My presence made the pain bearable, the daughter told me.

Respect is the third smooth stone. I think of the many volunteers on the team I lead who carry respect as a gift deep within. These volunteers share respect with folks who are different from the people they would ordinarily meet at church or anywhere else they frequent in this town. Carrying their own deep faith and personally treasured values but with no need to twist any arms, they respect differences in culture, family systems, and lifestyle. Such respect builds bridges of friendship and gratitude, and opens up unforeseen opportunities for the chaplain to pray. No one is ever pushed into the kingdom of God; believers are drawn in by the felt presence of an inviting and respectful Spirit.

Excellence is the fourth smooth stone. I witnessed excellence in action one day when I responded to a summons to the emergency room. Almost simultaneously, another page asked me to address another urgent need in the hospital. Lynnette, a former licensed school social worker turned into volunteer hospital chaplain, was handy; she followed me into the emergency department. The call, it turned out, was for a colleague who worked here at the hospital. She was in shock, for she had just witnessed the death of her husband as a result of a massive heart attack. He had entered the door of their home, and with his hand still on the doorknob, had fallen—as three grandchildren, ages 6 through 12, and their neighbor friends looked on in shock. I left the traumatized children and their grandmother in Lynnette's capable hands and went on my other mission.

I found out later that Lynnette's counseling and pastoral gifts were fully employed that day. She maintained a great sense of balance while surveying the intense emotional landscape and relating closely with the three grandchildren and their mother, who had come in to see what had happened to their grandfather. They also brought in pictures they had made about this experience. Lynnette knew just what to do to draw them out into open conversation. With excellence, she helped the entire family process their grief and dismay and facilitated their decision making regarding next steps. The episode graduated Lynnette from a spiritual care visitor to an on-call chaplain who responds to emergencies.

Wisdom is the fifth smooth stone we need in order to slay the giant. Wisdom is the judicious application of knowledge. It entails exercising the gift of discernment, using good judgment, and being able to see what one needs in order to face the situation at hand effectively. When I think of wisdom, my mind turns to something that happened when one of the new volunteer chaplains was shadowing me. Together we entered a room filled with stoic Amish women. The patient had just given birth, and the baby had been rushed to a children's hospital. No one was sure the baby was going to make it. The young mother, with no baby in her arms, was trying to act grown up, in the presence of friends and relatives chatting away as if the crisis were no big deal. The new volunteer, sizing up the situation, took a stuffed animal from the bedside stand and offered it to the deeply distraught mother. "Here," she said, "you need something to hold in your arms right about now. Hold it as if this is your baby." The floodgates burst open with a great release of tears. The chattering stopped. The women started connecting with one another and acknowledging what was really going on. My new volunteer had demonstrated her wisdom.

As these examples demonstrate, volunteer chaplains, through their carefully honed skills, provide deep spiritual care within our hospital. The people we minister to certainly care about how much we know, but most of all, they want to know how much we care. These smooth stones of CARE—compassion, accountability, respect, excellence,[8] laced with wisdom—will help us day by day confront the giant of intense spiritual needs and opportunities.

---

[8] CARE is Goshen Health System's acronym for its core values: compassion, accountability, respect, excellence.

Appendix

I have found the questions below to be effective when woven into conversations with patients in the hospital, in hospice care, and in extended care settings. They contribute to the goal of improving quality of care while addressing needs or issues in the spiritual and emotional dimensions of patients' lives. The trained chaplain volunteers at Goshen General Hospital who help me do initial assessment of spiritual, emotional, and relational needs have come to appreciate the value of these questions during initial and follow-up visits.

Keeping in mind that some patients at our facilities have no formal connections to any church or pastor, I avoid using confusing or lofty "spiritual" language as much as possible. These questions may differ from those pastors ask when offering spiritual care or spiritual direction to members of their congregation.

I urge volunteers to keep several other things in mind. First, body language, pacing, inflection, and tone of voice have greater significance than the exact words one uses. Perhaps even most important, the patient should be allowed to set the agenda. In other words, we must be selective and discerning about how many and which questions to employ. For an initial assessment visit as one is establishing a relationship, it is best to err on the side of keeping it short. Under these circumstances, I suggest focusing primarily on the beginning and the end of the list (questions 1, 2, and 11–15).

Enhancing the patient visit by asking good questions[9]

1. Tell me, _____, what's it been like for you lately? How has dealing with this illness been affecting you (and your family?)
2. Who comes to visit you now? Is there anyone else you hope will come and visit soon? (For those with end-stage illness or those who are dying, also ask:) When you reflect on your whole life journey, with whom did you have your most meaningful relationships? And, what were they like?
3. Have you been experiencing a great deal of suffering? (Note: Some may not be suffering, even if at the end-stage and dying. I feel it's OK to give room to those who want to use denial as a defense against suffering. Don't push if they answer no. For those who say yes, follow up by asking:) Are there things that help distract you from feeling bad or make it more tolerable?
4. What (or who) most gives you a sense of meaning and purpose in your life?
5. What gives you personal motivation, or hope, for your future?
6. Have you had any thoughts about God lately? If so, could you tell me about them?

---

[9] Clair Hochstetler, Spiritual Care Department (Goshen, IN: Goshen Health System, 2005).

7. If you consider yourself a spiritual person, in what ways do you like to express that? (Another way to get at this is: Are there particular ways that practicing your faith has helped you cope with this illness? Or any important rituals that you'd like to maintain?)

8. Is prayer important in your life? (If so:) Are there things you normally like to do (or places you like to go) that help make it easier to pray or express your faith?

9. (For those with end-stage illness, or who are reflecting about their possible death:) What does dying mean, for you? (Follow up with:) Who/What do you think is there for you, after this life?

10. Are there things you would like to say to anyone that you haven't had a chance to say? (If yes, then ask:) Is anything standing in the way that keeps you from saying these things? (Note: The response could lead into a problem-solving discussion to remove these barriers. Also keep in mind that, especially for those "actively dying," the issues most people commonly have a strong desire to communicate before death are: Thank-you ..., I'm sorry ..., Forgive me ..., I forgive you ..., I love you ..., Goodbye ...)

11. Are you connected to any particular church (or place of worship) these days? (If yes:) Could you tell me a bit more about that congregation and how you are involved? (Follow this up with:) Does anyone from your church come to visit you? (If the response is no, move on to the next question.)

12. Is there anyone who provides you with spiritual support whom you would like me to notify? (If yes, tell them you will do so right after this visit, unless that person/pastor is already aware. If no, tell them: "That's OK, we will be here for you, whenever you need us." We try to help make connections for those who do have a spiritual caregiver.)

13. (Please ask those without any obvious spiritual support in their life:) Would you like to have more chaplain visits while you are here?

14. How can I (we) best support you during these days? (To follow up, you could be proactive and ask permission to offer spiritual support—now!) Would you like prayer, or a blessing, for yourself now, or might you like me to read a favorite scripture passage?

15. (End the visit with some variation of the following question:) Is there anything else I can do today—to help address any spiritual issues or feelings that you have?

The chaplain as bearer and giver of blessing

Helen Wells O'Brien

The hospital chaplain is one of many strangers that people encounter in a hospital when they are in crisis and extremely vulnerable. My colleagues and I serve as staff chaplains in a level one trauma and burn center. We are charged with tending the soul in chaos, honoring the humanity of both patient and family, and providing hospitality to those who are literally and figuratively lost. Robert Dykstra, writing about his experience as chaplain in the medical center at Princeton, characterizes the chaplain as *intimate stranger*,[1] one who is allowed to sojourn with those who are thrust suddenly and inexplicably into life-threatening or soul-threatening experiences.

The priestly presence and function of the chaplain

One of the first roles the chaplain assumes is that of host, providing hospitality to those who are newly arrived in a chaotic and foreign experience. When I enter the family room of the emergency department or the burn center, I am often met with ashy faces, startled eyes, shaky voices, angry or fearful demeanors, and a general state of bewilderment. People sometimes cannot recall their own names or the names of their closest family members. They literally cannot tell me how they arrived or where exactly they are. One of the most common statements I hear is, "I don't know how this happened." These words are a perfect litany of disbelief.

My role at such a time is to create as much sanctuary as the family will allow, to assure them that they will not be left alone, to somehow, in the words of Henri Nouwen, "convert the *hostis* into a *hospes*, the enemy into the guest and to create the free and fearless space where ... the stranger can enter and become a friend."[2] There are many ways of providing hospitality. In emergency cases, I explain to families my role as a liaison between them and the medical team. I can serve as their temporary host, providing

Helen Wells O'Brien is a staff chaplain, Regions Hospital and Gillette Children's Specialty Healthcare, St.Paul, Minnesota.

[1] Robert Dykstra, "Intimate Strangers: The Role of the Hospital Chaplain in Situations of Sudden Traumatic Loss," *The Journal of Pastoral Care*, 44 (Summer 1990): 139–52.

[2] Henri J. M. Nouwen, *Reaching Out: The Three Movements of the Spiritual Life* (New York: Doubleday, 1975), 46.

essentials such as water, coffee, directions, and assistance with phone calls. My responsibility is to be with them until they receive the information they need to assess the next step. Like every chaplain, I find myself allowed into the most intimate and sacred experiences of life and death. If I am able to make a connection by creating sanctuary and by providing hospitality during this initial experience in the hospital setting, my shared experience with the family creates a common ground for continuing spiritual care during their sojourn in the hospital.

I have been humbled by my encounters with people of different faiths who have expressed their confidence that chaplaincy may be of spiritual support to them during their hospital stay. One spiritual value that emerges out of many faith traditions in times of crisis is the value of our common humanity and the need for the presence of a compassionate listener—a companion—to witness our grief and distress.

I am indebted to an elderly Vietnamese man for allowing me into his life during the time of his wife's dying. I was called to the critical care unit on Christmas Eve day, because this man was expressing distress that the medical staff could not understand. When I came up to the unit, he was sitting in the family room. I asked if I could speak to him and asked if he would like an interpreter. He declined an interpreter and in fact spoke fluent English. I asked him if he would be willing to tell me about his wife and about any concerns he had about her care and the care of his family. I explained to him my role as spiritual care provider. He told me that he realized the next day was an important religious holiday, and he did not know if he could care for his wife by himself. As we talked more, I realized that he believed all of the staff would go home for Christmas, and no medical staff would remain in the hospital to care for his wife.

I assured him that many of us would be working on Christmas Day, including myself. He said to me, "But you are a follower of Christ, aren't you?" I told him I was. I told him it seemed the right thing to do to work in the hospital as a follower of Christ on his birthday. He told me that in his opinion, Jesus was like a lotus flower, the least of all flowers in the world, but the most beautiful. My encounter with this devout Buddhist man was perhaps the greatest gift I received that Christmas.

One does not have to dig deeply to find that most chaplains who love their work and feel a strong sense of call to chaplaincy are people who have themselves been shattered by tragedy. They are often people who have spent a lifetime pondering and seeking the meaning of that tragedy in their own lives. They are folks who wrestle daily with God, who understand life and death through images and dreams, who do not fit in nicely with their own religious traditions or prescriptions. Finally, many of them—many of us—have decided to connect our vocation with the lives of other pilgrims. We have joined the mass of silent pilgrims who are marked and marred by tragedy, by illness, injury, dying, and death. We have embraced lamentation as an appropriate religious response and found that, with the psalmist, we can still praise God while asking the unanswerable question, Why?

How do you do your work? people ask me. Sometimes I have no answer. How can I say that I feel peculiarly at home among the shattered, that I find comfort among the bereaved, that I like working in a place where life's tragic surprises are viewed as the norm instead of something that most of us could escape if we just lived well? I find it moving to rejoice with those who have restructured their lives in the face of a life-changing event, who allow me the privilege of seeing their faces a year—two years, many years—out from the event. I find it crucial to remember those who did not restructure their lives but lost them through cruel circumstances.

As Lorraine Matties's poem, "Night Passages," conveys, chaplains are people who "risk remembering what memory mercifully declines to recall."[3] Chaplains face daily the reality that not every story has a hopeful ending and that God does not always seem fair or good. William Bonadio, a twenty-year veteran of emergency pediatric medicine, suggests that our work as chaplains is simply to keep the watch faithfully, to be there when tragedy strikes, to help the ones we care for prevail spiritually over forces that seem larger than we are.[4]

The chaplain as bearer and giver of blessing

The role and function of the chaplain as priest is to mediate between the great tragedies of life and the spiritual human need to feel blessed and assured that God has not abandoned creation and the created ones. Blessing others is a way of acknowledging the sacredness of their existence. In the hospital setting, where people become vulnerable by losing privacy, control, routine, and daily relationships, the act of blessing is powerful medicine, indeed. In Marilynn Robinson's novel *Gilead*, narrator Reverend Ames reflects on being a bearer of blessing.

> There is a reality in blessing…. It doesn't enhance sacred-
> ness, but it acknowledges it, and there is a power in that.
> I have felt it pass through me, so to speak. The sensation
> is of really knowing a creature—I mean really feeling its
> mysterious life and your own mysterious life at the same
> time. I don't wish to be urging the ministry on you, but
> there are some advantages to it you might not know to take
> account of if I did not point them out. Not that you have
> to be a minister to confer blessing. You are simply much
> more likely to find yourself in that position. It's a thing

---

[3] Lorraine Matties, "Night Passages," in *Born Giving Birth* (Newton, KS: Faith & Life Press, 1991), 47.

[4] William Bonadio, *Julia's Mother* (New York: St. Martin's Press, 2000), 181.

people expect of you. I don't know why there is so little about this aspect of the calling in the literature.[5]

In working as a chaplain in a level one trauma and burn center, I often encounter people who have been wounded by the very elements that represent the sacred in many religious traditions: fire and water. When someone is injured by fire or drowned by water, they experience grave bodily harm by elements necessary for human survival and used in countless religious rituals for blessing, affirmation, and symbolic representation of the sacred.

My own experience of this negation of the sacred was in the aftermath of an arson fire that destroyed my family's automobile, garage, and many precious possessions stored there. The fire threatened to burn our home, where my infant son and I were sleeping. The traumatic impact of this fire made it difficult for me to be near a candle flame for a long time. I struggled with the image of God in the burning bush. Open fires, such as a campfire, evoked a sense of panic. The smell of burning made my heart pound. I was cut off, for several years, from the spiritual nurture of Christmas Eve candlelight services, romantic candlelit dinners, and family campfires. However, in the mysterious way of the sacred, I was provided some healing for these terrors through the experience of teaching in an Ojibwa school in St. Paul, where every Monday morning we gathered around the sacred fire to burn sweetgrass and offer sage and prayers to the Creator.

In *Holy the Firm*, Annie Dillard writes these words of lamentation after hearing of the airplane accident that resulted in the severe burning of her seven-year-old neighbor, Julie Norwich: "It is November 19 and no wind, and no hope of heaven, and no wish for heaven, since the meanest of people show more mercy than hounding and terrorist gods."[6]

Lamentation is a very human and appropriate response to an event that contains the seeds of abandonment and betrayal by the divine. Part of the chaplain's role and function is to incline a human ear to the lamentation of those struck by tragic, injurious events; to risk remembering their stories, and to leave a blessing on those who feel abandoned and betrayed by life itself.

Final words and final blessing

Early one morning, the clerk on the burn unit paged me. She said a patient on the unit needed a Bible. Unsuspectingly, I took the Bible to the desk and asked for the patient's name. I was told that this patient was dying from burns she sustained when she set herself on fire after dousing herself with gasoline. She was asking for a pastor.

I will never forget the scene in her room. Her eyes beseeched me out of her charred face and connected with mine. I was barely cognizant of the

---

[5] Marilynne Robinson, *Gilead* (New York: Farrar, Straus, and Giroux, 2004), 22.

[6] Annie Dillard, *Holy the Firm* (New York: Harper & Row, 1977), 36.

clenching of my stomach and my mind screaming NO! It was her eyes that saved me, that entreated me to lean toward her, to incline my ear to her and to stay beside her. She knew she was dying. She wanted to die. She did not want any intervention, only medication for pain.

She wanted to speak to a pastor. Any pastor. Her final words were whispered to a stranger bending over her bed. She asked me to pray for her, and I did. She died a few minutes later. I have thought of her many, many times in the ensuing years. She suffered her final moments in my presence. I carry her with me now, changed by the act of having blessed her. Being a bearer of blessing is mysteriously a two-way street.

Naming as blessing

In my role as chaplain, I often think of the passage of comfort from Isaiah 43:1 that reminds us, "Do not fear, for I have redeemed you; I have called you by name, you are mine." Speaking someone's name can be an act of blessing, especially when that person has been taken out of everyday routines and confronted with life-changing circumstances. People who are faced with illness or injury often express the belief that they have become strangers to themselves, that they do not recognize themselves in their present condition. Having our names called can be an important reminder of who we are, or who we hope to be, in the midst of life-changing events.

Early in my hospital career, I encountered a sixteen-year-old young man who had a life-threatening condition that was progressively disabling him. He was scared and dying. He was essentially orphaned, living with an extended family member and her children when he was able to be home. During one of his frequent hospitalizations, he became understandably noncommunicative. I could not get this young man to speak to me, and the rest of the staff had the same experience. I do not know how I hit upon the idea of looking up his name in my concordance. In the small congregation that I had served for twelve years as pastor, we had always celebrated the "coming of age" of each child as she or he reached the age of twelve. I would prepare a meditation on each child's name, talking about the meaning of their name and their uniqueness.

Going on this shred of pastoral experience, I looked up my patient's name in the concordance, wrote it on a Post-it note with the Greek spelling underneath and added the meaning of it, which was "light-giving." I took it to him, and when I showed it to him I saw the first glint of engagement and connection in his eyes. "I draw names!" he blurted out in an excited voice. "What do you mean?" I said, hardly daring to hope he would tell me. "I like to take someone's name and make it into a piece of art," he replied. And thus we embarked upon many hours of conversation that would span our relationship for the next months.

As it turned out, he had been raised as a young child by his grandmother, had attended her Baptist congregation and been baptized there. He remembered his baptism in great detail. This young man and I discovered two similarities: we shared the same birthday, and both our names mean "light," from the Greek. He died two weeks after our birthday in 1999, at the age of seventeen. On my bulletin board at work, I have a photograph of an artist's rendition of a baptism in a river. The artwork depicts light streaming from the sky, reflected on the water and suffusing the baptismal congregation with its brightness. Underneath, I have a Post-it note that bears his name in English and in Greek. I was blessed to have encountered this young man, the light-giver, in my work.

Often chaplains are called to participate in the naming and blessing of a newborn. In our chaplaincy department, we use a service of naming and commendation for fetal or infant deaths. Naming a newborn is a way of acknowledging the reality of this new person, even if she or he lived only for a brief period of time. Naming is somehow powerfully linked to remembering. I always ask parents who have experienced a fetal or infant loss whether they want to name their baby. Below is the simple service of naming and commendation I have used in the blessing of an infant who has died. The pronouns in the service below are female; we also have the service printed with male pronouns.

A service of commendation and naming

Gathering

We gather together in the name of the Creator, who loves us and who called this little one into being. We gather to name this child and to commend your baby into the eternal care of the Creator and to ask for healing and help for you in this time of loss.

Commendation

Creator God, it was you who formed this child in the womb. She was not hidden from you when she was being made. Your eyes beheld her unformed substance. She is fearfully and wonderfully made. We entrust this child, who shall be named [baby's name] to your mercies, commending her to your eternal love.

Commitment to remember

In the rising of the sun and in its going down,
we will remember her.
In the blowing of the wind and in the chill of winter,
we will remember her.
In the opening of buds and in the rebirth of spring,
we will remember her.
In the blueness of the sky and in the warmth of summer,
we will remember her.
In the rustling of leaves and in the beauty of autumn,

we will remember her.
In the beginning of the year and when it ends,
we will remember her.
As long as we live, she, too, shall live,
for she is now a part of us as we remember her.

Prayer of assurance

God, be with those here who are grieving. May they experience
your love and support through the love of family and friends, and
through the ministrations of our staff. May they grieve without
shame. May they experience healing and new hope as the days
and weeks pass. Even in the most despairing times, we are not
separated from you. May your strength and mercies go with this
family [or use names of parents, family members].

Our chaplaincy department holds quarterly remembrance services for the patients who died at our hospital over a three-month period of time. Each patient's family is invited to send or bring a card with their loved one's name on it, so that the name can be read aloud during our service. Reading the names of those who died is a hallowed time in which the deceased are remembered in their uniqueness. I often find that the hearing or reading of their names is a way of releasing the ones we have cared for in the past few months.

Blessing and the creation of memories

I have learned many important things in working alongside our child-life specialists. Child-life specialists are a part of the medical team in pediatric hospitals. They have special training and education in helping children cope with the stress of hospitalization. When a child or young person dies in our hospital, the child-life specialist and chaplain help families create memories in the hours before or after death. We offer to make with or for them hand moldings, handprints (sometimes footprints), locks of hair twisted or braided and tied with ribbon, as well as photographs as appropriate, if family desires.

The creation of these memories is always presented as a choice. Some families decline for a variety of reasons. Some families want us to create the memories for them. Some families want to join staff in the making of these memories. Making hand moldings and handprints becomes an opportunity to hold their loved one's hand, to look at each finger, to consider the indentation of their hand or the uniqueness of their fingerprints. Sometimes in the intimacy and the focus on the activity, families begin to shed tears, tell stories, laugh, and reminisce. Whatever is created is placed lovingly and carefully in memory boxes that we provide, which are covered with handmade paper and closed with ribbon. These boxes are sent home as a tangible blessing from our staff to the families that have allowed us into their lives in the holiest and most awful of times.

The blessing of staff

A significant part of our ministry as chaplains is to the staff of the institutions we serve. In a large level one trauma and burn center, it takes time to build relationships of trust with staff. However, chaplaincy can be a source of blessing and healing for staff who are hard pressed each day to do their work in timely, professional, and compassionate ways.

In addition to the day-to-day listening and support we provide, our chaplaincy department leads regular critical incident stress-management debriefings for staff after the death of a pediatric patient or a critical incident involving a patient of any age. These debriefings can open up an opportunity for staff to provide affirmation and blessing of one another during the course of sharing their experiences, thoughts, and feelings. The confidential nature of the debriefing creates a covenant of trust, which makes this blessing possible even between staff members who do not know one another well but have shared a critical incident.

At the conclusion of a pediatric debriefing, I bring out an old blue pottery bowl that I use as a blessing bowl. I explain that this old bowl is like life itself: chipped, missing its handle, and seriously cracked down the middle. I cannot use it anymore for the pancake batter I used to mix in it for family breakfasts. But it can still hold blessings. I invite staff, before they leave the debriefing, to write on a small square of paper a blessing to the child or teen who has died, to fold the paper, and to place it in the bowl. I promise them that no one will read their blessing, but that I will burn them, along with other blessings, and scatter the ashes in a garden.

Another way we bless staff is through the blessing of hands, a blessing that is not unique to our chaplaincy department. We, like many chaplains, have been invited to perform a blessing of the hands for nursing day. Some chaplaincy departments have done this by going to nursing units and offering the blessing to nurses, housekeepers, technicians, physicians—to all staff who, through the work of their hands, provide comfort, service, and healing for others. We have done this ritual in a variety of ways: through symbolic hand washing and drying, through anointing hands with oil, or through simply taking a staff person's hands in ours and speaking a blessing over their hands.

Several years ago, many of our inpatient nursing units moved from an older part of our facility into a newly built addition to the hospital. During the move, staff struggled with the demands of learning to do their work in a very different physical environment. Even though moving into a new facility was perceived as a good thing, it was still a stressful event and a significant transition and change in the daily routine of staff. One unit moved from an old nursing circle, where they could all see and assist one another easily to a new curving, linear unit which provided more patient privacy but made it difficult for staff to see one another. The move threatened their sense of being a tightly knit community.

In light of the stresses, our chaplaincy department offered a number of brief services that acknowledged the transition and blessed the new workspaces. My colleague Adrienne Schlosser-Hall created a service for staff during which participants were invited to pick up a small stone, offer a hope or blessing for the transition and new space, and drop it into a glass vase provided for the new unit. The stones were of many different shapes, colors, and sizes. These vases of stones, holding our hopes and dreams, can still be found in the staff workrooms of these units several years later.

The chaplain as recipient of blessing

Blessings, as I observed earlier, form a mysterious connection between people, a connection that is an acknowledgement of the divine. The blessings I have received from patients and families down through the years are too numerous to recall here, but I would like to share a few of the blessings I have received as memories of sacred connections in my life.

On my first night as a chaplain resident on call, I was paged to the emergency department for what would turn out to be a fatal accident involving a sixteen-year-old youth. He had overturned an all-terrain vehicle and sustained a brain injury. His large family began to gather in the two small family rooms of our emergency department for agonizing updates on his medical condition.

Sometime in the middle of a very long night, the women of his family—his mother and grandmothers, aunts and cousins—all gravitated to the smallest family room. I came into the room quietly when I saw that they were praying, and one of the aunts pulled me gently down beside her. They were praying the rosary: the Hail Mary and the Lord's Prayer repeated over and over. As I settled into the midst of these women, the cadence of their prayers cradled my own anxiety, and I began to listen to the words: "Hail Mary, full of grace, the Lord is with thee. Blessed art thou among women and blessed is the fruit of thy womb Jesus. Holy Mary, Mother of God, pray for us sinners, now and at the hour of our death. Amen."

I came away from that night mysteriously moved by this prayer and the circumstances in which it was prayed. From that time on, I have found myself saying the Hail Mary when I am very anxious or afraid, drawing on the image of the Mother of God to sustain and strengthen me.

In *The Secret Life of Bees*, Sue Monk Kidd writes eloquently of finding this same comfort through the image of Mary: "I feel her in unexpected moments, Her Assumption into heaven happening in places inside me. She will suddenly rise, and when she does, she does not go up, up into the sky, but further and further inside me. August says she goes into the holes life has gouged out of us."[7]

Life does gouge holes in us. Down through my years as a chaplain, I have had the privilege of caring for patients who have sustained large physical wounds that require months to heal. Several women for whom I have provided spiritual care during their months-long hospitalizations have shared with me stories of horrendous abuse in their lives. In light of my experience, I have pictured their wounds as the physical manifestation of terrible wounds to the heart and soul.

As we have woven a connection of trust, there have been many opportunities for these women to articulate the blessings they need in order to survive. One woman needed to communicate with her son, who was in prison. In response to her letter, he asked the prison staff to help him make a videotape of himself for his mother. In the videotape, he sat and faced the camera, speaking profound words of blessing to her. We watched the image of her son together, and by the end, we were both weeping.

Another woman knitted and knitted during her hospitalization, literally weaving strands together as she reviewed her life, the abuse that she had suffered, and the love she had found. When I was married last Thanksgiving, this patient gave my colleague Lisa a scarf that she had knitted for me. Lisa brought it to me on the day of my wedding, saying that this woman "wanted you to have this so you would be warmed on your wedding day." She had even woven little pockets into the ends of the scarf so I would have a place for tissues for my tears of joy.

I often say that I will do this work as long as I can, and one day it will be done. In the meantime, I will keep watch along with my colleagues in behalf of those whose lives are shattered. They bring to us, within their shattered lives, a mysterious power. The blessings I have received as a chaplain from patients and families stretch out behind me like jewels on a rosary that I pick up and finger whenever I am discouraged or sick at heart. Each jewel contains a particular story and the hard prism of rock that is its blessing. This blessing reflects the radiant light of the divine presence. I am richly blessed.

---

[7] Sue Monk Kidd, *The Secret Life of Bees* (New York: Viking Press, 2002), 302.

Chaplaincy in public and religiously affiliated hospitals

Cornel G. Rempel

Chaplaincy is a profession endorsed by religious bodies, recognized by the healthcare industry, and regulated by professional associations. Not only a service, chaplaincy is a discipline with defined internal and external accountability, a common code of ethics, and professional standards that promote excellence. Similar standards apply to chaplaincy in all institutions, so one cannot always draw a sharp line between chaplaincy in public and in religiously affiliated institutions. However, some distinctions are possible. In this essay, the term *public institutions* will refer to the broad range of government-operated and university teaching hospitals, for-profit hospitals, and community-based not-for-profit hospitals. *Institutions with religious affiliation* will refer to healthcare facilities in which a religious body has the controlling interest. Although the term *faith-based* is common, this term could be interpreted to define the character of the institution, which is not the central issue in this essay. I wish to focus on how public versus religious sponsorship may affect the face and function of chaplaincy.

The difference between chaplaincy in institutions with religious affiliation and public institutions is more subtle than obvious. The similarities are greater than the differences, for several reasons. Public hospitals are not devoid of spiritual awareness, and religiously affiliated hospitals deal with the same fiscal, ethical, and management issues that public hospitals face. Furthermore, the significance of spiritual factors in healing is broadly recognized today apart from specific religious affiliation. Many staff members in public institutions are people of faith who are concerned about patients' spiritual well-being. Moreover, the provision of spiritual care is mandated for all healthcare institutions by hospital accrediting bodies, so the provision of religious services is by no means exclusive to institutions with religious affiliation.

In the rest of this essay, I reflect on how public versus religious sponsorship may affect chaplaincy, with regard to application of professional standards, the

Cornel G. Rempel is recently retired as a chaplain and Clinical Pastoral Education supervisor, Philhaven Behavioral Healthcare Services, Mount Gretna, Pennsylvania.

chaplain's place in the system, levels of accountability, the chaplain's image, the chaplain's use of authority, and integration of the chaplain's role in the institution. I wish to comment on similarities as well as differences.

Professional standards

Professionals in most fields are certified by a professional association and, as such, are accountable not only to their employer but also to their professional association. The same cannot be said for clergy. Most pastors are accountable to their denominations. Some are accountable only to their congregations. Some ministers are self-appointed. Because of the absence of common standards of practice among clergy, healthcare institutions for too long did not know what to expect from them. Consequently, the spiritual needs of patients were often neglected. The Association of Professional Chaplains (APC) in the United States and the Canadian Association for Pastoral Practice and Education (CAPPE) in Canada are the major professional associations that promote and grant board certification in order to assure a common standard of practice, even though chaplains' religious affiliations and roles will differ from institution to institution. Certification requirements include having completed a Masters of Divinity (M.Div.) or equivalent, ordination or endorsement for specialized ministry from a religious body, a minimum of four units of Clinical Pastoral Education, and demonstration of ministerial and professional competence through a certification process. Maintaining certification calls for adherence to the professional code of ethics and engaging in ongoing professional development.

Employing certified chaplains is in the best interest of a healthcare institution, because doing so assures that the candidate's religious endorsement and professional competence have already been recognized. Certification is also in the best interest of the larger faith community, because it assures that the chaplain is able to function appropriately in a multicultural and multifaith context. Major public medical centers are almost certain to hire only board-certified chaplains in order to avoid the need to establish their own standards for chaplaincy, and in order to offer a level of service in spiritual care that is consistent with the standards of other disciplines in their institutions. For economic reasons, prisons, nursing homes, and retirement centers often opt to hire part-time chaplains without requiring certification. Religiously affiliated facilities may place their emphasis on the chaplain's character and religious affiliation without regard for certification. Hiring uncertified chaplains may perpetuate a lack of clarity regarding what to expect from a chaplain. The specialized ministry to the spiritual needs of people from a wide range of religious backgrounds at a vulnerable time in their lives requires specialized preparation, ongoing professional development, and appropriate accountability in both public and religiously affiliated healthcare institutions.

Place in the system

Public institutions, whether for-profit or not-for-profit entities, are presumably established to fill a need in the community. Religiously affiliated healthcare and social services, on the other hand, have not been established for the sake of profit or on need alone. Rather, they are driven by a moral imperative. This imperative will flow from the sponsoring body's identity and may express itself in offering added value to patient services or providing for the underserved who would otherwise be neglected. The reason for the institution's existence, in addition to its own particular origin and history, will affect chaplaincy in the institution in reference to the chain of command, the allocation of space, the integration of spiritual care in the system, and the scope of expected services.

Religious motivation and history shape medical and spiritual care. This effect is illustrated by the following two examples. Roman Catholic sisters driven by a defined mission to care for the indigent and people with disabilities or addictions have a long history of providing a vast range of healthcare services across the United States and Canada. These healthcare initiatives were unquestionably focused on providing for the underserved and included generous provision of spiritual care on a volunteer basis. A second example is Mennonite initiative to establish mental health centers after World War II, in response to the appeal of Mennonite young men who served as conscientious objectors in the overcrowded and understaffed state hospitals. These men came back to their home communities saying, "There must be a better way." Their persistence and motivation resulted in the establishment of seven community mental health centers across the United States and one in Manitoba, Canada. Chaplaincy in these centers focuses not only on providing spiritual care for clients but also on resourcing staff so that best practice in behavioral sciences would be offered in the spirit of Jesus' ministry.

The mission of public hospitals may be driven by humanitarian values; the mission of hospitals with religious affiliation is presumably driven by the moral and spiritual motivation of their founders. Therefore, the chaplain and administration in the latter are more likely to speak a common language. Spiritual care will be more central to the institution's mission and may be less subject to the vagaries of administrative changes. In a public hospital, transitions in administrative leadership pose a particular risk for chaplaincy. The department of spiritual care may need to revalidate itself each time administrative leadership changes, unless the department is secure by virtue of the institution's mission. For example, pastoral services may fall victim to a budget crunch when seen as a support rather than an essential service. By contrast, in a hospital with religious affiliation, the director of pastoral services is more likely to report to the chief executive officer (CEO), because the CEO shapes and defends the mission of the institution. This relationship gives pastoral service a more direct link to the institution's mission than in a public hospital. In a public hospital, the chaplain is more likely to report to a lower ranking official whose responsibility for a variety of services or departments may place the pastoral services budget at greater risk.

Another subtle difference is that, in public hospitals, chaplaincy is treated as a profession, which functions as a discipline alongside other disciplines. However, hospitals with religious affiliation are more likely to view chaplaincy as a calling. About twenty years ago, when chaplains in a university teaching hospital in Winnipeg were negotiating work schedules, salary, and benefits, hospital administration encouraged them to join an existing union in order to standardize negotiations, because virtually all other staff were unionized. By doing so, the chaplains gained negotiating power. In a hospital with religious affiliation, however, unionizing would undoubtedly be seen as secularization. Adding volunteer on-call time to regular work hours would be the more likely expectation, by virtue of the chaplain's calling. Institutions with religious affiliation typically have the added expectation that the chaplain will represent the mission of the sponsoring faith group and help to keep the institution's mission consistent with the religious values of the sponsoring constituency.

One would expect the significance an institution attaches to spiritual care to be reflected in the allocation of office and chapel space as well. Given the competition for space that exists in most healthcare institutions, it is striking that many public hospitals have given prominent visibility to chapel and chaplain's departments. This may be owing to the chaplain's public relations role and to a concern to make the chaplain as available to the public as possible in a time of crisis.

Accountability

Because chaplains typically serve in a multifaith context in both public institutions and those with religious affiliation, many people assume that chaplains in public hospitals must compromise personal conviction in the interest of nondiscrimination, and that chaplains in an institution with religious affiliation are prone to impose a religious bias. Chaplains themselves are often unclear on these matters. Indeed, chaplains do serve people of all faiths (including nonreligious faiths). The question is, how? Does spiritual caregiving necessitate compromise? Examining the issue of accountability in chaplaincy can provide an answer to these questions.

Most professions maintain accountability and exercise authority based on two factors: their professional credentials and their employment contract. However, in the chaplain's role, regardless of the type of institution, two additional dimensions of accountability apply. If respected, these aspects of accountability can minimize frustration and confusion. One such dimension is personal authority derived from the chaplain's sense of call. Another is ecclesiastical authority granted by the chaplain's faith community. The third and fourth dimensions parallel accountability in other professions: professional authority achieved through credentialing from a professional association, and administrative authority based on the chaplain's job description.

While each of these dimensions provides the chaplain with the authority to function in a prescribed role, each also defines the chaplain's lines of accountability. Exercising personal accountability demands integrity in reference to the chaplain's personal convictions and God's guidance in a given caregiving event. Ecclesiastic accountability calls for appropriate adherence to the chaplain's religious tradition. Professional accountability has to do with maintaining competency and ethical standards of practice. Administrative accountability calls for responsibly to fulfill the employment contract. Proper application of accountability is essential in both secular and faith-based chaplaincy, because religious authority is not the primary concern of the institution. Such accountability serves to assure competent professional practice, to avoid compromise of conviction on the part of the chaplain, and yet to provide comprehensive, consistent, and reliable service.

By way of example, let us suppose that a chaplain scheduled for on-call duty is called to neonatal care because a newborn is at risk, but the chaplain does not show up. The failure to respond is a breach of agreement and therefore subject to administrative accountability. It is an issue to be dealt with by the administration. If, on the other hand, the chaplain appears but gets into an argument with medical staff about the treatment plan, this is a professional issue that not only the administration but also peer supervision must address, because the matter pertains to professional practice. If the chaplain comes and is asked to baptize the infant but declares that offering the sacrament is not appropriate, then the religious affiliation of the chaplain and that of the infant's family come into play. If the chaplain's religious affiliation differs from that of the family, and the chaplain lacks the authority to baptize, then the chaplain is professionally obliged to refer to someone who is able to provide the service. If, however, the chaplain and the family are of the same denomination and the chaplain determines that the circumstances prevailing in this situation do not permit providing baptism, then neither hospital administration nor professional peers can insist that the service should have been provided. This is an ecclesiastical issue that must be handled by the chaplain's supervising ecclesiastical authority. Proper differentiation of authority in both public and religiously affiliated hospitals assures the provision of nondiscriminatory religious services while preserving the chaplain's integrity.

In a hospital with religious affiliation, there is a fifth, albeit subtle, level of accountability, to the faith community that sponsors the institution. I spent time as a chaplain in a Catholic hospital in Winnipeg owned by the Grey Nuns. The influence of the order and of the archbishop of the diocese was much in evidence. Their involvement was supportive, and their expectations were not burdensome. They strongly undergirded spiritual care and expected chaplains to support the moral code of the founders. Later, in my position in a Mennonite behavioral health center in Pennsylvania, I met regularly with the religious welfare committee of the center's board of directors. The committee was made up of three bishops who represented the sponsoring Mennonite conference. Again, this level of consultation and accountability had significant real as well as symbolic value. Accountability is not burdensome when chaplains appropriately distinguish between the administrative, professional, and ecclesiastical spheres in their practice of ministry. On the contrary, it provides structure that authorizes chaplains to function with full integrity in public hospitals and those with religious affiliation.

The chaplain's image

In both public hospitals and those with religious affiliation, the chaplain is seen as one who provides religious services and spiritual care. However, in a public hospital, the pastoral identity may actually remain in sharper focus because the chaplain tends to be seen more exclusively as the keeper of the spiritual keys. When an invocation is needed, the chaplain is called on to offer it. When a conflict of a religious nature arises in patient care, the chaplain is likely to be consulted. In an institution that is deeply rooted in a religious tradition, however, the chaplain's role in reference to spiritual services is less exclusive. Other staff may be just as likely to offer the invocation. They may claim equal authority in spiritual matters and have the freedom to exercise it. Integration in clinical practice is to be applauded. Yet, when clinical staff is encouraged to address spiritual issues in the patient's life in the interest of integration, the chaplain's expertise may inadvertently be underutilized. In both types of hospitals, the chaplain will likely need to take initiative to function collaboratively with medical staff, even though the focus for that initiative may be different in a public hospital setting than in one with religious affiliation.

As already stated, the chaplain is more clearly linked to the founding mission of the institution in a hospital with religious affiliation than in a public institution. This connection no doubt affects how the patient or client may view the chaplain. In my experience in Catholic hospitals, patients expected the sisters to make initial visits without a prior request for spiritual care. The visits were seen as hospitality calls with the intent of welcoming the patient into their care. That practice applies to other centers with religious affiliation as well. In contrast, in a public hospital the patient may initially suspect that the motive of an unsolicited visit is evangelization or bringing bad news. The chaplain in the public institution may also be seen as having a personal mission, while the chaplain in a hospital with religious affiliation may be seen to represent the mission of the sponsoring faith community. This representation function could have a positive or negative effect, depending on the patient's image of the institution's sponsoring body.

Chaplains must always pay careful attention to the use of power. Chaplaincy in any institution functions by virtue of power that is derived both formally and informally. Informal authority or power evolves from trust that is earned through relationships. Formal authority or power is derived from the chaplain's position in the system. In a hospital with religious affiliation, the chaplain may derive additional authority from the sponsoring faith group, which can add weight to the chaplain's role. However, if the chaplain exploits this conferred authority by converting it to personal power, that move can raise resistance in staff, particularly when clinical decisions outside the realm of the chaplain's expertise are involved. Over-spiritualizing a psychiatric diagnosis in a behavioral healthcare setting would be a case in point. Another example: in a hospital where abortions are not provided, on moral grounds, the patient may not trust the chaplain to offer an unbiased hearing on a personal dilemma regarding her pregnancy.

Power and authority, whether derived formally or informally, must be used wisely and with discretion. The chaplain, in best practice, is actively engaged in the system, yet separate enough from the system to be a safe listener, a support, an advisor, and a confidant not only for patients and their families but also for staff. I often marvel at the depth of trust that can be earned and the range of influence a chaplain can exert at many levels in the system. In the course of a day, the chaplain may offer spiritual support to critically ill patients, support families in grief or in the dilemma of making difficult treatment decisions, participate in clinical care conferences, offer consultation to a parish pastor, encourage a member of housekeeping staff, participate in bioethical decision making, conduct a memorial service, and respond to emergency codes. Acceptance and effectiveness grow through wise use of professional authority.

Integration of the chaplain's role

Neither chaplains in hospitals with religious affiliation nor those in public institutions expect or demand a common expression of faith from patients. Both are equally concerned about the patients' spiritual welfare. The difference in type of employing institution is not in the chaplains' motivation or role but in how they are perceived in the institution and how compatible their role is with its mission. In hospitals with religious affiliation, such compatibility is assumed. In public hospitals, participation in ethics committees has resulted in increased credibility of chaplains in the system.

Chaplaincy at its best does not function in isolation; rather, it is integrated into the system, whether in public or religious institutions.[1] Such integration

---

[1] For further discussion of functional integration, see chapters 3 and 15 of the present volume: "Interdisciplinary Teamwork: The Place and Role of the Chaplain as a Caregiver among Medical and Other Caregivers," by Jerry Nussbaum, and "Building Therapeutic Community: The Chaplain as Caregiver for Staff," by Robin Weldon Walton.

is achieved, first, by a well-defined referral system, in which the profession of chaplaincy is fully accepted as a discipline among disciplines. A second dimension of integration derives from the involvement of community clergy in the care of their parishioners while in the hospital and in follow-up care. A third dimension of integration goes beyond viewing spiritual care as a support service, to the intentional integration of spiritual care in the treatment or therapy process itself. Two case studies illustrate dimensions of integration.

The first example comes from the medical unit of a general hospital. Bob (not his real name) was a forty-five-year-old male. His diabetes had reached a critical stage. Infection in his toes had set in, to the extent that amputation might become necessary. However, Bob was denying that he needed help and refused all medication and treatment. He rebuffed all attempts of persuasion from the physician and nurse, who were unable to treat him without consent. Recognizing that Bob was a religious person, the physician consulted the chaplain. The patient's record indicated that Bob's religious affiliation was with a Protestant charismatic group. The chaplain offered to visit Bob without identifying the visit as a referral, in order to avoid being dismissed on suspicion of collusion with medical staff. The chaplain perceived the key issue to be Bob's need for healing, not the physician's need for Bob's compliance.

Bob welcomed the chaplain and volunteered that he was an itinerant minister in aboriginal communities in northern Canada. When the reason for Bob's admission to the hospital came up in conversation, the chaplain discerned that Bob was dealing with a crisis of faith. Bob proceeded to tell the chaplain:

> The doctor is trying to convince me that I have diabetes, but I don't believe that.
>
> *You find it hard to accept what the doctor is saying.*
>
> I don't think it is serious. Besides, I have no need for a doctor. God can heal me without a physician.
>
> *So you want to entrust yourself to God for healing.*
>
> Yes. And if my faith is unwavering, it will happen.
>
> *Are you saying that accepting medical treatment would represent lack of faith on your part?*
>
> God has promised to do whatever we ask in faith. That is what I preach every Sunday.
>
> *And now you want to practice what you preach as a testimony to your faith.*

And I expect God to keep his promise.

Bob, you go from one community to another in the north to preach the gospel. Why do you do that?

God has called me so that the people can hear the gospel message and be saved.

Why doesn't God save them without you?

[emphatically] God called me to proclaim his word. That is how God works. If I didn't preach, they would stay in their lost condition.

You believe that God won't save the people without your preaching but expect God to heal you without the physician. Do you suppose the physician could represent the hand of God in your healing just like God's message of salvation comes to the people through your preaching?

The chaplain left Bob to contemplate the question. On his visit the next day, the chaplain found that Bob was accepting treatment.

The second example is from a behavioral health context: Troubled by guilt, Jan (not her real name) came to a therapist. She was twenty-four years of age and engaged to be married. Now that she anticipated marriage and a family, she was deeply troubled by a decision she had made at the age of eighteen to terminate a pregnancy. During the series of therapy sessions, it became evident that Jan was dealing not just with psychological issues but also with a crisis of faith. The therapist dealt with spiritual and psychological dynamics in helping Jan come to terms with her guilt, but it appeared that Jan needed to seal in her heart what she had come to terms with in her mind.

The therapist was a man of faith who could have initiated a religious ritual of closure, but he recognized that involving a chaplain at this point would introduce an added dimension of spiritual authority. With Jan's permission, the therapist discussed her situation with the chaplain. The chaplain then arranged for Jan and her fiancé to come to the meditation chapel and bring an object that would represent the lost fetus. He also suggested that she prepare a written statement or a prayer to express what she felt she needed to say. The chaplain invited the therapist to be present for support and as a sign that the therapy sessions and religious ritual were components of the same therapeutic process, rather than separate events. The ritual included carefully selected scripture readings and prayers. At a given point, Jan approached the altar and addressed God and her terminated fetus with a tearful confession. Then she placed the rose she had brought at the foot of the cross and left it there as a symbolic act of leaving her lost fetus in the care of a loving God. This act was followed by the chaplain's words of absolution and assurance of forgiveness.

To regard Jan's burden only as a spiritual issue would have been ineffective, because a premature ritual of closure would not have resolved her conflict. The psychological issues also needed to be addressed. However, cognitive therapy alone was not enough to assure healing either. The therapist's recognition that the issue was both psychological and spiritual made Jan's healing more complete. Neither the therapist nor the chaplain acted in isolation. This event represented wholesome integration of the spiritual in the private therapy sessions. It also integrated psychotherapy into pastoral care.

In the first example, separation between the chaplain and the physician was needed to neutralize Bob's resistance. In Jan's case, the presence of the therapist in the ritual of closure was important to symbolize the integration of the psychological and the spiritual in the healing process. Such integration may happen more naturally in a facility with religious affiliation, but it can happen in a public hospital as well. In the first, it may fit into the institutional culture. In the second, it can follow from relationships built between chaplains and the clinical staff.

Conclusion

Chaplaincy focuses on providing spiritual care, not in reference to a particular tradition, but in reference to people's need. However, the religious and cultural orientation of an institution affects the face and function of the spiritual care it provides. Differences in the delivery of spiritual care between public hospitals and institutions with religious affiliation are more subtle than obvious, because of common standards of training for chaplaincy and common standards of professional practice. Furthermore, all institutions that serve the public are expected to be nondiscriminatory.

In the future, increased attention to cultural diversity is likely to result in differences that are more noticeable between institutions of different types. Some public hospitals, for example, already have chapels that feature a worship center for a number of major religious traditions. Chapels in hospitals with religious affiliation will more likely continue to reflect the tradition that sponsors the institution, without denying others the opportunity to worship. Corresponding differences will likely be reflected in the delivery of services. Public hospitals will tend to focus on *spiritual* care more generically, while hospitals with religious affiliation will likely retain a more specific focus on *pastoral* care.[2] Nevertheless, with growing public interest in alternative medicine, a general shift away from a narrow focus on religious doctrine, and a greater interest in spirituality, chaplaincy in institutions of both kinds will continue to have a significant role in the healing arts in the years ahead.

---

[2] For more on the distinction between *spiritual* and *pastoral* care, see the introduction to this book.

Intercultural awareness in spiritual caregiving

An invitation to dance with God

Luis Elier Rodríguez

In the last four years, I have come to see myself as a dancer. Normally, I go twice a week to a studio to dance and learn different steps. These steps are connected; they reflect the unity between my dancing partner and me. Each dance has its own significance. For example, salsa and merengue are related to my country, Puerto Rico, and my culture. I have learned the fox-trot, swing, cumbia, and country western dances. They are evidence of cultural diversity and have become a bridge between my culture and other cultures. I have learned some of the dances of the Pueblo Indians of New Mexico and so forged a connection with Native American culture. I have practiced the tango, which symbolizes the passion and suffering of European immigrants to Argentina. They danced because they felt the suffering of exile. Likewise, I dance the tango when I feel nostalgia for my country. I left Puerto Rico as a pilgrim, and I do not know if I will ever go back home.

I feel interconnectedness with humanity when I dance. For this reason, for me the image of dancer represents the challenges and joys of spiritual caregiving. Both the confusion and frustration of learning new dance steps as well as the rewards and fruits of communicating well with one's partner suggest dynamics that are at work within caregiving relationships. Caregiving, like dancing, is sometimes difficult and requires much effort. Spiritual caregiving in the hospital is one special dance within the broader community of care. We might say that it has a unique place in the studio of the universe. Each step connects to the larger harmony of the dance as a whole.

Dancing with the creator

God, as creator of the cosmos,[1] has established interconnection between all things in the universe. Galaxies depend on one another through gravity.[2] Electromagnetic and nuclear equilibrium sustains the symphony of the uni-

---

Luis Elier Rodríguez is a chaplain and CPE supervisor of Harris County Hospital District, Houston, Texas.

[1] Genesis 1.

[2] Leonardo Boff, *Cry of the Earth, Cry of the Poor* (New York: Maryknoll, 1997), 159–61.

verse, preventing chaotic events from destroying the harmonic whole.[3] Such interconnection inspires beings to communicate with one another. Living creatures listen to one another's voices and hear the story that each tells in a process spanning billions of years.[4] Listening to the voice of the other is not merely a metaphor; it is grounded in human nature. Moisés Lopes, a Mennonite Indian pastor from Guatemala without formal education, explains: "The mountain hears the voice of the wind and interaction is established between the two—the wind with the trees, the trees with the animals, the animals with the atmosphere, and the human being, holistically, with all these beings, events, and so forth."[5] One responds to the other, keeping the dynamic equilibrium established between them.

This manner of listening to stories evokes the experiences of my formation as a chaplain and CPE supervisor. Each of us has a family and social story that affects our lives. I have a son with muscular dystrophy. This has been a source of much suffering. It is a sad story. Every time I see him losing more of his physical capacities, I feel like the earth is calling him. Yet the best experience of my life has been to know and love him. When I talk about my son's situation, I feel that I am dancing with both sadness and gratitude to God for letting us find each other. In the same way, I am present with patients so that they can express their stories; I listen as the mountain listens to the voice of the wind.

Having five sisters and four brothers has helped me appreciate theological and ideological diversity. My father attended a Pentecostal church. My mother also attended but had a close relationship with a Catholic group as well. My sisters attended a Baptist church, and one brother associated with an independent movement. My oldest brother declared himself a humanist, and the third and fourth brothers said they did not care for any discourse about God, because the most important aspect of any religion is simply the practice of love toward one's neighbor. When I was twelve years old, my father asked me if I believed in God; I told him, "Yes." Then he asked me if I wanted to continue going church; I said, "No." My father understood and gave me permission not to attend church anymore. Every night before I went to sleep, my mother came to my bedside, and we prayed the Lord's Prayer. These experiences have led me to see God as the creator of the dance of diversity.

Celebrating diversity

According to Brazilian theologian Leonardo Boff, a Franciscan, nothing is as contrary to the nature of the universe as homogeneity—imposing on the world a single idea, a single conviction, a single way of living together, or a

---

[3] Ibid., 163.

[4] Leonardo Boff, El Despertar del Águila (Madrid: Editorial Trotta, 2000), 74.

[5] Moisés Lopes, personal communication.

single way of praying and speaking of God.[6] Just as we respect biodiversity, we must also accept religious diversity and ideological diversity. Boff also suggests that God created interdependence as the sustaining structure of the universe, whereby the unity of the cosmos, the earth, and humanity is made up of a variety of cultures and peoples.[7] The perspective that diversity is a given informs me as a CPE supervisor, as I welcome students of different ages, ethnicities, gender, sexual orientation, ideology, and religious background. Respect for diversity is a key to developing multicultural competence and understanding the cultural beliefs and values of others.

As a spiritual caregiver, I ask myself, "How can we be culturally aware and competent?" The Standards Manual of the Association for Clinical Pastoral Education (ACPE), revised in 2005, now requires multicultural competency in spiritual caregiving.[8] The common *Code of Ethics* for chaplains, pastoral educators, and students of Clinical Pastoral Education (CPE) delineates the ethical principles to be upheld when relating to patients and families. Students and supervisors of CPE must demonstrate respect for the cultural and religious values of those they serve and refrain from imposing their own values and beliefs on them.

From my perspective, the new focus on intercultural competence challenges us to reflect on how we can provide empathetic and effective spiritual care in the midst of cross-cultural differences. These objectives address issues of cultural and spiritual sensitivity. They include factors such as ethnicity, language, geographical and historical location, values and ideals, habits of thinking, artistic expression, patterns of social and interpersonal relationships, and customs and norms. Our challenge is to have genuine respect for the differences among members of the healthcare team, as well as among patients and families. Such respect builds bridges between us and others. Competent spiritual caregivers pay attention to cross-cultural dynamics as these dynamics emerge in caregiving situations. Caregivers take time to identify aspects of the patient's culture, such as rituals, concepts of power, and family history, that play a role in the caregiving interaction. I suggest two possible approaches to the practice of intercultural awareness:

- Provide patients with the opportunity to speak about their culture and about how they think it might influence their struggle with illness or their stay at the hospital.
- Ask patients if there are particular ways the hospital staff can communicate respect and understanding in light of their cultural context.

---

[6] Boff, *Cry of the Earth*, 159–61.

[7] Ibid., 163.

[8] See the appendix at the end of this chapter for specific multicultural competency objectives.

David Augsburger, in *Pastoral Counseling across Cultures*, distinguishes five measurable and teachable characteristics that protect the counselor, the counselee, and the counseling process from being culturally oppressive:[9]

- Culturally aware counselors have a clear understanding of their own values and basic assumptions.
- Culturally aware counselors have a capacity for welcoming, entering into, and prizing other worldviews.
- Culturally aware counselors see sources of influence in both the person and the context, both the individual instance and the environment.
- Culturally aware counselors are able to move beyond counseling theory, orientation, or technique, to be effective humans.
- Culturally aware counselors see themselves as universal citizens, related to all humans as well as distinct from all of them.

I agree with Augsburger that the terms *diversity* and *multiculturalism* imply that a plurality of cultures exists and that cultures are themselves heterogeneous. I wish to go a step further and emphasize the importance of acknowledging and valuing the voices of the *othered*, that is, those who are ethnically or culturally different and who are marginalized and under-represented. Intercultural competence requires the disposition to care and the skills to communicate with others, especially with those who have been under-represented, under-valued, neglected, ignored, exploited, and cruelly treated. I think that our challenge as educators and spiritual caregivers is to refine the concept of multiculturalism to focus on the othered or marginalized cultures. In order to afford minority cultures a livable space, the dominant culture must not only accommodate but also welcome the people of these cultures in ways that allow for mutual transformation.

According to Robert Muller, the multiplicity of beings, the biodiversity, and the diversity of the constructive energies in the universe point to the diversified activity of the Spirit who values difference.[10] Within human community, the Spirit grants many talents and enters the Christian community through many charismas, as St. Paul attests (1 Cor. 12:7-11). Jürgen Moltmann states, "What is valid for the community of faith is valid for the cosmic, planetary, and human community. It is like this because there exists a relationship between cosmic community and community of faith. One can not live without the other."[11] In other words, the harmonizing work of the Spirit is manifest in both the cosmos and the church.

---

[9] Augsburger, *Pastoral Counseling across Cultures* (Philadelphia: Westminster Press, 1986), 20–22.

[10] Robert Muller, *El Nacimiento de la Civilización Global* (San Paulo: Aquariana, 1993), 80–83.

[11] Jürgen Moltmann, *God in Creation: A New Theology of Creation and the Spirit of God* (San Francisco: Harper & Row, 1985), 159.

Appreciation of the range of the Spirit's gifts and expressions grows out of coming to know oneself in relationships with others. For example, Chris was a CPE student from a Catholic background. Chris had converted to Protestantism a number of years ago in a Baptist church and had begun to feel persecuted by members of his family. Chris admitted that he had a negative view of Catholicism. Having Arthur, a Catholic deacon, as a peer helped Chris revise his perceptions and redirect his attitude toward Catholics. As a result of interactions with Arthur in the CPE group, Chris learned to appreciate and respect Arthur and his Catholic tradition.

Liberation Theology has much in common with ecological discourse. These perspectives argue that we must treat the poor, minorities, women, and children, as well as flora, fauna, and the ecosystem, with respect, care, and dignity.[12] We must acknowledge that the wound of poverty breaks the social fabric of many millions of people around the world. Another wound, the systematic assault on the Earth, breaks down the balance of the planet, currently threatened by the plundering development practiced by our global society. Each of these wounds has as its starting point a cry: the cry of the poor for life, freedom, and beauty (Exod. 3:7) and the cry of the earth groaning from oppression (Rom. 8:22-23).

It is common knowledge that a small percent of the human population, especially in the highly industrialized countries, consumes the large majority of the earth's resources. Millions of children die of hunger related to disease before they are five days old, and many more are under-nourished or go hungry all the time. Such injustice is paralleled by the great number of Hispanics living in the United States who do not have access to healthcare because of the language barrier or lack of economic resources.

These same barriers block many Hispanics in the United States from access to the services of a chaplain who speaks their native language. For example, 82 percent of the patients at Baptist Medical Center in San Antonio, Texas, are Hispanic, yet the hospital has no CPE resident who speaks Spanish. It is common to see chaplains there offering spiritual care to Hispanics in English, with a translator next to them. The population of San Antonio is 75 percent Hispanic, yet at this time there is no CPE program in Spanish. In spite of the fact that Hispanics are the largest minority in the United States, CPE is offered in Spanish in only a handful of U.S. locations. This reality has shaped my role as a supervisor; it calls me to continue offering CPE in Spanish, so that students and patients can speak their primary psychological, emotional, and spiritual language. The need for chaplains who can speak to patients in the language they understand challenges me to encourage students from other cultures and minorities to consider CPE and to become certified chaplains.

---

[12] Boff, *El Despertar*, 74.

I offer one example of the challenging diversity that occurred in a unit of Spanish CPE that I taught at Baptist Health System. I provided supervision to students from Brazil, Colombia, Texas, and Ecuador. This was a trilingual unit, in which participants spoke English, Spanish, and Portuguese. On various occasions, I asked Anna to speak first in Portuguese and then tell me in English what occurred inside her. I suggested this approach because I understood that at that moment she was feeling profound emotions. I knew that expressing herself in her primary emotional, psychological, and theological language would benefit her. This practice contributed to a developing sensitivity to the diversity of languages within the group. In this situation, the CPE group functioned as a kind of ecosystem where we needed one another, gave support and affirmation, confronted one another, and danced with diversity.

My experience working at Harris County Hospital District in Houston, where we have department translators for fifty-two languages, helps me understand that we are living in a multicultural society with new faces and new languages, accents, and intonations. More than 250 languages are spoken in the United States today. This multicultural reality motivated me to start a Spanish-speaking CPE unit in Houston, because this city has a large population of Hispanics; Caucasians are becoming a minority in Texas. I chose a multicultural composition of participants for this residency program, accepting two Africans, one Asian, one Hispanic, one African American, and two Caucasians.

The dance of communication

Communication provides another illustration of the image of God as a dancer. To communicate means to open ourselves, break the closed circle of our own identity, and welcome the other. Communication is a process of self-transcendence. The Holy Spirit enables this communication and the establishment of relationship in all directions. In the words of Martin Buber, "All actual life is encounter."[13] For these reasons, the human spirit seeks socialization and communication. It always coexists as a mode of relationship; the self is constituted on the basis of interplay with others, with whom it engages in reciprocity and complementarity. This awareness helps me as a chaplain and supervisor to put more effort into my communication with patients and students. For example, during a session of individual supervision with Martin, I stopped in the midst of our conversation, because I had the impression that Martin was not listening to my life history. We were able to renegotiate the conversation and begin again. I was able to communicate to Martin what I perceived and to confront him. I felt that God was present in our renegotiations and in my authority to confront him.

I went to the Southwest Region Certification Committee in March 2002, requesting a translator from the region, because I understood the

---

[13] Martin Buber, I and Thou (New York: Scribner, 1970), 64.

importance of guaranteeing clear communication. I did this as a way of affirming theologically that God is manifest in different cultures, languages, and ethnicities. I challenged them to continue to become multilingual. As a result, the Southwest Region accepted the responsibility of opening itself to a new history and to the generation of CPE minorities. During my meeting with the Certification Committee, I was able to express the importance of my ethnicity in my work as a supervisor.

Dancing with God as creator of *ruach*

God relates to human beings and to the universe as dancer and creator of *ruach*, a feminine noun that is the Hebrew word for "spirit." The spirit is what makes us human. According to Judeo-Christian tradition, humans—male and female—have been created in the image and likeness of God (Gen. 1:26-27).

Christians view and yearn for full humanity in the light of Jesus, whose life and ministry demonstrated the way of wholeness, including healthy relationships between women and men. All of Jesus's dynamism, his option for the poor, and his courage to confront the opposition, even to his death, reveal his commitment to this vision of wholeness. Therefore, it is no wonder that he established caring relationships with the women he met; some became his disciples. According to the Gospels, Jesus had a special concern for people who were in need, oppressed, marginalized, sick, and sinful—women as well as men. He declared his wish to unite the children of Jerusalem as a hen gathers her chicks under her wings. One might suggest that a feminine dimension belonged to Jesus' humanity as much as did a masculine dimension.[14]

As chaplain and CPE supervisor, I am inspired to promote pastoral and educational companionship and collegiality between women and men as patients and as CPE students. For example, I listened to the pain of Mirta, who said she wanted to be a pastor but her denomination would not support women as pastors. I invited her to dream about her desire to be a minister and to use the group as a resource for discovering her ministerial possibilities. I seek to promote equality between men and women and to be in solidarity with the feminist movement. This is why I agree with Judith Plant when she states that the earth has been raped and that men have similarly mistreated women and made them feel inferior.[15] As CPE supervisor, I promote equality among students. I invite them to experience the constructive anger, guilt, and grief that are appropriate when they become aware of the continuing rape of the earth and the violence of inequality between women and men.

---

[14] For a systematic theological anthropology of the feminine, see Leonardo Boff, *The Maternal Face of God: The Feminine and its Religious Expressions* (San Francisco: Harper & Row, 1987), 61–100.

[15] Judith Plant, *Healing the Wounds: The Promise of Ecofeminism* (Philadelphia: New Society Publishers, 1989), 58–60.

It has been a struggle for me to feel the freedom to cry, to feel compassion, and to guide the learning process of students, for I come from a family in which I never saw my father cry, except when my mother died. To the extent that I can integrate within myself masculine and feminine characteristics, I become a more competent chaplain and supervisor. I can thus share my own pain and empathize with those who suffer. For example, when a student in a group narrated that she had been molested and that she was still suffering, I felt connected to her in her pain and was able to cry with her.

In addition to the meaning of *ruach* as spirit, the word also connotes meaning. Everything that human beings encounter can be meaningful. A fact is never merely a fact; it is something to be interpreted. The human being is capable of symbolizing, adding something to what is given, and seeing the phenomenon as a bearer of manifest or hidden meaning. I practice this process in my chaplaincy experience by constantly asking myself what the experience I am living means to me. Sometimes I ask my patients or students what their tears mean in order to help them become aware of what is going on. For example, Dominick expected a lot from himself. He battered himself emotionally and spiritually, assuming that he could never please God. By exploring the nature of his perfectionism, he realized that he perceived God as a super-teacher who gave him assignments that he could not fulfill. Dominick then considered the meaning of grace, and integrated grace more adequately into his life. He was eventually able to transform the image of such a strict and demanding God.

Dancing with the peacemaker

God calls us to relate to one another through action and reflection. For example, an Anabaptist saying states that the only way to know Jesus is by following him in actual life, by living according to the way of love, peace, and justice.[16] For Mennonites and other Anabaptist groups, the normative nucleus of human relationship centers on the Sermon on the Mount, in which love, service, justice, and truth are declared to constitute the fundamental axis of human relationships. Such a summons for peace *(shalom)* certainly includes the call to care for our planet.

John Howard Yoder, Mennonite theologian, in *The Politics of Jesus*, observes that the biblical concept of shalom includes peace, justice, welfare, and salvation in an intimate relationship with the symbol of God's kingdom. For Yoder, peace has to do with relationships of welfare and not simply tranquility of the spirit or serenity. Yoder states that peace, justice, and salvation are

---

[16] The saying originates with Hans Denck, who stated that it is impossible to know Christ unless one follows Jesus daily and, conversely, it is not possible to follow him if one does not know him. Walter Klaassen, *Anabaptism: Neither Catholic nor Protestant* (Waterloo: Conrad Press, 1973), 19–27.

synonyms for the general welfare of human relationships and for creation.[17] I would point out that shalom includes an intimate relationship with our planet's ecosystem. The concept of shalom has helped me develop a model of supervision underlined by democratic leadership. On occasion, I ask the CPE group to talk about who has dominated the session and how power has been distributed among the group. In one instance, this helped Adam to understand and form awareness of his tendency to dominate conversation in the group. When the group was not talking about him, he felt bored. Eventually he became aware that his tendency to talk all the time distanced him from the group and prevented him from hearing what the group had to say. Shalom suggests that leadership will be democratic, because it is leadership concerned with justice.

In *Community and Commitment*, Mennonite theologian John Driver presents shalom as an essential element of relationship between human beings and God.[18] Shalom includes health and human welfare in its spiritual and material aspects. Shalom is created when we strive for the common good and when we treat people with justice and respect. Similarly, when there is greed for unjust gain, when there are not equal opportunities for all, or when economic oppression causes suffering, we cannot say there is peace. When I read the prophets' call for economic justice, I think of John Driver's words. Those biblical and theological sources are indispensable to the development of a ministerial ecology.

As a Mennonite, I share my theological tradition when I promote the value of respect for neighbor in honor of the diversity of creation, and when I work for relationships of peace. This tradition has helped me as a chaplain and supervisor in my interactions with three supervisors in training (SIT) members who are in the army and come to the SIT meetings in their military uniforms. To be with three soldiers in the CPE context has helped me see the SIT group as a kind of ecosystem. The friendships that I have developed with them and my learning from them have been profound. I have also been able to supervise Hugh, a student whose goal is to be a military chaplain in the United States Army. My experience in the refugee camps of Honduras and Nicaragua in the 1980s helped me develop openness to others regardless of their beliefs, because we received any people who had been wounded, whether by the guerrillas or by the contras (the army). Peace means respect in the midst of diversity. It does not mean that we have to agree theologically but that we remain open to establishing and maintaining relationships with people of different perspectives.

---

[17] John H. Yoder, *The Politics of Jesus* (Grand Rapids: Eerdmans, 1972), 80–100.

[18] John Driver, *Community and Commitment* (Scottdale: Herald Press, 1976), 71.

Dancing our cultural competencies in spiritual care

Based on my reading and reflections on my experience as a professional chaplain and CPE supervisor, I consider the following specific competencies essential for professional chaplains, CPE students, and CPE supervisors. As spiritual caregivers become more skillful dancers, they provide support and empathic presence, with an awareness of and sensitivity to cultural and contextual issues. Competent caregivers demonstrate the following skills:

- Ability to narrate stories within a cultural framework and to have a sense of one's own personal cultural profile, to research one's family tree, and to learn more about the cultures of one's ancestry. Becoming aware of one's own assumptions is of utmost importance if one is to appreciate the cultural and spiritual values and customs of others.[19]

- Awareness of biases, stereotypes, and prejudices. When racist attitudes are uncovered, it is possible to experience new learnings for the sake of racial justice."[20]

- Ability to assess patients' spiritual condition, including the role of culture, and patients' sense of finding sustenance or aggravation in the struggle.

- Understanding of ethnic identity and the distinctive path of identity formation in minority and majority contexts. For example, in some cultures, family includes non-blood relationships such as those with godparents or neighbors. It is necessary to determine how patients define *family.*

- Practice of respect and cultural sensitivity towards people of all religious customs and beliefs.

- Awareness of minorities' experiences of institutional barriers.

- Willingness to facilitate referrals when culturally appropriate.

- Awareness of bias or discrimination in response to language and accents.

- Caution in exercising nonverbal signals and cues, which may have different meanings in another culture.

- Use of simple language in cases of translation into another language. Avoidance of jargon, slang, and idioms.

- Awareness of potentially hostile environments for people who are gay, lesbian, bisexual, or transgender. They have the right to a non-hostile environment. Competent spiritual caregivers have the

---

[19] Gerald Corey and Marianne Schneider Corey, eds., *Issues and Ethics in the Helping Profession* (Pacific Grove: Brooks/Cole, 2003), 36–50.

[20] "Social Strata Inventory," in Katherine R. Allen, Stacey M. Floyd-Thomas, and Laura Gillman, "Teaching to Transform: From Volatility to Solidarity in an Interdisciplinary Family Studies Classroom," *Family Relations* 50, no. 4 (October 2001): 324–25.

courage to talk with, or provide spiritual support to, someone whose sexual orientation is different from their own.

* Awareness of patients' perceptions of power and the implications for spiritual care. People's power perceptions may vary because of cultural differences, tending toward either high power distance or low power distance. High power distance is the typical perspective of the powerless; they perceive that they cannot change the system, and they accept inequality as a given in life. At the other extreme, proponents of low power distance think that inequality can and should be minimized. They feel powerful and close to power; they believe that they can gain more power, for example, through education. Competent spiritual caregivers are aware of culture's impact on perceptions of power and of how culture influences spiritual care.[21]

These intercultural competencies help us provide spiritual care and CPE supervision to people of any gender, sexual orientation, age, race, ideology, and religious background. Such skills challenge us to increase our sensitivity and to accept that intercultural understanding takes time, attention, and self-awareness. Welcome to this multicultural learning process!

Appendix

Association for Clinical Pastoral Education
Standards for Multicultural Competency[22]

Code of Ethics	101.4 Avoid the imposition of theology or *cultural values* on those served or supervised
Level I	311.2 Pastoral Formation: identify and discuss major life events, relationships and *cultural contexts* that influence personal identity as expressed in pastoral functioning.
	311.7 Pastoral Competence: initiate helping relationships *within and across diverse populations*
Level II	312:2 Pastoral Competence: provide pastoral ministry to diverse people, taking into consideration multiple elements of *cultural and ethnic differences*, social conditions, systems, and justice issues without imposing one's own perspectives

---

[21] For a full description of high and low power distance see Geert H. Hofstede, *Culture's Consequences: International Differences in Work-Related Values* (Beverly Hills: Sage Publications, 1984), 70–108.

[22] The following information comes from *Standards of the Association for Clinical Pastoral Education, Inc., 2005* (Decatur: ACPE, 2005), 2, 9-13. emphasis added.

312.6 Pastoral Competence: demonstrate competent use of self in ministry and administrative function which includes: emotional availability, *cultural humility*, appropriate self-disclosure, positive use of power and authority, a non-anxious and non-judgmental presence, and clear and responsible boundaries.

CPE Supervisor

315.6 Competence as Pastoral Supervisor: Awareness of *how one's culture affects* professional and personal identity, pastoral practice, the supervisory relationship, and student learning.

316.3 Competence in Theories of Supervision: Articulate rationale for *multicultural competence*, integrating the theory of practice of CPE, which is based on and congruent with one's theology.

317.5 Competence in the Practice of CPE Supervision. Use one's personality and personal, religious and *cultural history* as a teaching resource in shaping a personal supervisory style.

Principles and practices of self-care

Myra Raab

The well-known author Norman Vincent Peale states: "The first person one must learn to love is oneself. If you do not respect and esteem yourself, you will not be able to love anyone else.[1]

Self-care in ministry sounds like an oxymoron because *self-care* focuses on the minister, and *ministry* focuses on the other. How can a chaplain do both at the same time? This essay starts with the premise that self-care in ministry is not an either-or option. Rather, ministry and self-care should happen in tandem and in balance. Excessive focus on self-care leads to narcissism and missed opportunities for ministry. Exclusive focus on ministry without self-care becomes empty and rote, leading to stress and burnout.

Caring for oneself needs to be as holistic as caring extended to others. Holistic care stems from the recognition that a person has physical, emotional, mental, and spiritual needs. In *The Wounded Healer*, Henri Nouwen challenges those who hope to care competently for others to take responsibility for all aspects of their own being. Nouwen asserts that those who are able to articulate their own experience can offer themselves to others as a source of orientation.[2] Ministry with integrity calls us to continued growth, both personally and professionally. Such growth means discovering all that God intended us to be, in order to help others discover all that God intended them to be.

Self-care while caring for others

Self-care means practicing what we preach as we encourage patients to allow their bodies to heal. Self-care can prevent us from becoming patients ourselves as we step out of the mainstream of life and allow our physical body to catch up with our mind and emotions, so to speak. In this way, we become whole again.

Myra Raab is a chaplain and manager, Center for Spiritual Care, Saint John's Health System, Anderson, Indiana.

[1] Norman Vincent Peale, *A Treasury of Courage and Confidence* (New York: Peale Center for Christian Living, 1996), 106.

[2] Henri Nouwen, *The Wounded Healer* (New York: Doubleday, 1972), 38.

Recently a patient was talking to me about his faith and patterns of rela-tionship. In our conversation, he quoted the saying of Jesus, "It is more blessed to give than to receive."[3] When taken out of context, this statement may seem to negate the need for awareness of one's own needs and to focus only on taking care of the need of others. The verse, no doubt, unconsciously and consciously shapes the theology of many caregivers, often to the extent that caregivers find receiving unnatural and embarrassing. A misinterpretation of these words occurs when we fail to include ourselves among those on the receiving end of our care. No one knows better what we need than we our-selves. It is appropriate and necessary to give to ourselves life-giving gifts.

Failure to care for ourselves or to ask for and welcome care from others while we continue giving leads to a loss of vision. We lose track of why we do what we do and whom we are doing it for. Eventually, lack of self-care also leads to emotional, mental, physical, and spiritual exhaustion. Perhaps the patient above was repeating to himself, "It is more blessed to give than to receive," and this mantra contributed to his need for hospitalization. Who knows?

· If the fuel in an oil lamp is not replenished, the light becomes dim and eventually fails to serve its purpose. Similarly, our caring burns dim without replenishment. Caring for others and caring for oneself need not contradict each other. The two efforts become partners in the dance of spiritual care-giving.

Recognizing needs is the first step toward self-care. Most caregivers make decisions based on what they value rather than on the logic of a situation. For example, in my intense care for others, the question sometimes arises, "Do I take time to go to the bathroom now, or do I move on to the need that is waiting for me in the emergency room?" To make a decision based on what I value dictates that my bladder can hold a little more urine, because the grieving, scared patient or family member is waiting impatiently for me to come. Considering the logic of the situation, I realize the patient or family member likely has lost a sense of time, a nurse or volunteer is present with them until I get there and, if I take the time to go to the bathroom, I will be more comfortable as I minister to that patient and the family. Further, taking time to go to the bathroom and pause for a drink of water may reduce the number of bladder infections I will suffer. Thus, taking care of ourselves at the simplest level starts with a practice that is symbolic of self-care in the early years of life, namely, going to the bathroom. Such an elementary, intentional act reflects a basic spiritual caregiving principle. It is a kind of emptying of self so that we can be present to others.

A more complex need caregivers must recognize is their need to come to terms with the trauma that we witness. Some years ago, when I was beginning my chaplaincy ministry, I interviewed a chaplain who had recently retired. I

---

[3] Acts 20:35.

do not remember the question I asked her, but I do remember her response. She started telling me a story about ministering to a mother and father after the death of their child. As she told me the story, tears began running down her cheeks. At an appropriate time, I asked her, "How long ago did this happen?" She said, "Twenty years ago. I haven't thought about that incident in a very long time." Her response caught me by surprise because the tears spoke of a memory that was alive and potent in her being, despite the passage of many years. Her response also suggested to me that the experiences we have as chaplains—even when we feel we have processed them and have taken care of ourselves—often hide from the self-examining inner eye.

When flashbacks of ministry situations occur, it is helpful to let the memory surface and to reflect on how this experience has shaped one's life and ministry. A scene from the morgue—a teenage girl who had died while trying to climb out of a wrecked car—rushes through my mind. Rigor mortis had set in before the accident scene was discovered. When I saw her, she lay on a stainless steel morgue table in the same climbing position she was in at the time of her death. As I looked at her lifeless body, my mind rehearsed the panic, the fear, the cries for help, and the numbness of the accident itself that may have been hers before she died. My thoughts turned toward her parents, whom authorities had advised not to see their daughter in these circumstances but rather to wait to see her body at the funeral home. In the midst of recalling this trauma, my maternal instinct wonders about my own daughter's safety and feels my need to hug her. "Lord, have mercy" becomes the prayer of my heart.

Hospital chaplains, more than other ministering persons, are frequently exposed to trauma. As we minister to the traumatized, we are likely to experience trauma. Pat Sheehan suggests that those who counsel victims and survivors of trauma pay a price for having their hearts open to so much pain. She believes caring professionals know cognitively and intuitively that traumatized people need authentic connection with another human being: "Staying in a detached professional position will not be effective. As our hearts go out to those we minister to in traumatic situations, we also open our hearts, minds, and bodies to the horror, the tragedy, and the evil they have experienced. We thereby run the risk of compassion fatigue."[4] Sheehan uses the term *compassion fatigue* to describe the secondary traumatic stress syndrome that results from exposure to others' traumatic stories and from wanting to help traumatized people. As caregivers, we cannot know precisely the impact a given situation will have on our emotions and our soul.

---

[4] Pat Sheehan, "Healing the Healer: Identifying and Recovering from Compassion Fatigue" (workshop presentation, Kindred Spirits on the Edge, Indianapolis, Indiana, 20–22 March 1998). The event was sponsored by the Association of Humanistic Psychology, the Institute of Noetic Sciences, Indianapolis Gestalt Institute, Peace Works International Network for the Dances of Universal Peace, and *Personal Transformation* magazine.

In ministering to others, we encounter fear, anger, and sadness that mirror our own fear, anger, and sadness. In the best case, we welcome intense caregiving experience as a way to further understand and integrate our sense of identity and vocation in relation to God and others. In the worst case, we ignore or disregard the impact that ministry with others has on us. The cost to us continues to mount, and eventually, in the name of Christ, we die giving our life for others. It may be that our death is not physical but emotional, mental, or spiritual, characterized by depression, isolation, numbness, joylessness, judgmentalism, and lack of compassion or connection.

Holistic self-care

Chaplaincy ministry has shaped me more than I have shaped it. I simply try to honor the same life-giving principles that Jesus practiced when he healed the ill, the broken-hearted, the demon-possessed, and those held by a captivity of their own making. In so doing, I grapple with these words of Jesus: "'You shall love the Lord your God with all your heart, and with all your soul, and with all your mind.' This is the greatest and first commandment. And a second is like it: 'You shall love your neighbor as yourself.' On these two commandments hang all the law and the prophets." [5]

Self-care starts with understanding what it means to love the neighbor as oneself. Scripture introduces the commandment to love self and neighbor in the words to the Israelites about holiness in personal conduct, found in the book of Leviticus. As rationale for their obedience, God says, "You must be holy because I the Lord am holy." [6] Holiness and holistic health care begin with loving God, self, and others.

To understand self-love, it is essential to understand love itself. Self-love is not romantic love, nor is it narcissistic love, in which one is enamored with a total concern for self. Gerald May captures the essence of love when he describes it as "the fundamental energy of the human spirit, the fuel on which we run, the wellspring of our vitality." He adds that grace, "the flowing creative activity of love itself," makes loving possible. [7] Loving self can be an act of grace that gives life and restores to wholeness.

Both self-love and caregiving are rooted in the understanding that the caregiver and the one cared for are created in the image of God. God is love, and love is as essential to our whole being as blood is to our physical bodies. Love is an energy that flows through us and gives life. This energy within us is essential to our answering God's call to re-present divine love to others. Through love, all dimensions of grace—redemption, transformation, and sustenance—are possible. Healing and love for ourselves and our neighbors

---

[5] Matt. 22:37-40.

[6] See Leviticus 19:2, 18.

[7] Gerald G. May, *The Awakened Heart* (San Francisco: Harper Collins, 1991), 3.

are God's salvation at work. Salvation is the experience of wholeness and of God's holiness.

To extend love to self requires self-awareness. May suggests that when we accept the invitation of love, our minds awaken to our hearts.[8] Self-awareness is intentional; it requires deliberately paying attention to the patterns of our mind, our emotions, our bodies, our souls, and how they interact, so that our words and actions may better represent God's love and healing in the world.

Failure to spend such time with oneself and lack of healthy personal boundaries are two obstacles to deepening self-awareness. Maintaining healthy boundaries is essential in caring for oneself while caring for others. A boundary is the invisible line that surrounds me—the line that distinguishes me from another person. Boundaries serve to define, protect, and guide us. They are not meant as fences that divide and keep us separate from other people and their needs. Boundaries help us recognize which issues are ours and which belong to other people. They help us discern what God invites us to do in caring for the other. Charles L. Whitfield's book, *Boundaries and Relationships*, is particularly helpful for understanding the role boundaries play in healthy relationships.[9] When caregivers have little awareness of who they are in relation to God, self, and others, they may live in a frenzy of trying to meet every need that presents itself, because they experience each need as their own.

To care for self and others requires an awareness of where one's personal reality begins and ends. A nurse commented about a CPE student's ministry during a time of crisis, "He did a really great job. He knew when to move in to be with the family and when to step back." Her remark affirms the appropriate operation of self-awareness and boundaries in ministry. Without an adequate sense of self and a sense of the other's needs, it is difficult to stay separate and objective in order to be a helping presence in a time of crisis. Remaining separate allowed this chaplain to take care of himself while showing great sensitivity to the needs of the patient's family.

The person being cared for is not responsible to set healthy boundaries for the caregiver. Healthy self-care is dependent on caregivers knowing their inner life and setting healthy boundaries. Without such boundaries, caregivers soon experience burnout and stress. Recognizing their symptoms of burnout or stress can help caregivers reexamine boundaries. Marion J. Heisey has identified the following symptoms of burnout and stress:[10]

---

[8] Ibid., 49, 68.

[9] Charles L. Whitfield, *Boundaries and Relationships* (Deerfield, IL: Health Communications, 1993). This book includes a boundary inventory that elicits helpful reflection about one's sense of boundaries.

[10] Marion J. Heisey, Mennonite Health Assembly seminar, "The Care Giving Dilemma," March 23, 2001, Albuquerque, New Mexico.

- Burnout is a defense characterized by disengagement.
  Stress is characterized by over-engagement.
- In burnout, the emotions become blunted.
  In stress, the emotions become over-reactive.
- In burnout, emotional damage is primary.
  In stress, physical damage is primary.
- The exhaustion of burnout affects motivation and drive.
  The exhaustion of stress affects physical energy.
- Burnout produces demoralization.
  Stress produces disintegration.
- Burnout can best be understood as a loss of ideals and hope.
  Stress can best be understood as a loss of fuel and energy.
- Burnout produces a sense of helplessness and hopelessness.
  Stress produces a sense of urgency and hyperactivity.
- Burnout produces paranoia, depersonalization, and detachment.
  Stress produces panic, phobic, and anxiety-type disorders.
- Burnout may never kill caregivers, but their long life may not
  seem worth living.
  Stress may kill caregivers prematurely, and they will not have
  enough time to finish what they have started.

Either burnout or stress may lead to poor decisionmaking. In the last five years, I have seen two talented and gifted chaplains make poor decisions with legal ramifications that led to loss of jobs they loved. In essence, burnout and stress caused these chaplains to lose sight of who they were as persons, chaplains, and ministers, and to lose their motivation and sense of purpose about what they were doing. Burnout and stress were key factors in their loss of vision for their life's work.

Chaplaincy that contributes to healing is an intense ministry. Time away and time to rest are essential to a chaplain's ongoing ministry. Antidotes to stress and burnout include taking time out to reflect and regain a sense of our identity (who we are), our purpose (why we do what we do), and our vision (what we are supposed to be doing). In short, we must practice Sabbath.[11] Jesus modeled Sabbath keeping when he retreated after delivering the Sermon on the Mount, feeding five thousand people,[12] and healing many others.[13]

Sabbath does not come easily for caregivers. It competes with many needs before us and requires an intentional decision on our part. Lack of time or money, fear of being alone with our thoughts and emotions, and our definition of Sabbath are common barriers that keep us from caring for ourselves. Sabbath calls us to reflection, which deepens our awareness of God, self, and others. It enables us to grow beyond our illusions and to delight in the way

---

[11] See Wayne Muller, *Sabbath* (New York: Bantam Books, 1999).

[12] Matt. 14:23.

[13] Mark 1:35.

things are. Sabbath enables us to open our hearts and minds to receive the nourishment that comes when we are connected to the source of our being. Caregivers then become like trees planted by the river of life, giving shade to those being scorched by the heat of life, offering protection for those being tossed around by the storms of life, relaying the whisper of the divine voice for a troubled heart and mind, and sharing the beauty of God's creation. Sabbath renews in our being the energy of love for God, self, and neighbor. Thus transformed, we are able to go forth and offer this same transforming love to others.

Self-care as stewardship

Caring for oneself involves being a good steward of the resource God has given to the world in the person one is. It is caring for our mind, emotions, body, and spirit. In so doing, we enjoy and share a vibrant quality of life. Such care is being a good shepherd of our being. Self-care may thus involve observing and being aware of our latest addiction, striking dream, troubling mood, or crisis of faith. The good shepherd Jesus sought the sheep that had strayed. We too are to seek the part of us that has strayed and bring it home to ourselves, so that we may be whole, one with God and with ourselves.

In *Care of the Soul*, Thomas Moore distinguishes cure from care: to cure is to put an end to that which troubles, whereas to care for the soul is to give ourselves ongoing attention.[14] This ongoing attention includes recognition that the sources of conflict or tension in our lives may never be fully resolved. In other words, self-care is not a once-and-for-all fix but a process needed wherever we are in our life journey. Moore compares care of the soul with cultivating fields:

> Cultivation of the soul implies a lifelong husbanding of raw
> materials. Farmers cultivate their fields. All of us cultivate
> our souls. The aim of soul work therefore is not adjust-
> ment to accepted norms or to an image of the statistically
> healthy individual. Rather, the goal is a richly elaborate
> life, connected to society and nature—woven into the
> culture of family, nation, and globe. The idea is not to be
> superficially adjusted, but to be profoundly connected in
> the heart to ancestors, and to living brothers and sisters in
> all communities that claim our hearts.[15]

Caring for self cultivates the soul. It breaks the ground that has become hardened and baked by the sun and allows it to breathe. The spirit of God that hovered over the world at creation is hovering over us, waiting and wanting to revitalize the soil of our being. That which is germinating within us yearns

---

[14] Thomas Moore, *Care of the Soul* (San Francisco: Harper Collins, 1992), 18–19.
[15] Ibid., xvii.

to push forth and become nourishment for those we care for, including self. The aim of self-care then is to be grounded in the source of our being. It is also to be in communion with those who have gone before us and with our neighbors in all communities that fill us with life and the passion to care.

Moore defines *soul* as a quality or a dimension of experiencing life and ourselves. It has to do with depth, value, relatedness, heart, and personal substance.[16] Self-care is not merely providing care for something—the soul—within us. Self-care is facilitating a way of life that deepens our spiritual connection with God, self, and others. Self-care is treating ourselves with respect, dignity, and value. It is coming home to ourselves.

Self-care requires us to become aware of our inner world and needs and to know where we begin and end in relation to others, so that we may maintain a healthy connectedness with them and with ourselves. To care for ourselves is to practice love for ourselves.

Let us reiterate that this is not a love rooted in narcissistic fixation, however. Gene Outka suggests in his book *Agape: An Ethical Analysis* that the love of wholesome self-care is a love of self that respects our integrity. Such love is rooted in an endeavor to stay connected with our own insights and commitments.[17] The resulting personal integrity and conscious affirmation of ourselves makes it possible for us to remain differentiated from others, from our mission, and from our ministry.

Such differentiation, however, does not mean separating ourselves from community. All of us participate in communities that affect, and are affected by, the people within them. Communities come in many shapes and forms. In northern Indiana, chaplains gather every other month for a time of fellowship and sharing, and peer review groups offer support and accountability. Family may be another type of community. The healthcare institution itself is a community of people working together towards the same end. Community may also mean the group of people we regularly interact with in school or in our neighborhood. Chaplains sometimes have difficulty finding a community that nourishes the soul. Such a community is one that orients our heart and passion, helps us better understand the holy and sacred in our life, and fills us with the breath of God.

Interacting with a community that nourishes the soul is vital to understanding who we are in the give-and-take of love, forgiveness, and grace. Community is the context where we connect with our own belief system, where we are fed and nourished, and where we receive the support of others. Communal life provides a dimension of connecting to the sacred. It allows our imaginations to ponder the mysteries of the divine. Our human relationships manifest the grace of God's immanence, suggests Gerald May. This grace, together with the grace of God's transcendence, deepens our experience of

---

[16] Ibid., 5–6.

[17] Gene Outka, *Agape: An Ethical Analysis* (New Haven: Yale University Press, 1972), 35.

love.[18] Participation in a faith community allows the hands and heart of God to minister to us as we become God's hands and heart in ministering to others. Choosing to be part of a caring community is an expression of self-love that can enable us to see ourselves, as it were, with the eyes of God as mirrored in the community of believers.

Practices of self-care

I cannot begin to identify all the ways our spirits might find nourishment. Each of us is unique. We have unique patterns of gathering information, making decisions, being energized, living life, practicing ministry, and understanding God. What I offer here are a few ideas that I and others have found helpful in caring for self.

A change of scenery can be refreshing. As I complete this essay, I am attending the symposium, "Spirituality in the Workplace," in beautiful Scottsdale, Arizona. It is energizing to experience more of God's creation through a landscape different from that of my home in the Midwest. There are no cornfields, but mountains and desert with cactus and sand. The brown landscape reminds me that life is not always green. A change of scenery from what one normally experiences provides different images that evoke the beautiful diversity of life itself. Such a change also brings a change in routine. Time away takes us away from house and property, so that while we are caring for ourselves, we are not tempted to mow the grass, clean the house, or other everyday activities. While doing these things may also be a path to spiritual renewal, I am proposing that we balance *doing* with *being*. Too much doing can distract us from time spent getting to know ourselves and becoming more aware of patterns of our inner world that motivate our actions.

At the conference I am attending, Andre Delbecq presented the practice of Lectio Divina as a form of self-care.[19] Lectio Divina (sacred reading) involves contemplative reflection on sources such as scripture, spiritual writings, the newspaper, nature, or a life event. The Lectio process begins with silent preparation, asking for the grace of quiet, moving into the presence of God, calming body and mind, and becoming open to surprise as a disciple of Christ. The second step is to read short passages slowly two times with an intention to listen and become aware of sensations, feeling, thoughts, or images, and then to return to a word, phrase, or sentence that stands out from the entire passage. A third step is to meditate and reflect on the word, phrase, or paragraph that particularly catches our attention. We allow ourselves to be drawn to what resonates, noting sensations, feelings, and images that surface. We sit with thoughts and feelings that emerge, and look for deeper

---

[18] May, *The Awakened Heart*, 130.

[19] Andre L. Delbecq is director of the Institute for the Spirituality of Organizational Leadership, Leavey School of Business, Santa Clara University, Santa Clara, CA. The Institute explores issues of spirituality within organizations.

meanings that may illumine our life situation. We also accept questions that come, and we wait with watchful anticipation.

The fourth step of Lectio Divina requires honesty before God. In prayer, we admit the less attractive side of ourselves, which may include anger, fear, jealousy, desire for revenge, and so on. Our prayer may include the classic expressions of awe and adoration, thanksgiving and delight, supplication or petition, and contrition. We accept the mystery, the paradoxes, and the imperfections of life while avoiding "God lust" (that is, wanting to be God). Finally, we rest with God by setting aside judgment and analysis. We prayerfully open our heart to God.

Lectio Divina is one practice that may bring a deep sense of refreshment and an opportunity to step away from the false self and the need to control. It may help one learn dependence, surrender, emptiness, and acceptance. Lectio Divina is a circular process rather than a linear endeavor in which one strives to achieve. It is circular in that the steps start with self and bring the self back home, renewed with glimpses of the mystery and love of God.

Another practice of self-care is mindfulness. Being mindful is a way to slow down. When under stress we often forget to breathe deeply. Three minutes of deep breathing will slow the heart rate and decrease blood pressure. We can practice mindfulness in the act of eating. Consider eating a meal in silence, deliberately savoring the food you are eating. Pay attention to the texture on your tongue and in your mouth. You may want to try this exercise by starting with a raisin. Allow the raisin to be in your mouth. Roll it around with your tongue. Feel the ridges as they fade and the raisin is restored to the plumpness of a grape. Then slowly begin to chew it. Reflect on the nature of what just happened and what you learned.

When I first practiced mindful walking, I had to work intentionally at slowing myself down. The pace of mindful walking is like a bride walking down the aisle or a graduate on graduation day. Slow movement allows for attention to and absorption of the sights, sounds, smells, and feelings of our surroundings. We breathe in the freshness of nature while exhaling the stresses of life.

Physical exercise is an important practice of self-care. Many forms of exercise are possible. Running and walking tapes are readily available. Clothing for every form of exercise from swimming to other strenuous workouts is accessible. Exercise equipment can be purchased for use in the home, while membership at a fitness club provides the opportunity to exercise along with other people. Mindful exercise, such as yoga or tai chi, enables conscious awareness of thought and breathing and works to integrate mind and body.

Tom Reid and Kathy Johnson recognize an essential connection between our deepest values and practices of self-care. They write, "Fundamentally, the impetus to pursue positive energy rituals and to build physical, mental, emotional and spiritual energies is grounded in our sense of life, mission and passion. It is easiest to develop discipline when we are working in service of our personal vision which inevitably carries us beyond ourselves." They suggest the following questions for reflection as we develop a routine of self-care:[20]

- What is my fundamental mission?
- When do I feel most connected? When am I most able to give and receive love?
- Whose life do I most admire?
- What are some of the barriers that are hindering me in fulfilling my mission?
- What other rituals might I consider adding in the future?
- Some of the experiences that are most life giving to me are ...
- One ritual of self-care I can initiate today is ...

In conclusion, stewardship is rooted in care taking, that is, managing well the abundance of gifts and goodness each of us has been given in life. Self-care is a necessary expression of love of self and others meant to increase awareness and to foster integrity. In light of the greatest commandments,[21] self-care is a joyful and grateful response to the invitation to live a life worthy of the vocation we have received.[22]

---

[20] Tom Reid and Kathy Johnson, "The Reid Group E-Letter," 2 August 2005.

[21] Mark 12:30-31.

[22] Eph. 4:1.

Part 2
**The chaplain
as caregiver in
specific settings**

Spiritual caregiving in the emergency room

Norma Lelless

My experience in the emergency room (ER) has spanned five years of sporadic on-calls in four different hospitals and one and a half years of part-time work at one particular hospital. Although the number of cases I have attended in the ER is small compared to my work elsewhere in the hospital, I feel I have benefited greatly from the experience. Over time, my eyes, ears, and heart have opened wider. My spiritual assessment and communication skills are continually developing. I have learned to laugh as much as cry and to be deliberate about practicing self-care.

As I prepared this essay, I found that the recall of my ER experiences released some emotional memories that surprised and fatigued me, while the spiritual analysis in every case was strengthening and revitalizing. I have selected examples containing cultural and religious variety[1] that challenged me to think of spirituality beyond the Christian tradition. The diversity has stretched my limitations, enriched my understanding of spiritual needs and sensibilities, and increased my capacity for compassion, the heart of genuine Christianity. I remain a committed Christian and necessarily view, interpret, and understand situations from my Christian perspective.

Death of a loved one

Receiving news that a loved one has been rushed to the emergency room because of critical illness sets off all sorts of internal alarms. Anxious family members and friends arrive at the hospital already in some stage of anticipatory grief, which transforms into various emotions on receiving word of their loved one's condition. When death occurs, the grief response may be extreme, complex, and require lengthy attention. In order to offer the best care, crisis workers, social workers, and chaplains specializing in grief work may support the ER staff. The chaplain generally is perceived as a calming and sensitive

---

Norma Lelless is a chaplain, North York General Hospital, North York, Ontario.

[1] For the sake of privacy, I changed names and did not identify the hospital locations. The length of the presentation of each experience varies, because I strove to concentrate only on information that characterizes the variety of roles of chaplaincy and to highlight the spiritual dimension in each.

companion, capable of identifying and responding appropriately to spiritual needs beyond emotional and psychosocial disorientation.

Abe's family

At 11:00 p.m., I received a call from the ER asking me to escort Abe's family—his wife, Ada, and three children—to the room where Abe's lifeless body lay. He had been pronounced dead on arrival. While I headed toward the ER, I prayed for sensitivity and wisdom; took deep calming breaths; and picked up a pen, a pastoral care record, and literature on funeral arrangements and bereavement support.

The nurse on duty offered more details: "53 years old, collapsed during a volleyball game, the paramedics were unable to resuscitate him. Please support the family and keep them confined to this area of the crowded ER."

Abe's lifeless body, draped with a sheet, lay on a gurney in a bare room next to the ambulance entrance. As I brought in chairs and boxes of tissues, I wondered for a moment what kind of person Abe had been and what his life had been like. I wondered what his family believed about death. (Very often, I have heard from people of various religious backgrounds that when one completes the task God has set for one to do, one dies.) Soon Ada, her children, and a couple of women arrived, followed by a couple of men. The children were in their teens. Ada grew tense before entering the room and screamed when she saw Abe, repeatedly calling his name and urging him to awaken, crying out, "No! No, I'm dreaming! This can't be happening." Everyone else wept. One stone-faced boy, looking numb, leaned against the wall and slid down to the floor.

The doctor came to speak with the family. I asked those who were not family to grant us privacy. When the doctor finished and left, I introduced myself as the chaplain. Through their tears, they spoke of shock and disbelief at this death and narrated the events of the evening. I listened attentively with empathy as they searched for understanding.

The room filled with wailing and laments. Ada stroked and kissed Abe's face. She kissed his hand, begged him to come back, to take her along, to trade places. She mixed her pleas with repeated descriptions of what he had been doing during the day and words he had spoken during their last conversation. She had noticed no discrepancy from the usual routine. In her ruminating scrutiny of her most recent memories of Abe, she was trying to make sense of this death. Ada spoke often to Abe and buried her head on his chest, sobbing, seeking comfort. I thought she might have been accustomed to turning to him for help in this way. She could not understand how he could die so suddenly.

Her sisters-in-law were tending to Ada's daughter and one son. Because they paid no attention to the other son, who remained apart, sitting on the floor against the wall, appearing shocked, I assumed he processed grief this way. Although the emotional intensity of the room fluctuated, this boy remained simply shocked.

During a quiet moment, I spoke gently to the group, "It's heart wrenching to hear so much wailing and to see so much pain. I can see this loss is huge. Abe is obviously well loved."

Ada responded by talking about Abe. She spoke of their deep love for each other and their family. She talked about Abe's popularity in his community and all the good works he had done for others. Then she returned to talking about this day, searching for a key to his death. "Everything had seemed normal." As far as she knew, his health was excellent. She felt this death was unjust. "He took care of himself. He took good care of his family. He loved life, enjoyed every minute, and loved his family and friends. He loved to have fun and laughed a lot." Then she said he taught good values to his children, even though he did not attend church except on Christmas and Easter. None of them did. They never had much time to get ready for church, especially with three small children. Nothing made sense. "Could they have overlooked something?" she wondered aloud.

Ada continued to repeat the details of Abe's last hours, interspersed with reasons for not attending church. She kept searching, scrutinizing, and justifying. When she assured me that they believe in Jesus, I said, "I can understand how difficult it must have been to get everyone organized on Sunday mornings. I suspect that God understands, too. You did what you could."

She started to identify the meaning of this loss. She characterized Abe as the heart of their family, the head of their household, a successful businessman, the chief decision maker, their advisor, and her closest friend. I listened attentively and responded supportively, nodding occasionally.

Friends and team members arrived. Their arrival captured Ada's and the children's attention. As the small room filled with more visitors, I stepped into the hallway, where a gathering of a few of Abe's friends and relatives spoke to me about Abe's good character, his true friendship, his community involvement, and his devotion to his family. I thought to myself, "My goodness, this feels like a day of judgment with everyone standing up to give their witness of this man's good character." I quickly set aside my thoughts and resumed listening carefully. Many of them easily expressed their thoughts and feelings. The team members expressed concern about whether they could have saved Abe. After they described how they had reacted to his sudden collapse, I said it sounded as if they had done all the right things, adding, "You must have felt helpless."

His brothers were concerned about the stress this shockingly unexpected death would create for his family, who now would need to take over Abe's business. Curious about Abe's quiet son, I asked one of Abe's brothers whether the boy normally was so withdrawn. "Richard never was much of a talker," he replied. "He's the oldest son and probably will help run the family business and guide his younger siblings where he can."

"Ah, I see. What responsibility for someone that age! Who will help him?" Abe's brother said he planned to do so, and of course, Ada would help too.

Back in the room, I slowly approached their oldest son. He did not twitch or show any discomfort about my being there, so I gently spoke, "How are you doing, Richard?" He shrugged his shoulders and turned away. "This is brutal," I said. He did not move or speak for some time. "I hope you'll let someone know what you're thinking," I suggested gently, "A teacher, a friend, anyone you can trust." He did not respond, so I retreated slowly, giving Richard the solitude he seemed to desire.

One of Abe's sisters-in-law asked me to say prayers, and Ada asked me to bless Abe. We gathered around Abe. I began by thanking God for this well-loved man. I repeated much of the praise I had heard, and I invited those present, if they wanted to, to thank Abe for something he had given to them or had done for them. I realized this was a difficult time. Many people cried. Ada promised lasting fidelity to Abe, because no one could ever replace him. Many of the others spoke in turn. Some chose not to speak. Everyone was patient, though tense. We recited the Lord's Prayer together. Next I drew their attention to the promise of eternal life with Jesus expressed in John 14:2-3 and concluded, first, by asking God to grant Abe eternal peace and the rewards promised by Jesus, and then by requesting peace in the hearts of everyone involved this evening, including the paramedics, his teammates, friends, and family. Finally, I asked God to give strength for this time of mourning and help when needed. "Amen" and "It was his time to go," echoed in the crowd.

As I stepped out of the room, I saw about twenty visitors arriving, so I stayed nearby to support the ER's request to keep this group in one general area. The ambulances came and left, breaking up the crowd each time a new patient arrived. The group started to leave. Most of them thanked me, and some even hugged me. Before Ada left, I gave her the information booklet, and she asked about storing Abe's clothing for a while. I helped make the arrangements. She hugged me, thanked me, and walked away. It was about 3:00 in the morning.

I reflected on this experience while filling out the pastoral care report. The impressions I received led me to believe that this family expressed their spirituality in their love for life and for one another. Their connection to extended family and community was strong. It was a close-knit community of loving support. I suspected that relatives and friends would provide attention and care during the family's adjustment to bereavement. Many promises were made to help Ada and her children carry on. I recalled how Ada seemed embarrassed about not maintaining regular church attendance and wondered if they had felt a higher need for family closeness than for public prayer. I was especially thankful that Ada did not linger with the notion that this death was punishment.

Ada seemed to draw on her internal strength. She talked about continuing their family life and conducting Abe's business in the ways Abe would want this done. She showed a capacity to trust and to ask for help when she needed it. Two months later, she returned for the clothing and told me that it had taken this long to arrange business matters, yet the most difficult moment was right now, when she had to look at the clothes Abe wore when he died. His clothing became a powerful symbol, first, of how things had been when Abe lived and social leisure formed part of their weekly routine, and second, of the moment of death when suddenly the family needed to restructure and redirect their energies in order to maintain their way of life. This family's system and social network functioned like a small faith community.

Most of the mourners who had participated in the prayer of blessing were able to express their gratitude to God for Abe's life, and they indicated their sense of helplessness when they agreed, "It was his time." This life-changing event was a sobering reminder of the fragility of life and the unpredictability of death. Growth takes place through the acknowledgement of vulnerability.

The family related to me, on a limited basis, as a bridge to the divine. This distance seemed to reflect their relationship with their religious tradition. In my prayers, I asked that the oldest son who stood apart from the others would be able to experience care. I also thanked God for close, loving families and supportive communities that call to mind the community of disciples and apostles that surrounded Jesus.

Death while in the hospital

Religious traditions may take on a dimension of power and authority beyond human history, where boundaries between the secular and the sacred become blurred. When, for example, the statement "Do this in memory of me" is spoken in different contexts, it takes on different spiritual meanings. The following experience led me to reflect on the healing power of memory when the people involved express no belief in God.

Mr. Mah's daughter

It was late evening when an elderly man named Mr. Mah succumbed to wounds from a motor scooter accident. The nurse in the ER asked me to sit with him as he lay dying, until his family arrived. The nurse felt he should not die alone. I took a few deep calming breaths, picked up a bereavement support brochure, and prayed for sensitivity and wisdom. The only occupied gurney in the trauma room held unconscious Mr. Mah. I sat beside him and spoke gently, introducing myself and expressing hope that he was comfortable. Very soon his daughter Carol arrived, escorted by the nurse, who introduced us to each other. The doctor followed, explaining Mr. Mah's injuries. He said that Mr. Mah was dying, and he offered his condolences.

Carol listened attentively, showing no emotion, and asked a few questions for clarification. After the doctor left, I said, "My heart sank when I heard the news." I asked if I could be of any assistance to her. She said she was not religious. I thought that she might prefer that I leave, but I hesitated to do so when Carol began to show me Mr. Mah's wounds and to talk about them. She spoke gently and respectfully, occasionally wiping blood from his nostrils. In response, I stayed and showed my interest.

She whispered in my direction about the accident, how she had suspected something was wrong when he had not returned home. I nodded gently and whispered, "You waited with fear." She repeated some statements, as if to persuade herself to accept what was happening. I remained attentive, nodding occasionally and paraphrasing some of her remarks: "You felt worried." "Yes, now he's here." "Uh-huh, you hope he's not suffering." She nodded. "He's your father and you have great respect for him. I can see this," I added. Carol lowered her eyes, looking embarrassed, and then she nodded.

Mr. Mah stopped breathing, and Carol searched for his pulse. I signaled the nurse, who joined us and confirmed that he probably had just died. The doctor would be here shortly to officially confirm this. The nurse left. Carol sighed heavily and then suddenly raised her voice, speaking directly to him. She cried and reproached her father for having made a mistake that caused his death. She protested about being left alone to raise her children without him. Then she regained her composure and in a calm voice thanked him for his paternal guidance. She promised to remember him and honor him by doing what he had taught her to do and keeping the honor of the family name for the sake of all their ancestors. I spoke, "Carol, you have been taking care of your dad. You seem kind and respectful. I can see your sadness, and I think that you will miss him." I was struggling with the sudden disappearance of Carol's emotions and unwittingly was trying to retrieve them. However, Carol was finished for now, so I said no more about her feelings.

We arranged for Carol to bring her children there. She returned in twenty minutes with two children: a girl about eleven years old and a boy around nine. With hunched shoulders, making timid steps toward the gurney, they looked frightened. Each in turn spoke politely, almost formally, but sincerely, to their grandfather. Holding back tears while saying good-bye, they thanked him for having been good to them and promised to honor his memory. The boy hesitated and struggled not to cry. When they finished, I waited for a moment and then said to them, "I feel sad for you, because your grandfather has died. It must have been hard to speak to him, but you were courageous and you spoke well. That touched me tenderly." Carol next asked about funeral arrangements, and I gave her more information. She thanked me for my help. I expressed my sincere condolences, "I am deeply moved by how much love and respect you have shown. Thank you for giving me the privilege of spending this time with you." Carol's sadness showed in her eyes. She nodded, said "Thank you," and they left.

While I filled out the pastoral report, I thought about Carol's careful listening to the doctor and her expression of heartfelt reproach and promise of loving respect. I thought of the extremes of fear and courage involved in such an experience. I also thought of how they honored Mr. Mah by their obedience to him and to their Chinese cultural tradition, evident in how politely they all spoke to him and the promises they made. Carol demonstrated that she was a loyal, devoted daughter who had taught her children, despite their feelings, to express thanks politely, to promise to maintain the family's honor, and to say good-bye.

Their spiritual need was to have closure, to demonstrate strength, and to grieve, while also honoring the deceased and their cultural heritage; their spirituality connects past, present, and future. The lives that continue carry forward the dignity of all the family members who precede them.

As a chaplain, I served Carol by remaining with her, affirming her feelings, and supporting her grief. I whispered when she whispered, and I nodded or uttered affirmation. I also let her know that I noticed her respect for her father. When she suddenly stopped crying and became calm, I only tried once to keep her in touch with those feelings. That was my weakness. Instead of letting her feelings rule her behavior, Carol chose to put them aside and attended to the children's obligation to their grandfather. I also responded to the children's feelings and praised their actions.

I felt privileged to have spent this time with them. My desire was to elevate the honoring above historical time and to appreciate it more deeply. I wanted to emphasize the value of Carol, Mr. Mah, and each of the children as precious individuals in their own right, with a claim equal to my own to eternal life at the end of time. I wished I could know what Carol believed about time—whether it ends. I wanted to discuss the significance of who they were and of all their ancestors being preserved into eternity. At the same time, I realized how seldom I see anything like this custom in my own ethnic and religious culture, where we seem, instead, to disconnect our own future behavior from our lineage. No Westerner has ever asked my permission for children to speak in a similar way to a deceased parent or grandparent.[2]

A suicide

In contrast to the previous story about maintaining the family honor through the ages, that is, of taking pride in one's ancestors, debilitating toxic shame enters the picture when the emotional dysfunction and moral failure of the

---

[2] There was one four-year-old child years ago who asked to see her deceased baby brother. The parents struggled with whether seeing the baby would emotionally harm this child, but she surprised us by speaking lovingly to the baby. In Abe's family, no one formally spoke directly to Abe about how they would maintain honor of the family name. Abe's legacy was not connected to his ancestors.

father falls onto subsequent generations. Without the sacrifice of the one for the all that Jesus represents, how does the shame that comes with unresolved offenses stop? How does atonement happen? I asked myself this theological question in the midst of reflection on the following experience.

Mr. Yee's children

Mr. Yee committed suicide because of his gambling debts. He succumbed to his self-inflicted wounds soon after arriving at the hospital. The police brought his children to the ER. I was paged to be with them. It was 2:00 a.m. Through other hospital experiences, I have seen the blow with which suicide strikes families—the helplessness, frustration, betrayal, anger, responsibility, and self-doubt that haunt those bereaved—the overwhelming, stinging wound. I thought my pastoral experiences had prepared me for this moment until the nurse offered one further detail: their mother, his wife, lay in another hospital, dying of cancer. My heart sank. The two children sitting in the waiting room, twelve and fourteen years old, were in a wretched predicament.

As I was about to enter the waiting room, a woman approached me, identifying herself as a pastoral counselor sent by their mother's doctor. She said she had nearly succeeded in converting their mother to Christianity. She was confident that this hospital was an important place for her to be at this moment. I told her that I appreciated her concern but felt that this was not the time or place to speak about Jesus. Definitely not now. It is never appropriate to take advantage of people's vulnerability, especially that of children.

The nurse led us into the room together. We introduced ourselves to the children. I identified myself as a Christian chaplain working for the hospital. The visiting counselor, Mrs. Lo, introduced herself, spoke about their mother, sat silently for a while, distributed her calling card, and left. The nurse also went out of the room.

The children were visibly shaken, looking helpless and lost. They remained speechless and fidgeted restlessly. "This is a nightmare," I said. The girl, Donna, agreed. I suggested it might help them to talk about what happened and asked if they felt like doing so. Donna started speaking immediately, and David filled in details. I listened attentively as they spoke angrily about their dad, his gambling debts, and his forcing Donna to give him her life savings and then losing it all. David talked about finding his dad unconscious, about trying to resuscitate him while Donna called 911, and about how quickly paramedics and the police arrived. Now that he was dead, David added, they felt shocked and angry. They never expected this to happen.

"You are amazing, so kind hearted," I offered, trying to console them. "You've been so hurt by him, and still you tried to save him. You did everything you could. It's not your fault that he died and not surprising that you feel so upset."

They looked surprised and continued to reason their way through the events, trying to determine whether they should have anticipated this event. "He often threatened to kill himself," Donna said. "This time didn't seem any different." She added that they did not want to see him again and immediately explained that her father's spirit was still in their home where he had died. "Oh dear," I said. She repeated that she did not want to see him. She was too afraid. "Uh huh," I responded supportively and gently. "Of course."

They resolved to stick together and wanted to be with their mom and to focus on taking care of her now, to help her get better. They expressed the slim hope that a bone marrow donor would be found to help her. They wanted to focus their energies on recruiting potential donors. I listened with genuine empathy. They continued repeating the events, showing frustration, disbelief, and anger with their dad. I fixed my attention on them. I nodded, affirmed, but did not speak while they ruminated and vented their feelings.

Then David moved to repercussions of this death: his dad's debts now would fall on him and Donna to pay. They were afraid the people whose money was lost would come after them. "What a burden!" I said. "Sometimes circumstances seem too big to control, but this is Canada! Children do not have to pay their parent's debts." I said that I believed their dad's debts should be cancelled. They could check with a social worker or a lawyer. Maybe a trusted teacher at school or a guidance counselor could help them find out. They did not seem to believe me.

Uncles and cousins arrived, visibly anxious. The nurse escorted the uncles to Mr. Yee's body. When they returned, one of them said something about not wanting to put out another penny for this man. He, too, was angry. When Donna and David reacted to his anger by bowing their heads and slouching, I thought they looked ashamed. I suggested to the uncle that they consider financial support from Social Services to pay for the funeral, and that the children could not be held responsible for their father's debts. The uncle glared at me, and I felt confused. (In hindsight, I wonder if their culture mandates that the children take on the debt of their father regardless of legal obligation, lest they bear even more shame in the eyes of those uncles). I asked where the children would stay now. They were young and vulnerable. Who would care for them? He said they could spend the night at his place, but then would need to return to their own home. He did not have enough space for them and his own family. Besides, he said, they were old enough to take care of themselves.

The nurse brought forms for the uncles to sign and discussed the need for an autopsy. When they finished, I said I hoped there would be some kind of trauma counseling available to help them get through this tragedy. I knew of a free counseling service for trauma victims. If they wanted me to, I would speak with the social worker in the morning and ask her to send them information. The children agreed, but the uncles declined and thanked me politely. I added, "I won't be able to forget this evening. I will hold you in my heart and sincerely wish you strength and peace." One uncle smiled and shook my hand. He simply said, "Thank you."

I left, feeling foolish. I had broken one of the rules of chaplaincy: not to involve myself in trying to fix what may seem wrong in another's life. I also felt certain I had missed something, a kind of subliminal message that I had not grasped. I should have realized that Mr. Yee might have owed money to his brothers, or that Mr. Yee's brothers feared they would be held responsible for the debts. However, I was reading this situation from my own expectations and my lack of experience with matters such as gambling and owing debts. There was a huge gap here, which I knew I was not able to bridge. Above all else, my heart ached for those children in this terrible chaos, and I needed to admit that the maternal drive in me was operating in full gear, even blinding me, at 2:00 in the morning.

The next morning, I spoke with our social worker, who is Asian. She drew my attention to the culture's sensitivity to privacy and the strong sense of shame that this family likely felt. She said that they probably would not let anyone know about this death and that the responsibility for the loans was a custom difficult to break. Because the social worker is the spouse of a Christian minister, she was able to talk about the well-intended actions of the pastoral visitor, Mrs. Lo.

I asked the social worker whether her husband's church would consider helping those children somehow. She laughed and said I did not understand. My intentions were good, but their customs and their high desire for privacy made it very difficult to help the children. I felt perplexed and, because I deeply respect this social worker, I trusted her wisdom. I was grateful for her honesty. Consulting with her helped me gain perspective on this experience and on myself. I recognized that my offer of outside resources may have unknowingly challenged the ability of the children and uncles to cope with their felt obligations to family honor, thus compounding their humiliation. I realized I needed to let go of the feelings this case evoked in me. I needed to understand how much I was judging these people and their choices by my own values.

When I looked beyond the pain and fear in these circumstances to the spiritual gifts offered, I noticed hope. The children had the opportunity to make free choices, if they wanted to do so. It seemed to me that they were trapped, metaphorically speaking, by a ghost that needed to be exorcised (the haunting stigma and toxic shame of debts and of suicide, not to mention their sense that their father's spirit was still in the house) and by further tragedy lurking on the horizon (their mother's death). But their situation may not have been so hopeless. They were young and strong, determined and willing to speak to strangers about their actions, their plans to care for their mother, if possible, their fears of incurring debt, and their wish never to see their dad again, thus dismissing the source of pain and shame. In fact, they showed me their hope by noting that there still was time to search for a bone marrow donor for their mom. They would likely be able to transfer the strength that they drew from being together, committed to a common cause (their mother's needs), to solving other problems as well.

Another insight was that resources were available in the people surrounding them—their mother's compassionate doctor, who showed concern for their welfare, and the two uncles and cousins who cared about them enough to be with them in the middle of the night. They might be able to lean on these people. Their uncle's anger may have been a manifestation of grief, not necessarily a response carved in stone. I prayed that the children would find all that they needed to heal from the pain of this experience, and that they would continue to be strong as this new chapter of their lives unfolded.

On further reflection, I felt embarrassed that I had unwittingly challenged the children and their uncle. Still, I felt glad that in my naiveté I had spoken truthfully. I had delivered a message that ways to resolve difficulties often emerge, ways that require courage to step out of one's box in order to effect healing. I hoped this message stayed with them as a seed planted for future cultivation. It certainly helped me understand my shortcomings here.

My role had been simply to show pastoral support, to listen with genuine concern, and to offer them freedom to process their feelings while also giving a voice to the spiritual strength they demonstrated. I realized I had fallen short of the mark. I also realized my presumptuousness and how difficult it was for me to separate my own fears from the broader reality of the situation. Because I lost sight of everyone's grief, helplessness, frustration, betrayal, anger, and disappointment, I failed to stand apart from the situation and respond pastorally to the uncles' needs.

I sometimes reflect on this experience and gratefully thank God for the insights into my limitations. I pray that I might find ways to be more sensitive, so that I do not add to the condition of shaming and oppression through insensitivity, when people most need tenderness. I also pray for eyes to behold mystery, ears to hear the whole truth impartially, a heart to feel lovingly, and a mouth that speaks only words that serve Christ.

Miscarriage

Miscarriages occur for various reasons in women of diverse ages and ethnic, cultural, economic, and religious backgrounds. Although each individual involved is a unique combination of physical, psychosocial, and spiritual needs, commonalities occur in the general pattern of grieving among women who miscarry. Their deep emotional and physical discomfort releases strong feelings, which they must process before they can begin to make sense of the experience.

Because the medical condition of the patient requires immediate attention, the time available for the chaplain's visit is short. Even shorter visits are called for if patients suffer so much physical discomfort that they cannot concentrate to hold a conversation. Generally, I inquire from the attending nurse whether the patient has seen the doctor already. If so, I speak with the patient and perhaps the baby's father, before medical treatment begins. If not, I wait. If I arrive before diagnosis, I may alarm the couple and may even provoke anger; if too late, I will have missed the opportunity to speak with them.

Often couples make emotionally laden statements that indicate their sense of connection to powers beyond human limitations. Some move quickly to discuss coping strategies. Careful listening enables the chaplain to construe their preferred God-image. To facilitate healing, one of the hospitals here offers a fetal burial service, free of charge and appropriate to several different religious and nonreligious backgrounds. A local funeral home and cemetery sponsor the service, which pastoral services designs and carries out at the gravesite, with the help of funeral personnel and hospital staff. The remains of the deceased little ones are cremated and buried in a common grave to which the couples may return to honor the life lost. The chaplain sometimes extends the invitation. Most parents are pleased to offer their baby a respectful burial. Some appreciate the related opportunity to bless and name their baby at birth.

Helen and Herb

For the American tourists Helen and Herb, the miscarriage of their first pregnancy far from home was both devastating and terrifying. The couple met my question, "How are you doing?" with a heartfelt characterization of how distraught they felt, mostly through laments expressed by Helen. "I hear your pain. I can tell you feel very sad," I murmured in support.

The miscarriage led them to wonder whether traveling had been a mistake. The prospect of not having any children terrified them. "Have you discussed your concerns with the doctor?" I asked gently.

"He doubts travel made the difference," Herb said.

"How do you feel about this?" I continued. They responded that they were worried that they might not be able to have children. "Oh dear, that's a horrible thought," I commented. "Not knowing makes you very anxious. What do you need to restore hope?"

They were silent. After a while, they asked me to pray for them.

"Would you like to pray together now?" I naively asked.

"Not now, but we'd appreciate your praying for us later," Herb said. According to their Orthodox Jewish faith, prayer *with* me was inappropriate, he explained; however, my prayer separately *for* them was not. They hoped God would give them strength to get through this loss and eventually would grant them children.

"Is it your belief that God decides about whether and when we have children?" I asked.

They nodded, replying, "Uh-huh, yes." I nodded, smiled, and promised to pray for them, for strength and for children. I added that I appreciated hearing Helen's laments and respected their faithfulness to their religious tradition, that I was grateful for their invitation to pray for them. They were kind to show confidence in my prayers. As I expected, they were not interested in our fetal burial program, preferring instead to follow their own religious tradition. They expressed sincere gratitude for my having listened to them with empathy.

It seemed to me that Helen and Herb drew strength from commitment to their faith. They obviously held family, community, and God in high regard, for these were the source of their hopes. Having their laments heard and validated by others at this time was also important, especially because they were alone in a strange place. Asking questions and requesting prayer was comforting and enabled them to cope better. Their image of God was clear and familiar to me. A component of my prayer for them accordingly addressed God's power over life and God's hearing and listening to petitions and laments.

In my work I meet Christian, Muslim, Hindu, and Jewish people who, believing in God, also believe that God hears everyone's prayers. For many, it is comforting to imagine a higher level than the human one, to which the collective petitions of all believers rise to be received by divine ears.

Varied responses to the disappointment of the loss of a baby, whether they are secular or religious, have inspired me to think about my own theology around such loss. Disappointment alerts parents to their limitations, a deeply upsetting experience. Some express lament and appeal to God as the highest authority, according to their tradition. They have an understandable need to know the cause of miscarriage. Some promise behavior that is more responsible in the future. They want to be sure that they did the right things.

It does not surprise me that it has taken humankind so long to validate the deep sadness and disappointment that accompany such an experience. Facing human limits is disturbing; we rarely take this step by our free choice. A miscarriage confronts couples and doctors with limits that they may not be able to transcend. Chaplains who serve those facing miscarriage also face limits. As long as the couple has reason to believe there may be something they can do with the help of medicine and with God's help, they remain optimistic.

Another response to miscarriage I have encountered is pessimism, along with insensitivity to the tiny life lost. Ironically, such a mood may accompany an overwhelming feeling of devastation if the woman has suffered multiple miscarriages, and the prospect of never being able to carry a child to term becomes a reality. In these circumstances, women have said to me, "I don't want to talk with God; I'm too angry." "I don't even want to see the child. I just want to get rid of *it*." "I was afraid I might lose the baby, so I didn't let myself feel anything for this child. I didn't even want to think about this pregnancy." Sadly, alienation from their experience often takes over. Many of them decline the chance to participate in the fetal burial program.

All these need tender care. The chaplain simply must stand with them in their pain. My prayer for such women is that God surround them with loving, sensitive, nurturing caregivers that support them appropriately and help them to move on. We also need to feel the deep sadness, admit our limitations, and remove the social stigma associated with such loss.

Possibility of death

In the emergency room, high anxiety caused by anticipatory grief distresses families and friends as they wait to hear about their loved one's condition. Family and friends may wander restlessly into and out of the ER. Every minute seems like an hour, and tragic scenarios may run endlessly through their minds. Tension mounts. Whether the prognosis is favorable or hopelessly negative, as soon as the news is delivered, an emotional catharsis takes place.

Lou, his family, and a friend

A young man on a motorcycle had collided with a truck. He was being examined for serious injuries. The police had not been able to find his mother, but his girlfriend and another young man were in the waiting room. The ER nurse asked me to sit with them. Before introducing myself to them, I explained that it is customary to send a chaplain to stay with a family while they wait. They introduced themselves as Lou's brother Rob, and Lou's friend Connie. I surmised that the patient's name was Lou.

Anxiety grew when a police constable from the provincial police came in to speak with the family. He gave few details and said that the city police would take over the case, because technically it had occurred on municipal property. Many witnesses had seen the accident. The constable identified the truck driver, who was being held in custody. The charges would depend on Lou's condition. The police were still trying to reach Lou's mother. However, they had reached his father, who was on his way from up north.

I thought to myself, "Families need to know the patient's condition before hearing who caused the accident. Drawing attention to the truck driver now almost suggests that vengeance is settling. This doesn't feel right." Yet I also understood that the police had limited time available, so they needed to fulfill their obligation to provide information to the family.

Long tense periods of silence followed, interrupted by Rob's efforts to phone a third brother, Alan, and their mother. A police constable from the Toronto police arrived and offered more details: no alcohol, no drugs on either driver. Rob pointed out that their mother, a religious leader, raised them not to do things like that.

Alan arrived, breathing heavily from rushing. "How's Lou?" he asked.

Rob said, "We don't know. Where's Mom?"

"She's on her way. She was teaching at one of the Salvation Army cita-
dels."

"Dad's coming, too," Rob added.

"Oh." Alan let out a deep breath.

Rob then explained to me his concern about their parents, Rita and Ed,
meeting for the first time after a bitter divorce. Their dad had remarried. Rob
then introduced Connie and me to Alan, who continued to ask questions.
He wondered whether their dad's new spouse was joining him.

Rob gulped, "I don't know."

"Oh dear," I interjected, reflecting their mood. Rob and Alan sat with
their heads downcast. Alan rubbed his eyes with the thumb and forefinger
of his right hand.

We sat in silence for a short time, and I wondered how painful the memories of their parents' split must have been, now coupled with fear about their
brother's condition. I could hear everyone breathing. Then their mother
arrived, breaking the silence. She explained how she had received word of
the accident and asked about Lou's condition.

"We're all still waiting to hear," Rob said. He introduced Connie and
me to his mother.

Rita asked me to lead a prayer, saying she felt an acknowledgement of
God's authority was necessary now. I suggested that I start; others could add
their own words, if they wanted to, and Rita could close. I prayed about not
knowing Lou's condition, trusting God, and wanting to offer God our hopes
and fears now. Rob and Alan expressed the desire for Lou's survival and
healing. Looking anxious, Connie remained silent. Rita appealed for Lou's
protection and healing. She asked God to guide the doctors.

A knock on the door interrupted her prayer. A doctor entered, bringing
news that Lou's condition was not critical. He had a few minor internal
injuries that were being monitored, and his arm needed to be set. He was
expected to recover fully. Immediately, the collective anxiety transformed
into a collective sigh of relief. The doctor told the family that they could
visit Lou now. His dad was already with him.

Alan, Rob, and Rita rushed to Lou's side, but Connie walked slowly behind. She indicated that she wanted to speak with me. I listened as she told
me that she did not know any of these people. She hardly knew Lou. This
was going to be their first date. Lou had planned to cook dinner for her, and
they were going to go to a movie. She asked what she should do.

"How are you feeling right now?" I asked.

Connie took a deep breath, released it, and said, "Well, I *was* feeling
partly responsible and worried about Lou's condition. Now I'm just scared
about meeting all these people."

"I can understand that. What would you do if they weren't here?"

She thought for a moment and replied, "I guess I'd visit him."

"Can you speak with him anyway?"

"I don't know," she replied. "I feel overwhelmed. There's just so many of them."

"Uh-huh. I guess you feel outnumbered and awkward. But I suspect saying hello won't imply more than showing respectful concern. If you hadn't given the police Lou's home number, they wouldn't have known who he was or where to look for his relatives. But the choice must be yours, and if you feel too awkward, then trust your instincts." I waited and then asked if it would help if I stayed with her. She said it would. She decided to enter the room after all. I followed her.

Rita was standing across from Ed, smiling and looking relieved. The men were laughing about the confused evening. Lou noticed Connie and said, "Connie! I never thought I'd be introducing my family to you under these circumstances, but here they are. Connie, this is my family. Family, Connie." They laughed and greeted each other.

Just as they said hello, another police constable arrived. He came directly to Lou and said, "You must be a believer. Were you ever protected! I'm glad you're okay. Lucky for the truck driver, too." Happy chuckles of relief sounded.

"Amen," I added.

Lou replied, "All I remember was the green light changing and slowly starting off. Suddenly I saw this truck coming straight at me. The next thing I know, I'm here. I must have passed out."

"You must have," the constable continued. "We found your backpack, but not your wallet. What the hell were you doing with a huge frozen fish in your backpack?"

Nervous laughter broke out, venting pent-up anxiety, and more discussion continued with more details. They recalled earlier stories of risk and adventure while fishing with their dad at his cottage.

In the barrage of words, I noticed that Connie and Rita remained quiet. Connie seemed subtly awkward and uncomfortable. At some point, Robert and Alan talked about leaving. Robert offered to drive Connie back to her place, and she accepted. I said I was glad Lou was going to be all right, and then I said good-bye to everyone, adding, "We can all say prayers of thanks tonight."

I stepped aside and spoke briefly with Connie, asking how she felt. "Relieved, thanks," she said. After they all departed, I filled out the appropriate report for Lou's chart.

In retrospect I realized I had felt a bit overwhelmed by the fluctuating emotions, too. My role had been defined by Alan and Rob's need of my support as spiritual caregiver, by Rita's request that I lead prayer, and by Connie's need for a confidante. I thought it was a gift to Connie to be able to see Lou as part of a wider context now and thus be able to understand him better—an insightful way to begin a dating relationship. It was a gift to the sons to see their parents together, not fighting, and a gift to Rita to see her ex-husband once again interacting with their sons in male-bonded camaraderie. Both parents cared enough for Lou to put aside their differences and come directly to his side. Ed went first to Lou, rather than to the family room. His new wife stayed at home, minimizing the possibility of drawing attention to that relationship. Ed kept his boundaries clear, thus maintaining the focus on Lou.

I thought of the contrast between the anxious silence of unknowing and the energetic talking when Lou's condition became known. I thought of the different signs of dignity: Lou's clean lifestyle, his brothers' admission of fear about their parents' meeting, their father's not joining the others in the family room, and Connie's coming to the hospital though she hardly knew Lou, and her honest disclosure of her thoughts and feelings. I thought of the sense of justice in how the accident turned out. Especially I thought of the many interruptions and twists in this whole episode. There were humorous surprises. The young men's mother and teacher, who had raised them, felt the need to recognize this event as taking place under God's sovereign will.

This family's bond, among the males in particular, demonstrated appropriate care and loving support for one another. They seemed to draw strength from within and to be respectful of the wisdom of good, clean fun. Except for Rita and one police constable, I did not hear any of them refer to God. Their mother may have provided connection to a church, which they seemed to respect, especially when she asked for prayer. Their prayers were brief, speaking their desire for Lou's good health. It was easy to see that this event would give them much to talk and laugh about. They did not indicate whether this event affected their view of life or of God. It simply triggered memories from previous adventures. They expressed their spirituality in continuity with their mother's moral guidance, embracing wholesomeness in life and supporting each other.

Once again, I realized that, regardless of circumstances, good character and commitment surrounded with genuine love bring out the best in people. I also noticed, as I have seen before, that when life-and-death issues confront people, most demonstrate their level of connection to the God of their deep beliefs, to the God they worship according to the way they live. I thanked God that the outcome for Lou and his family was good, said a prayer for the truck driver, and prayed for the best possible resolution for everyone involved.

Conclusion

The experiences I have described in this essay demonstrate how varied and complicated pastoral service may become in the ER. The chaplain may perform a number of auxiliary tasks but must always maintain eyes, ears, and a heart for spiritual care, which transcends but remains connected to psychosocial care. In the ER, I find myself usually joining anxious people in a cloud of unknowing, waiting, and wondering what lies ahead. I have felt like a personified echo that validates thought, feeling, and personal meaning. Through prayer, blessing, and support, I have served as a bridge to the divine that transcends the particulars of language and form. My eyes, ears, and heart have identified differences ranging between spiritual brokenness in people with strong religious affiliation and spiritual strength in people claiming none. By addressing the needs of patients, families, and staff, I have noticed many instances when the sacred was revealed in the secular, which has encouraged me to think through my own theological beliefs and understanding. My ER experiences have required a significant investment of energy, and have sometimes even left me emotionally drained, but I have found them well worth the investment. They have encouraged me to appreciate similarities and differences in religious convictions and thinking, regardless of denominations or creeds, and have deepened my understanding of grace and the truth in God's Word.

The chaplain's presence in crisis caregiving

Ruth M. Johnston

I have been asked many times why I chose chaplaincy ministry. Some people find it hard to fathom a life's work that includes responding to those in crisis, addressing the needs of the dying, or sitting at the bedside of someone with a new and serious diagnosis. Some have even implied that chaplaincy is a second choice for ministry and suggested that maybe one day I will be a "real pastor." However, God has called me to this unique ministry, and I have chosen this work intentionally. My work as a hospital chaplain has become so close to my heart that when I stop to reflect on it, I experience an overwhelming sense of gratitude for the gift this ministry is in my life. Almost every day, in one way or another, I am privileged to touch human vulnerability and divine mystery through my patients and their families. It is incredibly meaningful, humbling, and challenging work.

Entering with intentionality

When I am called to an emergency care situation, sometimes it is with individuals and families I have known and followed for days or weeks. Just as frequently, however, it is a situation I step into cold. I may be called to the death of a person who has just been transported by ambulance to the emergency room, or I may be called to care for a patient whose health is suddenly declining. Many chaplains love to develop longer-term relationships with patients and families, but we are called into any situation in which we are needed. We must gain the ability through training to step into intense situations with little grounding except our own faith, our experience, and our ministry skills.

As I move into an emergency, I do so with certain intentions already in mind. First, I enter with an awareness of God's love for me and for those in my care, and with a desire to embody that love under those circumstances. Second, I go to be fully present in whatever is unfolding and to get on board with this unfolding story. Third, I go in with the desire to be a connector. That is, carefully, and as it is appropriate, I explore how I can help the family connect with God through prayer (if they so desire), with people from

[1] Ruth M. Johnston is a chaplain, Methodist Hospital, St. Louis Park, Minnesota.

their own faith tradition, with their own family members not yet present, and perhaps eventually with other resources. If the family is in great distress, and especially if there is but a lone family member, part of my work may be to serve as link to a sense of reality amid grief that leads to disorientation. At times, the chaplain claims this role of anchor while the family weathers the news of a tragedy that will change their lives forever. Fourth, I seek to be a comforting presence. I comfort not by offering platitudes but by listening with love, by sitting with people in their grief until the early shock begins to lift, by helping them negotiate the confusing system that every hospital is, by advocating for them so that they may get answers to their questions, and by providing simple physical comforts such as water or tissues.

I offer the following family care situation as a means of reflecting on the role of the chaplain and the purpose of the chaplain's ministry in emergencies.

A ministry experience

On a busy summer day in the hospital, I was paged to an emergency in the intensive care unit. I arrived to find a patient rapidly declining. He and his wife had recently arrived from mainland China to visit their son and his family. The patient's son and daughter-in-law spoke fluent English, but his wife spoke virtually none. I offered myself to the family, but they were too distracted and anxious to engage much with me. I asked the patient's son if there was a faith community I could contact for them, and he indicated that there was not. Then the patient made a sudden turn for the worse, his blood pressure fell as he bled internally, and the doctors alerted the family that he had little time left. Sorrowfully, the two doctors present told the family there was nothing more they could do for him.

The family hurried to his bedside. I entered the room behind them and stood at the foot of the bed. The patient's wife wept and wailed. They huddled together at the bedside while her son interpreted into English all that she said. The doctors were mostly outside the room, the nurse was in and out, so I was the main person, outside her family, to receive the words of this woman. She begged that more be done to save him, she wailed and jumped up and down in anguish, anger, and helplessness. She lay across her husband and asked him not to let this happen. She blamed her son for a trip that was ending in disaster. Her agony was palpable in the many turns her mind took. In the privacy of a closed room, she expressed her grief, and her son interpreted every word urgently for anyone available to listen. I had become the primary listener. I stood present as the waves of grief ran through the room and renewed again when the patient's heart stopped.

After an hour or so, the terrible truth had begun to sink in, and the wailing began to subside. Eventually, the patient's son went to call a family member in another state, and his daughter-in law stepped out of the room. His wife stayed at the bedside talking to her deceased husband. I stepped out of the room as well, to give her privacy. After a while, I moved back inside, wondering how I could minister to this woman who spoke almost no English. As I approached the bed, she came slowly from the other side and met me. We stood at the patient's side. Though I felt we had few words in common, I took a risk and put my arm lightly around her shoulder. I told her, "I'm sorry." I am careful when initiating physical touch in my work, and I was especially aware that I was also crossing cultural boundaries I probably did not understand. To my surprise, I felt her leaning into me for a hug. When she pulled away, she looked at me and said, with a distinct accent, "Thank you." For me, this profound moment showed that she was aware of my presence and that despite all that separated us, we were nevertheless connected.

After this, she began, in Chinese, to tell me the story of what she had just gone through. She used hand signals to indicate the taking of blood pressure and then wrote a "20" with one finger on the palm of her hand. I remembered that shortly after I had arrived her husband's blood pressure had been down to 20. After this beginning, she went on in a stream of Chinese, talking to me as if I could understand but knowing that of course I could not. Yet I listened, and on some level, I did understand. I could not understand the words she said, but I understood that being with her husband of many years as he died was probably one of the most traumatic and significant experiences of her life and she would likely need to tell the story of this day many more times. She was beginning this process by telling me, a stranger who could not understand her language but who was present and had been present throughout her ordeal.

With common language and culture stripped away, I learned that the ability to minister through pure presence to another person remains—presence requires that I risk offering myself and that the other person risks receiving me. In this case, we were both able to take these risks, and a meaningful connection was created.

Initiating, engaging, and creating a safe place

As I entered this situation, I introduced myself and began to engage with the family. This process of engagement takes patience when a family is intensely focused on their loss or impending loss. It was important to let them know who I was and to be accessible to them. Some families may respond little to the chaplain in the beginning, as was true in this case. At this stage, almost any response is "normal," because there are many ways for people to express their grief and fear. At times, the chaplain may walk in the door only to have a family member fall upon her as if awaiting her arrival. People respond to crises in diverse ways, from extreme need and dependency to a lack of initial engagement, and everything in between. The chaplain offers her caring presence, beginning with this initial engagement.

As chaplains initiate a relationship with a patient or family, we model God's initiative in our own lives. Chaplains learn to offer themselves with a kind of graciousness that accepts whatever response they receive, free of conditions and expectations. We extend that graciousness with openness and acceptance of the unique needs found in each situation, each family, and each individual. Often we are well received, but sometimes we are not. Our presence may represent a reality a family wants to deny—an impending death. At other times, our presence may bring to mind a painful part of someone's history with the church, with another clergy person, or with God. These are responses that we respect. We continue to remain available (though not physically present) even if we are not immediately wanted. I believe we model God's initiative in this way. Nothing we can do or say removes us from the love of God, or from God's availability to us. However, God never forces us to accept it. Neither is anyone forced to accept a chaplain's presence. A cold response to initial engagement requires careful discernment about whether the family is so focused on their own grief that they cannot respond immediately or whether the family is uncomfortable with a chaplain's presence. In the ministry experience with the Chinese family, I sensed that the family was overwhelmed with the situation they were in, and I did not hear anything to indicate that they were uncomfortable with my presence; therefore I stayed in their midst, present to what was unfolding.

From the beginning of engagement, the chaplain also works to establish a safe place for the family or patient to do whatever they need to do in the moment. In the situation above, I monitored the door, keeping it closed for the privacy of the family inside, who needed to wail, weep, and speak out. This act also protected other patients and families on the intensive care unit from witnessing what they may not have wished to hear. Creating a safe place is about much more than closing doors, however. It is about watching over highly vulnerable people and providing them with adequate space and time to freely express their pain. It is sometimes about giving helpful direction to other staff or even to the bereaved person—if in grief their judgment seems impaired. Mostly, it is maintaining a culture of permission to weep, speak, and do what they need to do. Creating a safe place may include making sure there is a chance for good-byes, staying close during wracking tears, or asking a few opening questions about the life of the deceased in order to help less expressive families begin to share memories and feelings with each other. It may be about simply getting out of the way so that the bereaved family has the privacy they need. Perhaps a fitting image is that of helping a family rest under God's wings—hidden, safe, held.

Being a witness

Part of a chaplain's work includes witnessing the story unfolding before her. This is possibly the most difficult aspect of the ministry to articulate but is something of great meaning and importance. Human beings are innately social and cannot live without some kind of society. We need relationship. We were made in the image of a relational God—one who leads us from slavery (Exodus

14), struggles with us in the night (Genesis 32), and lifts us like infants to God's own cheek (Hosea 11)—a God who chose to walk the earth among us in human form. We know who we are largely through our relationships with others—with God, family, and friends. We readily identify ourselves by how we contribute to our society—as chef, construction worker, minister. In times of loss and distress, when no one can change what is happening or take away the pain, the need for another to witness our story remains. When others witness what we are going through, we are less alone, and our own experiences are confirmed. In a crazy-making situation, we come to know, as others acknowledge our experiences, that we are not crazy—rather, we are struggling in the momentary chaos. In the experience above, I became the primary witness to the family's pain and loss, to their confusion and anger, and to their eventual resignation. Their need for someone to witness their experience was made evident through the role the patient's son took in interpreting every word his mother said. He did not want the language barrier to rob her of witnesses. He wanted her thoughts and feelings, her experience, to be known. Furthermore, a witness can help carry on the meaning of the experience, as I have just done here.

One chaplain tells the story about a visit she made to the emergency room to see the parents of a young adult who had just died as a result of a car accident. These parents of five had lost two children to disease. The chaplain recounts the reaction of the father at the news of this son's death. She says, "I stayed in a room with the patient's father after he heard the news. He lay down on the floor in his grief and screamed. At that moment it was my job to be present with him as a witness." Because we belong to a relational God, we claim a witness to our everyday lives. We are never alone. But sometimes we forget that God is with us, or we are unable to feel that presence. As chaplains, we embody this aspect of God's care; we witness the realities of another's existence. Sometimes we are called on to witness others' excruciating pain. Sometimes we witness their joy. We face, with others, life's twists and turns and the limitations and resiliency of the human spirit. As witnesses, we represent communion in the broadest sense—belonging to God, to a community, and to all of creation. We witness to the hope that no human experience or endeavor occurs in isolation. We are all connected.

Listening with ears and heart: Welcoming the story

Throughout engagement and witnessing, we are always listening. The experience shared above recounts a time when listening needed to be done in both the traditional sense and in a more intuitive sense. I could understand much of what happened throughout the early part of the visit, because I understood everything said by staff and everything interpreted into English by the patient's son. In ministering directly to the patient's wife, something more was needed. I had to listen with my heart—to imagine what she had experienced and what some of the meaning of this event might be for her.

She had just suffered an incredible loss, and she was far from home and from all that was familiar to her. I thought of how vulnerable, afraid, and out of control this situation would make most people feel.

Whether or not there is a language barrier, listening on a deeper level is important. Patients and families cannot always express their experience with words, especially when they have the disorienting sense that their world is crumbling. The numbness that often sets in after the sudden news of a loved one's death can in and of itself become an obstacle to communication. Grief can rob us of our normal thinking processes. It is not unusual for a lone family member of a deceased patient to try desperately to remember just one relative or friend's phone number, with little success. Words needed to express thoughts and feelings may also seem to disappear as a person sits stunned by devastating news. Listening becomes an exercise in hearing what is said and what is unsaid. It may include reading the look on someone's face or in their fatigued form, suddenly so small in the chair. These may say more than the bereaved can themselves articulate. Insofar as it is possible, the chaplain listens with the ears and the heart and offers a response that integrates what she has heard on both levels.

When the time comes for words, the chaplain is open to and encourages the telling of the story. In the ministry experience above, I spoke to the patient's wife, saying simply, "I'm sorry." I did not know if she would understand, but I wanted to open up something between us. These words were a simple expression of my own feelings; they also served as an invitation for her to respond in kind. She began to tell me the story. Telling the story is the beginning of the process of making sense, finding meaning, and integrating the loss. When the patient's wife began to tell her story, it was a good sign, a sign that she was beginning to absorb this experience and accept its reality in her life. This would likely be a long process, but we can always invite its beginnings.

Receiving and listening to the stories of our lives is similar to what caring parents do for children as soon as they can string a sentence together. It is what we imagine God does for us as we pray about our lives. Story is important; Jesus used it in the form of parables as his primary mode of teaching. There are therapeutic benefits to simply telling our story to someone who really listens and cares. In fact, listening attentively and without judgment is a real ministry in and of itself. When we tell our story to someone with whom we feel safe, we can approach it honestly and may find ourselves sharing something we had never before told ourselves, something we had not previously recognized about our feelings, expectations, and motivations. When we are heard in this way, we feel fundamentally valued, and we have the chance to become transformed by new understandings. Listening to others' life stories is a fundamental part of our work as chaplains. Within this role, when there is opportunity, we interweave the patient or family's story with

God's bigger story. When serving those from a Judeo-Christian background, we may reflect back to them the connections we see between their story and the biblical narratives.

Holding prayerfully and offering touch

During the above visit, there were at least two things I offered the family that were not verbal interactions. One was my silent praying for them throughout the experience. This was one way of "holding" them during the time that I was unable to engage verbally with them. Such prayer is partly for my own benefit. It offers me a sense of peace, and it offers a purpose and focus when I want to stay present but do not have an obvious task at the moment. It offers the comfort I need in order to manage my own feelings around the pain I am witnessing, which sometimes makes me want to flee. In other words, prayer nourishes me so that I can be present for those to whom I minister. I also believe in prayer as a way of putting good intentions out into the world, and I believe in a God who listens and responds to our prayers. My hope and prayer is always for God's presence and transforming power in the situation at hand and in the days to come. I cannot demonstrate the effects on others of holding them in prayer; it is a matter of faith that loving intentions make a difference.

Second, I offered physical touch to the patient's wife in the form of an arm to her shoulder and a hug. Offering touch is so full of possible pitfalls that when I first started ministry I thought it might be easier to avoid it altogether. Before long, I realized that avoidance was not a good answer. It is of utmost importance to respect other's bodies and physical space. We never know who among us has been the victim of some kind of physical violence—including sexual violence. Furthermore, some people simply do not appreciate a stranger's hug. For others, it is uncomfortable because it was not a part of their cultural upbringing. Even if none of these is the case, in a moment of anger or disbelief, we may not want to be hugged! I have found that, insofar as it is possible to do so, it is best to ask before touching others. In the situation above, asking would have been very difficult because of the language barrier. I offered an arm to the shoulder lightly and in such a way that it could easily be declined by withdrawal. But I found it was exactly what was called for, as the patient's wife leaned into and curled up in my embrace for a moment.

Human touch can have amazing power. It goes beyond spoken language as a way of communicating care. It is more direct. It is a way of making our connection to another more concrete. For those who are very ill, holding a hand or offering a light touch to the shoulder to show you are there with them may be of real comfort. Many times, I have offered my hand and had patients or family members cling to it as if it were a lifeline. This can be a humbling experience. We are called to be God's hands and feet; we are called to embody God's love in this world—for what we do for the least in this world, we do for Christ. It therefore only makes sense that a part of this call to minister is to love one another through our bodies, through physical touch. For many people, touch or hugs are an early and important means of communicating love and care within the family, and they remain a direct and powerful form of comfort. I have found it to be a meaningful part of my own prayer life at times to envision God's arms around me, especially when I am hurting. We can be those divine arms for others, if we use care and sensitivity as we reach out to people.[1]

Blessing and letting go

There comes a time when chaplains must begin to disengage. Like engagement, disengagement takes discernment on the chaplain's part. For some of us, the tendency may be to leave the scene too soon—to protect ourselves from the frustration of trying to find our role in the midst of the chaos or to guard against the pain of witnessing raw emotions. For some of us, it is hard to leave. We may struggle to recognize the limitations of our role and to have the faith we need in order to let go. It is incumbent on us to remember that we are representatives of God's care, yet we do not even begin to possess God's ongoing work and love in the lives of those we serve. If it were not for my strong belief in God's initiative in our lives, from before birth to after death, I suppose the duties I perform and the endlessness of human need could deplete my energies. However, my belief that all of creation is within the sovereign care of God allows me to step into a crisis and step back out again. When the time to leave comes, a blessing and a prayer help me trust that this moment of crisis will not last forever. There is a time for moving on. Patients and families need to move on. I need to move on.

In the situation above, as the patient's wife began to share her story with me, in part through pantomime, I found it reassuring that a woman who had been wailing less than an hour earlier was already beginning to tell her story. The initial moment of crisis was moving into the next stage of grief. There is a time for every purpose under heaven (Eccles. 3:1-8). We can be thankful that the moments as well as the seasons of our lives change. A chaplain must read the story that is unfolding before her to sense when to step in and when to step out. As I say my good-byes, I always tell those in my care that I will continue to think about them and pray for them. This is a promise I take seriously. I know that after I leave, God will continue to care for them and others along the way. Therefore, with a blessing, we part ways.

The months and years after the family visit recounted here have brought many more visits with patients and families, as my work continues. Each visit is unique. Meeting with people in a wide variety of human situations is one

---

[1] For a helpful discussion about the healing power of touch and the dangers of misusing touch, see Cristina Traina, "Touch on Trial: Power and the Right to Physical Affection," *Journal of the Society of Christian Ethics* 25 (2005): 3–34.

of the most wonderful gifts of hospital ministry. The ways God has spoken into the lives of those I meet is a constant reminder to me that God is deeper and wider than I can ever imagine or understand. This work teaches me daily about how deeply God touches each of our lives—caring about us in body and spirit. It also teaches me about the vastness of God—working far beyond my humble ideas and aspirations. This work holds before me the mysteries that remain, the unanswerable questions, the pain of feeling God's absence, the wait for God's movement—a wait that can seem interminable. Chaplains often find themselves ministering to those facing hard questions and painful waiting. Chaplains represent in the thick of the struggle, in an imperfect yet important way, the love and hope of God—intangibles for which many patients and families are searching.

In Hebrews 2, we read that humans are made just a little lower than the angels. These words ring true as the resiliency of the human spirit makes itself known to me every day. It is undeniable that the human spirit is sometimes terribly wounded or broken. Yet so often I witness the human spiritual ability to be renewed, to heal, to grow and change, mirroring and even transcending the body's same abilities. As the Psalmist says, we have been "fearfully and wonderfully made; wonderful are [God's] works" (Ps. 139:14). What a gift it is to witness to this reality through the ministry of hospital chaplaincy.

Caring for people
who are terminally ill

Helen Kruger

Caring is at the heart of what it is to be human. One wounded human being reaching out to another nurtures and sustains humanity. Caring is the love and attention we give another person because that person is a child of God, just as we are.

People who are terminally ill often experience powerlessness, which may turn to self-rejection. The fear of being left alone, or of not being loved in this condition, may lead to a feeling of abandonment, even by God. Caring is the act that says to a dying person, "I am here with you, and I will accompany you to the end." That presence is a sign that God cares as well.

About a year and a half ago, when I first heard the diagnosis of cancer after my surgery and thought I might die from it, I had no idea how lonely I would feel. None of my friends and colleagues, who were going on with their jobs and their usual daily patterns of life and work, was on death's waiting list. I was the one, and it was scary. Most of the meaning in my life had come from helping others—teaching and walking a path that could lead others to become spiritual caregivers. This new journey was a lonesome valley, and I had to walk it by myself, pointing straight at myself. I had to feel the pain. I had to realize that my body had let me down. I had to stop caring primarily for others. I had to become centered in myself. Meaning had to come from inside, and I eventually came to the conviction that God had put everything into my life that I needed in order to face death, or life. I began walking with God in a different way. I shared with God a close relationship, a kinship that would carry me through. This image of kinship supported me and helped me gain insight and meaning. Even now, when there is no evidence of cancer, the image of closeness with God is reinforced and symbolized by those who were near me and really cared.

Three key questions

Perhaps the three most common questions that come up when we face terminal illness are: Why me? Where is God? Who am I? In the next paragraphs, I will consider these challenging questions.

Helen Kruger is a retired chaplain and spiritual care educator (Clinical Pastoral Education), St. Paul's Hospital, Saskatoon, Saskatchewan.

Why me?

For a person who is dying it can feel as though dying has never happened to anyone before. The question "Why me?" is a natural reaction to the impossibility of running away from disappointment, failure, and death. If we suffer because of illness, accident, or natural events, meaning can come out of suffering. In the Gospel according to John, we learn that suffering is associated with the opportunity for new life.[1] It is not a fault, or sin, but it can be an opportunity. It can destroy us or add meaning to our lives. We could hardly bear the pain and disappointment if we thought there was no sense behind it. After asking the question, "Why did this happen?" one might ask, "How am I going to respond?" The why question is really a cry for someone to hear the pain. When someone is willing to hear and acknowledge the pain, talking about the experience may lead to growth.

We often have the idea that life should be fair. When the unfairness of pain and suffering reaches us, we may be tempted to think that in the future our suffering will receive compensation. We may interpret our situation in terms of punishment and reward. If something bad happens, it must be a punishment. Therefore, cancer is a punishment. "What have I done that deserves this kind of punishment?"

In a nursing home, I met a fine elderly gentleman who lived with his wife in the independent living quarters. He became very ill and needed to go to the hospital; it was six months before he could return. Meanwhile his wife had a heart attack, died, and was buried. He was too ill to attend the funeral. When he finally came back, I went to see him.

Greatly disturbed, he said, "I don't agree with that sermon the minister preached today in chapel. He said the prodigal son received acceptance from the father, but the elder brother received no recognition. I don't agree. I don't understand that. The elder brother led a good life, and it's not fair that the other brother got all the attention." Tears rolled down his cheeks. As we talked, I realized that he was angry—very angry—at God, but he could not say that. This man felt he had been good all his life, but he had not received fair treatment. Why should this happen to him?

Life is not fair, and it is difficult to accept the purposeless things that happen to us. It is not good enough to say, "It's God's will." I do not believe that God wills for those things to happen. God does not send evil to create good.

A story from Ralph Milton, writer for the United Church of Canada, describes his feelings at the bedside of a suffering young man:

> I was standing with my sister at the bedside of her son who was dying from cancer. Such a short time before, he had been playing basketball. A tall, cheerful, bright young

---

[1] See, for instance, John 16:20-22.

man. And here, a skeleton covered in skin and sores was dying. It made no sense and I could only feel one emotion: anger. Jay had sung for years in the boys' choir at his church. And so to his deathbed, we had called the priest, his friend and pastor.

And as the priest came to his bed, I thought, "Please, don't try to be helpful. Don't try to make it right. Because. . . it is wrong! Please don't say anything helpful." The man was priest but also friend; he was mourning too. Perhaps also angry. And he did exactly what should be done at such times of anger and pain—he took his little book and in it he found the words we needed. Not little saccharine pieties, but the huge, soul-shaking lamentations of the Psalms. With passion and anger in his voice that reflected the passion and anger in our hearts, he cried to God those vast, unanswerable questions; he threw at God the anger of our souls; he brought to God the terror in our hearts.

And the words he spoke brought peace. Not resolution. Not answers. But peace. A sense that we were part of a community that had known these things before. We were not alone. We were not the first to shout out our anger and despair to God. For that moment, it was enough. It took many quiet, sometimes tearful conversations, many prayers, many caring friends, and time, to heal the wounds and make life possible again. The "why" was never really answered. Nor could it be, but God came into the pain to offer hope and healing. It was enough.[2]

Where is God when we suffer?

Among the heart-wrenching holocaust stories, Elie Wiesel tells this tragic tale: Forced to watch an innocent child being hanged in a death camp during World War II, the people asked, "Where is God now?" Wiesel, who was present, replied that he heard a voice within him say, "Where is he? Here he is—he is hanging here on this gallows."[3] God was revealed in a new role—not intervening to stop the suffering, but being present in suffering.

The book of Job challenges the idea that suffering is punishment. Job was an upright man who suffered and found no answer to suffering. When Jesus came to earth, he was always seeking to heal. He showed us that the divine

---

[2] Ralph Milton, *Sermon Seasonings* (Winfield, BC: Wood Lake Books, 1997), 52.

[3] Cited in Dennis, Sheila, and Matthew Linn, *Good Goats: Healing Our Image of God* (New York: Paulist Press, 1994), 30–31.

will is not to inflict suffering but to graciously make available joy and love to the fullest. Nevertheless, suffering is part of being mortal. Jesus was killed by those who rejected his way of life and sought to silence him; the cross was the sign of this tragedy. God was at the cross with the one who suffered. Our suffering does not please God. The gracious Spirit suffers with us and is present in the midst of pain. God never abandons us.

Who am I?

When terminally ill people no longer deny death and know they are dying, the "Who am I?" question connected to their inner selves may help them go on an inward journey. This question ends the routine of daily life and sharpens the focus on what life is all about. Because death is inevitable, when they learn they have a terminal illness, they may experience a new freedom to be themselves. Some people experience this as an awakening: no more hiding, no more masks, and honesty about the past. For caregivers, such awakening involves listening without judgment to the life stories of people as they struggle to explain the meaning of their experience.

> A forty-two year old businessman, divorced and remarried, hard working, ambitious and aggressive, discovered he had leukemia. After raging at fate, crying in fear and asking "Why?" he came to the point of self-discovery where he could say, "I hate to think of what would have happened to me if it were not for leukemia. I'm so lucky. I've discovered the deep love I have for my wife. I've been forced to spend time with her and have discovered her love for me. Lying in bed faced with death, I've had to examine my values. I was possessed with things. I still like conveniences and comfort, but they are not so important now. My wife and my children, my friends—they're important. I know what life means now. If I had to go through it all again, I would, because what I've discovered is the most wonderful thing in the world.[4]

Death sets a boundary to our existence, like a wall. One suddenly sees life as one's own, as meaningful and real. This can happen when someone such as a chaplain allows the dying person to go into the chaos and despair, while being supported by the listener, until God's love comes through into meaning and purpose for the sufferer.

Suffering is a time that invites the caring and love of people around the sufferer. It is important to have trained people who can listen to the sick one's question "Why?" without asking more questions or giving answers. A

---

[4] Colin Johnstone, "On Asking the Right Question," *The Journal of Pastoral Care* 35 (September 1981): 175.

caregiver must be ready to suffer in empathy, which means putting ourselves in the sufferer's place but still maintaining our own identity. We must not give answers when there are none. We do not need to defend God. God can handle anger and doubt and does not need to be justified. Those who suffer must express emotions and tell their stories to discover their depths of feeling before beginning to see themselves the way they really are. In the presence of one who supports and loves, this transformation of self can happen.

Community context

I stood at the bedside of a man who had suffered for many months. As he lay in palliative care awaiting death, he seemed utterly exhausted. His family seemed to be tired too. After they all had left, he turned to me. "What is really bothering you?" I asked.

"I'm so tired," he said. "I can't hang on. I can't keep my faith. I am totally exhausted."

I took his hand and answered him. "Your community of faith will pray for you. They will keep faith with you. Your loved ones will pray for you. And I will pray for you." He relaxed and went to sleep.

There is a place for the community to uphold dying members of the church. Brothers and sisters of the faith can pray for them. It is important that the community uphold those who are suffering, whose strength is depleted. Ministers of the community of faith must equip the church to become a caring and healing community. In the process, they must discern who has necessary gifts and who may have potentially problematic, self-centered motivations. Some may have a need to help another who is in worse straits than they are, as a way to make themselves feel better. The community should be an active part of praying and should be ready to help in concrete ways at all times. The physical being affects the spiritual. As illustrated by this young man's experience, physical issues may keep a person from being able to hold on. The dying one should never suffer alone. This is a time to support the one who is dying as well as the family. Fear of becoming a burden to loved ones is one of the greatest worries of dying people. Care may be demanding, because it takes emotional energy and often lasts a long time. Family members may be fatigued to the point of desperation.

Sharing these duties can lighten the load and give blessing to more helpers. This is a time of sacred responsibility. Relationship with a person confronting the mystery of life and death is an opportunity for members of a community to come closer to one another and realize the experience of centeredness as a community. The caregiver, the family, and the community have a healing potential that affects each one involved. For me, personally, participation in such a community brought about my decision to become an ordained minister, to bless and to be blessed by those in need, to study theology and to attain certification as a chaplain and teaching supervisor.

Society and the cultural milieu often add to the suffering of the terminally ill. The appearance of someone without hair, maybe without breasts,
skin stretched over bones, is not our idea of beauty. Not being able to care
for basic needs such as going to the bathroom, losing control of bladder or
bowels, or increasing dementia and weakness bring on a feeling of shame
and dependence. When we see the *person* as the disease—blind, cancerous,
or paralyzed—the result may be loss of dignity for that patient.

A man in the last stages of cancer wrote this description of himself:

> A scrawny, hairless man. Those formerly marvelous, mara-
> thoning muscles just hang on bones of unproductive and
> depleted marrow. The bright blue eyes are bloodshot. They
> peek out through tiny slits where my eyelids have glued
> themselves to each other. This skinny man is bent over,
> divided by an angry, red scar that looks like an N-gauge
> model railroad track…. My lips are red and puffy, like a sad
> circus clown. That's the view through the eyes of reality.
>
> Then there are the eyes of love. My wife sighs, "Every time
> I look at you, I fall in love all over again." My daughters say,
> "Remember what good times we had when we were little
> girls and you lay down on the sofa after supper and we'd
> sit on the back of it and roll you off with our feet? You're
> the best dad ever." My teammates call to say, "Hurry back.
> Nobody else has the reflexes to play third base as close to
> the batter as you do." A woman tells me, "I'd be dead except
> for the hope you gave me." A now grown man tells me,
> "You have no idea how important you were to all of us on
> campus in the sixties. You made us believe we could make
> a difference." God says, "I love you just the way you are."
> Those aren't the eyes of reality; those are the eyes of love.
> They see me as I want to be and yet, for them, already am.
> Now that I have cancer, I can see myself through their eyes.
> I like seeing me through the eyes of love."[5]

Death and dying with dignity

The personal growth often experienced by persons who are dying suggests
that those who are dying have a dignity of their own, a dignity that cannot
be taken away, regardless of circumstances. This is the dignity of a child of
God. Caregiving involves first and foremost seeing the face of Jesus in the
person one is helping.

---

[5] Robert McFarland, *Now that I Have Cancer I Am Whole* (Kansas City: Andrews and Mc-
Meel, 1993), 11–12.

The negative attitude of our society toward sickness and death is evident in practices that distance people, especially children, from death. The ill person is kept at a safer distance when turned over to the hospital, an institution that is geared to making people well. Dying is a threat to this role. Doctors and nurses may experience guilt when someone dies. They are under pressure not to make mistakes. They can be held accountable if they do not attempt every possible procedure geared toward sustaining life. Often patients expect a certain medication or intervention to help. The emphasis is primarily on physical needs. The role of a spiritual caregiver may help broaden such a constricted focus. Spiritual care can bring ethics into consideration, which may focus support for a patient's process of dying without subjecting the person to painful and demeaning procedures.

In my first year of chaplaincy, a ninety-three-year-old woman who was being subjected to many tests pleaded with me to get the tests stopped. She said they were painful, and she did not want them. I thought it appropriate to tell this to her daughter, unaware that the daughter was the one who was pushing for any and all tests in a vain attempt to keep her mother alive. We do not need to play God in keeping people alive, nor in allowing them to die. The patient should have a voice, and nature should be allowed to take its course when that is the person's desire.

The procedure of making living wills (advanced directives) should be followed for all people, old or young. In Canada, they become legal if witnessed and signed. They designate power of attorney in order to give authority to another who can make decisions when the patient is no longer able to do so. They also state the person's clear wishes in the matter of treatment such as feeding tubes or intubation. Chaplains can help patients fill out such a document if patients do not possess one when they come to the hospital.

Because society does a poor job of dealing with death, even churches have few sermons dealing with this sobering topic. As a result, people lack skills for dealing with death or grief. Indeed, there is little preparation for the experience of death.

As chaplain of a large hospital, I was called to the neo-natal unit when triplets were born prematurely. They were very small, and in a week, the first one died. In a matter of days, the second died. I received a phone call from the father, who asked to talk to me. He told me that he was not able to work. Many people were phoning him, and he could not help crying and breaking down. What concerned him most was that he could not carry out his working duties because he was becoming so upset. He was completely unprepared for death and did not know how to deal with his emotions. I tried to help him recognize his emotions and his need for time and support to deal with his pain and grief. Recognizing these needs and reassessing his priorities stopped him from rushing past this important time in his life.

Death must be accepted, as hard as it may be to do so. Such acceptance can be the means of reaching out to others. Accepting death can give love and caring a chance to come to the center of our universe. Spiritual care can integrate technology and rationality with intuition and imagination in the search for truth and the divine.

I believe that patients should be given the choice to die at home, if possible. This is a great opportunity for spiritual growth, and for nurturing love, strength, and community, even though care for the dying may not fit into daily schedules of the home. Those who die at home may enjoy companionship with their families, receive acceptance from them for the persons they have always been, and welcome familiar things around them such as photos, plants, music, and even food. This experience can open doors of insight and love, and even provide a glimpse of the eternal.

Palliative care

Most hospitals now have palliative care units or rooms for palliation. Regardless of where terminally ill patients are placed, the same principles apply. The philosophy of palliative care is that the patient has a right to information and services from a team of trained professionals and volunteers. This team includes social workers, chaplains, doctors, volunteers, and others. A chaplain on the team is in charge of coordinating services. The chaplain may facilitate making knowledgeable decisions by helping identify options and advocating for the patient's wishes. Perhaps the patient has confided in the chaplain, "I want to go home," "I don't want to be alone," or "I don't want any more tests." In a family conference, the chaplain may speak on behalf of the patient who is unable to hold his or her own in such a setting.

A decision for palliation means that deliberate attention is given to social and emotional support for the terminally ill individual. The patient should receive shelter from the stress of illness, help in relieving symptoms, and assistance to maintain function and comfort. Many palliative care units have a cot in the room for a friend or relative to spend the night. Palliation does not cease to provide physical support but adds to it psychological and spiritual support. The atmosphere is relaxed; a volunteer may be baking cookies in the kitchen, and family members may visit at all hours. For a woman who longed to see her pet cat one more time, an exception to the no-pets rule was made. Music, books, and videos are available, as is a clown. It is common to hear laughter from a room. The acceptance of death can be seen as natural, and the inevitable allows humor—even partying.

A young businesswoman whom I met in palliative care was sitting on her bed, phoning instructions to her office. When we talked, she told me about the party she was planning for the evening, in the hospital, for her minister and her church friends. She died within the week, in a peaceful frame of mind. Death does not need to defeat us. Whether we are actively living or have entered the actively dying stage, chaplain and patient can participate in the knowledge that death is a natural consequence of living and maybe even the joy of a new beginning. Henri Nouwen's book *Life of the Beloved* is an excellent tool to prepare for death and the discussions around it.[6] If the person asks about life after death, caring conversation about the topic is important. We have the assurance that God has prepared for us a place in which God is present and loves us. Scripture passages such as 1 Corinthians 13, 2 Corinthians 15, John 14:1-6, and Psalm 23 can be reassuring and foster the sense of communion with God.

Ethical issues

Euthanasia is an ethical issue that accompanies terminal care. Anabaptists have tended to oppose the intentional termination of life, whether by suicide or euthanasia. It is necessary that people in despair have continual access to a spiritual caregiver, one who can support and offer a presence of hope and faith, one who understands their physical needs and how these may affect their coping abilities.

A story in *Good Goats: Healing Our Image of God* tells of a minister comforting a mother whose son has taken his own life. She is afraid that God will condemn her son. The minister asks her to role-play God when the son comes to the judgment seat. "What would you do?" he asks her. "Oh!" she exclaims, with tears running down her cheeks, for she sees her son coming, looking lonely and empty, "I would put my arms around him and say, 'I love you.'" "Well," the minister responds, "do you think God loves us less than a mother?"[7] This image of God is not vengeful. Our God understands the human situation and knows that life may end in trying to mentally resolve problems, just as cancer ends the physical life when people cannot force themselves to live on.

Managing pain

Pain is often what persons fear most in terminal illness. Pain is almost always a combination of physical and psychological factors, and often the spiritual enters in as well. Sometimes emotional pain stems from acts that have been committed and cannot be erased but can be forgiven. It is important for the chaplain who gains the trust of the patient to listen to these stories, so that sharing, praying, and forgiveness can happen.

A man began to manifest symptoms of acute pain. He had been carrying feelings of inadequacy as a parent because of certain paths his child had chosen. When he allowed himself to speak about the cause of his years of suffering, worry, and self-blame, he was able to identify the responsibility that belonged to his child, to begin the process of forgiving himself, and to

---

[6] Henri J. M. Nouwen, *Life of the Beloved: Spiritual Living in a Secular World* (New York: Crossroad Publishing Co., 2002).

[7] Linn, *Good Goats*, 30–31.

submit his emotional reactions to a more objective self-examination. Dying is a unique opportunity to come to terms with the truth of one's own reality and to process it with family members, who may make peace and offer forgiveness where necessary.

Some physical pains are difficult to control. As a nurse, I had to face the effect of morphine, which I gave for pain but which also shortened the days of the patient. Ethics is based on intention: I gave morphine to control pain, not to shorten life, which was a side effect. Patients' wishes to remove tubes and respirators deserve respect when they have been diagnosed with terminal illness and do not wish to have these interventions. Those who are actively dying have a right to dignity and comfort.

Family dynamics

Dealing with emotions of family members as dying progresses is a part of the chaplain's concern. I recall a twenty-two-year-old man who was dying of cancer. His parents came from a distance to be at his bedside. As soon as I walked in and introduced myself as the chaplain, they asked for prayer; they seemed in deep distress. We went to the quiet room and I began to pray, talking to God about the son. The father interrupted me. "No, no," he said. "We want you to pray that he will be healed." I continued my prayer and committed this young man to God. Then I had a long conversation with the parents. The father was very upset. Their son had not been baptized, and the father knew that the son would be buried outside the cemetery in his hometown if he had not been baptized. Then I spoke to the young man. He expressed his readiness to be baptized, but not by his home priest. We arranged for a baptism. As the hospital priest and I talked and supported the family, peace with God came to them, and they were able to accept the coming death.

Family tensions often erupt when old roles in the family reemerge in the face of questions about who should take charge. At the bedside of a dying grandmother, the adult children fell into their earlier pattern of the oldest one taking charge in making various arrangements, and the younger ones following. Yet after the death, it became clear that the youngest siblings were taking charge of the funeral arrangements. Together we worked out a plan whereby the funeral would be held at the funeral home, in order to avoid a squabble about which church to use; family members were Catholic and Protestant. The oldest son called me several times, because he was deeply offended at not being in charge of funeral decisions. At first, he would not cooperate with his siblings. After several counseling sessions, he was able to resolve his feelings and collaborate with them.

In the final hours of this grandmother's life, grandchildren were present with her. I have always encouraged children to be present at death unless the death is very difficult, or the children really do not wish to be part of the group. Children need to say goodbye. If they see what is happening, they will not need to reconstruct scenes in their imagination, of what might have been happening when grandma died.

Death and illness bring out deep feelings and high tensions. Each family member may have a different interpretation of the crisis. When emotions are high, a more objective person, such as the chaplain, can be someone to whom all relate as they work to express feelings and articulate thoughts.

Another example of the mix of emotions at the bedside of a terminally ill person involved a father and mother with their forty-year-old son who was dying of cancer. Staff had informed me that the parents had never discussed the son's condition or his imminent death. When I arrived in the room, the mother stood up and began telling me about all the mistakes that had been made. The cancer had not been detected in time. No treatment had helped. Her anger hung in the room. She came close to me as she was talking, looked intently at my face, and said, "And how do you know that you don't have cancer in that wart on your face?" God gave me the grace to be quiet. I looked toward her husband, who was crying as he looked at his son lying motionless on the bed. "Have you had an opportunity to tell your son how much you love him, and have you said goodbye?" I asked. He immediately went to the bedside, encircled his son's face with his hands, telling him how much he cared about him and what he had meant to them. The mother slowly walked to the other side of the bed and began to whisper in his ear and stroke his hand. The son was clearly aware of them as he pressed their hands and tears rolled down his cheeks.

Phases and faces of the dying process

Elisabeth Kübler-Ross has identified five emotional stages through which a dying person (and loved ones) may pass.[8] These stages do not occur in any set order or pattern; not all may be experienced, and several may appear at once. The five phases are denial, anger, bargaining, depression, and acceptance.

Denial is helpful when it protects the self from a reality that is too painful to face. When the person is ready to face reality, he or she at that time needs someone present to listen and absorb. Often the family is in denial, making it difficult and lonely for the patient who is ready to move on. When this is the situation, the patient may somehow take the opportunity to die when all the family members have left the room. The caregiver must be responsive when the patient wishes to know the truth, even though it is up to the medical personnel to share this news.

The baby of a single mother whom I visited every day was not responding to treatment and was judged to be terminally ill. I was asked to break the news to the mother. Every day she greeted me in the same way. "Don't you think he is a better color today? He smiled at me today." I helped her enjoy her baby; I could not bring myself to tell her that he was dying. I felt intuitively

---

[8] Elisabeth Kübler-Ross, *On Death and Dying* (New York: Macmillan, 1969).

that she had built a wall and did not want it to be broken down. The baby died. I led the funeral. A month later, the mother called me and asked if we could go out for coffee. "I want to know," she said, "how was it that you supported me and helped me enjoy the short life of my little boy? I knew he was dying, but I wanted to have a happy time with him. How did you know never to put my hopes down?" I did not know what to say. Finally, I told her that God gave me the right words at the right time so that she could enjoy her baby and appreciate his short life.

Sometimes we need denial to protect us, at least temporarily. As a rule, however, it is healthier for both patients and families to be realistic to the extent that they can bear it.

Anger is common, particularly in men, because they have been socialized to express anger rather than fear. Sometimes anger is heaped on the caregiver and other times on staff. Patients may feel anger at God, but they are often afraid to say that. In any event, anger is an emotion that is not good or bad until the person invests it for some purpose. Anger may help patients cope with the underlying fear until they can face it.

Bargaining often takes the form of promising God something in return for longer life. It is often private, but the good listener allows the expression of the bargaining process. It may signify hope and desire, though somewhat unrealistically.

Depression is common when the reality of the situation becomes clear. Symptoms of depression may include sleeping a lot, and crying. If patients feel guilty about being a burden, feel unattractive, or even feel that money is being wasted on them, the caregiver can listen and be supportive and reassuring. However, if the losses are overwhelming or the future is just too hard to accept, it may be better to let a person grieve in silence. Holding hands or just sitting with the patient may be enough.

In the best-case scenario, the patient reaches the phase of *acceptance* before family or friends begin to think that they are being rejected. They may not understand that the patient is trying to be realistic, separating from all that is happening, and preparing for the next stage. Quiet time to be alone needs to be respected.

Needs of the dying patient

To summarize, the needs of the dying patient would normally include the following:

- Opportunity to discuss the process of dying, body changes, losing control, and what happens after death
- Involvement in decision making
- Acceptance as the person they have always been (and the need not to feel that they are a burden but are needed)
- Choice to die in the setting most appropriate for them

- The dignity of dying in the presence of significant others (that is, the need not to die alone)
- Opportunity to express feelings
- To be pain free
- To be cared for and know that they will be remembered with respect

These needs determine the goals the chaplain keeps in mind. Help is available from other resources—trained hospital personnel, family, and the minister of the patient, as well as the community of faith. The chaplain is the one who coordinates these resources and remains on call. The chaplain brings together the treatment, the hospital scene, and the private wishes of the patient. Visits from the patient's minister, if the patient has one, can be reassuring, and may involve planning the funeral.

There are meaningful activities that dying people can carry out with minimal help. If they can tell their story, it can be recorded, videotaped, or audiotaped. Reminiscing with the chaplain or with friends can thus be preserved. Special events can be celebrated, in the institution or by making short-term arrangements elsewhere. Meaningful objects, such as symbols, music, and books, should be made available. The process of forgiveness can occur by letter or face-to-face encounter; the real issues and feelings need to come out. Writing a letter about hurt feelings, more for release than for confrontation, may also be helpful. It need not be mailed; just the writing of it will give insight. The dying person who longs to be part of the future of the family may record messages for future events, such as graduations, weddings, births, or Christmas.

A strong sense of spirituality is the best coping resource for the dying process. Spirituality is a way of living in relationship to oneself, to others, and to God. In suffering, human responsibility to continue living with integrity may be strengthened by divine assistance. Religious resources may provide a way through which people can discover meaning for their life. Worship and religious rituals can be important to bring the sense of a higher presence to the dying person. Such rituals might include anointing with oil, celebrating communion with members of the church community, or practicing continual prayer, with the participation of the patient if possible. These rituals and practices may neutralize anxiety about the afterlife and point to freedom from pain as well as the promise of ultimate wholeness. Finally, our faith can supply a way to make sense of loss and suffering even in the face of death. Our faith can help us recover meaning and hope, which are essential to the ongoing process of facing death.

Each day, even for the terminally ill, hope for relief and quality of life can be available. Praying to a God who cares, responds, and walks with us may contribute to a sense of peace. Gratitude is perhaps the most powerful disposition behind joy and positive attitudes. The caregiver can lead in this exercise.

Viktor Frankl, through his experience in the death camps of World War II, has described the primary motivation for life as searching for and discovering meaning, which gives us hope, and without which the will to live weakens.[9] Prayer can strengthen hope and allow the terminally ill person to bear suffering with a sense of purpose and meaning.

It is the chaplain's privilege to respect those who are dying and offer compassion with honesty and genuineness, with empathy, and without pity. Most people are more willing to share with a stranger whom they can trust, than with people who belong to their inner circle. In hospitals, this is a well-recognized fact and seems to be especially the case with those who are dying. All people should have access to such a service, which allows them the freedom to discover themselves and enhance their relationship with others and their sense of communion with God.

The goal of caring for the terminally ill is not to cure or to continue to prolong life as long as possible. The goal is wholeness; the purpose of our being is becoming whole each minute of our lives, whether our days are many or few. The aim is to be healed by becoming whole. Wholesome spirituality integrates love of God with love of those around us; both are essential dimensions of our wholeness.

---

[9] Viktor E. Frankl, Man's Search for Meaning: An Introduction to Logotherapy (Boston: Beacon Press, 1963).

The chaplain as minister of comfort

CarolSue H. Borkholder

It was Saturday evening as I began my twenty-four-hour weekend shift, making rounds on all the units. The critical care unit was full, and there were several referrals from the nurses. Mark, a registered nurse, met me at the desk and said, "You might want to check on the family of Mrs. Brown in room 16. She's not in good shape." When I inquired about the details, he explained that the patient was seventy years old and had had an emergency appendectomy with many complications. "Oh, and she is Doug Brown's mother," Mark added.[1]

Doug is a respiratory therapist in our emergency department. During the past months, I had had several conversations with him about his mother, Donna. His mother's physical and mental health was declining. Her memory was deteriorating, and she often got things confused. Doug also suspected her substance abuse had increased. He attempted to talk with her about it, but she always changed the subject. Doug took it all in stride, "After all these years, I can't change her."

I proceeded to room 16 and knocked on the door. When I entered, Donna was restless and agitated. I introduced myself as the hospital chaplain on duty to a man sitting in a chair by the window. After explaining that I was doing my rounds, visiting patients and their families, he got up and came to the bedside. "So you must know Donna's son, Doug?"

"Yes, I do know Doug and have worked with him several times in the emergency room. He is an excellent respiratory therapist. And you are …?"

"I am Ray, Donna's husband."

"I'm pleased to meet you, Ray. I'm so sorry Donna is going through all this." He smiled politely and said, "We'll just have to get her through it."

We talked a bit more about the details of the surgery, and he stayed clear of any emotional responses. After multiple references to Doug as "her" son, I was careful not to assume that Ray was Doug's father and made a mental note to continue to be sensitive to that dynamic.

CarolSue H. Borkholder is a chaplain, Battle Creek Health System, Battle Creek, Michigan.

[1] All the names that appear in this chapter have been changed to protect privacy.

I informed Ray that I would be available throughout the night and the following day, and then wished him peace and a restful night. He told me that Doug had gone home to sleep and would be back to work the following day, and that Doug would be glad to talk with me.

His quick deferral to Doug as the one who would want to talk with me, and his reluctance to share his feelings, had me reflecting later on our conversation. I wondered if I had missed something. Ray had not shared his feelings; I would continue to be respectful of that.

The next morning, when I rounded through the emergency department, I waited for Doug to finish with a patient and then expressed my support for him and his family. I acknowledged that it is always complicated to be a healthcare professional and the son of a patient. "Yes," he said with a look of gratitude on his face. He expressed the wish that Ray would make his mother a "No Code"[2] and asked me to talk with him and her nurse to see if that could be written as an order before something happened.

I returned to critical care and spoke with Karen, Donna's nurse for this shift. Karen informed me that the "No Code" was already in place as a result of a discussion with the doctor that morning. She wondered aloud, however, whether Mrs. Brown's husband was being realistic and recognizing the seriousness of Donna's condition. Through the blinds, I saw Ray standing by the patient's bed, so I quietly entered the room. Mrs. Brown's restlessness had ceased, and she was no longer responsive.

"Good morning, Ray. Did you get some sleep?" He responded briefly and appeared more somber. We chatted some more before I commented that as chaplains, we like to check with families about the code status. I wondered what the family had been thinking and if they had reached a decision on the code status. He told me they had made Donna a "No Code" and how it had come to be. "I think it is best for her. If she can't pull out of this, she wouldn't want to live on a machine. We'll just have to wait and see." I affirmed his choice to honor her wishes and validated their struggle.

About 2:00 in the afternoon, my pager went off with a message to call the emergency department. When I walked through the emergency department earlier, it had been calm, but things can change quickly in that area. Perhaps this was a trauma coming in. I dialed the number and the voice that answered, "Hello, emergency department," seemed hesitant.

"Hello, this is CarolSue with pastoral care. I was paged. How may I help you?"

---

[2] The code status provides guidance for medical staff in the event that the patient's heart suddenly stops. "Full Code" means that staff administers cardiopulmonary resuscitation and takes all measures to revive the patient and sustain her breathing, on a ventilator, if necessary. "No Code" means that they will keep the patient as comfortable as possible and not extend efforts to revive her if her heart stops. It is important that the staff knows the status in advance, so they can provide care appropriate to the patient's wishes.

There was a pause before I heard, "This is Doug. Can you come down and see me please?"

"I'll be right there, Doug," I replied.

As I walked down the stairs, I wondered if his mother had taken a turn for the worse. Maybe he wanted to talk more in depth about how he was feeling. I met him in the hall, and we went in a small exam room for privacy. He was trying to keep his composure, so I waited until he spoke. "It's my little sister. Can you please talk to her?"

I was puzzled, trying to sort out if his mother was worse, or what had happened. I knew nothing about a sister but quickly answered, "Sure, if she wants to talk with me." Doug continued, "Well, Deb is very religious, and she just isn't dealing well with this. She's always been so religious and … she doesn't know what will happen to Mom. I told her about you and that I thought it would help to talk with you."

"OK. Where is Deb now?" I asked.

"She's up in the room."

"Well, I will go up there and meet her."

As I walked up the stairs to critical care unit, I wondered about this "little sister." Did she really want to talk with me as much as her brother thought she needed to talk with me? What did Doug mean by "so religious"? Maybe Deb's talk of not knowing what would happen to Mom was a way to express worry about whether her mother was "saved." I sighed, expressing my discomfort when family members want the chaplain to be the judge and to assure them of their loved one's salvation.

I entered Mrs. Brown's room and found the patient's husband and another woman and man by the bedside. I introduced myself and simply stated that I wanted to meet Doug's sister. I was careful not to state the brother's agenda, which would make Deb more uncomfortable if she did not really want to talk. The woman quickly identified herself as Deb and introduced her husband Bob.

"I'm happy to meet you." I paused and moved toward the patient, gently touching her hand. "Your mother doesn't appear to be in pain. It's been an exhausting several days for her and all of you. How are you doing, Deb?"

"It's hard … so hard," she mumbled, trying to hold back the tears.

I moved over closer to her and placed my hand on her arm. We stood in silence looking at her mom. "It is hard…. There is no other way to walk through it. Everyone has to do it in their own way. Deb, have you had time alone with her?" I inquired.

"Yes, I have."

At this point, her husband spoke up, "Deb, would you like time alone with the chaplain?" I felt relief that he introduced the idea without my needing to bring it up.

Deb glanced at me and then at Bob.

I let her know that I would be open to that. "This is a very difficult time and brings up many issues. I would be willing to process things with you, and I would keep our conversation confidential." I wanted to assure her that I would not run back to her brother to report what we talked about. "If you'd like, we could go to the chapel. It is peaceful and quiet there." If she was religious, I thought the chapel setting, rather than the waiting room, might comfort her spirit. "We could go now if you'd like, or you could have the nurse page me later." This offer gave her an out if she preferred not to talk with me and felt uncomfortable declining to do so.

Her husband interjected with, "It's fine to go now, Deb. I'll go get some coffee."

Deb hesitated and then said, "I'd like to talk now."

"We can do that. Bob, would you like to walk with us to the lower level where the chapel is? It's beside the cafeteria, so you can get coffee and wait until we're finished."

They agreed, and we chatted on the way to the chapel. I breathed a prayer, "May the Spirit guide me and minister to her."

The chapel offered a welcoming reverence, which also felt supportive to me. I pulled two chairs together, and we sat facing the cross. "Oh Deb, I'm so sorry you have to deal with all of this. Where would you like to start?"

"I'm just not ready to have her die. I'm not ready." She burst into tears. "I don't know if she is ready." She paused, crying, and then continued. "It's all happening so fast."

"It is happening fast, and that's part of what makes it difficult for our minds to grasp it all," I responded. "It is understandable that you aren't ready to let go. We only know life with our parents. It is difficult to imagine life without them. And maybe you had things you wanted to do yet. Or say to her."

"She has things she should say. She should say she is sorry for the way she has acted. She should ask God to forgive her. I don't know if she is at peace with God."

"And that leaves you not feeling at peace."

"Yes. I want her to go to heaven. She hasn't always been this way. My mother used to take us to church, but she stopped when we were older. Then these last years, with her habits, she has been so ... so difficult. And if she dies now ..."

Deb was crying, and I waited a while before I spoke. I did not feel that this was the time to explore the question of Deb's relationship with her mother, in spite of her passionate insistence that her mother needed forgiveness. "Deb, I wish she was alert enough now for you to talk about this with her, but she isn't. This is where we really have to trust. It is so mysterious how the human spirit communicates with God. Even though the physical body is fading, the spirit may not be. We don't know what kind of connection your mom and God are having right now as she lies there. She isn't responsive to us, but her spirit still can respond to God. Maybe they are sorting things through, and your mother is asking for forgiveness now."

"Is that in the Bible? What if is it too late?"

"We don't really know." I could tell this perspective did not really ease Deb's fears. "The Bible doesn't tell us much about the dying process. But we can trust in God's mercy and desire for all to come to peace." Because Deb asked about the Bible, I realized that scripture must be important to her. Therefore, I decided that sharing some resources from scripture might be fitting.

"There is a story in the Bible that speaks of God's invitation and promises. There was a farmer who had a vineyard and wanted workers to come tend the crop. So he advertised and said he'd pay them a certain amount for a day of work. Well, some responded and came first thing in the morning and worked all day. Others came before lunch and worked the rest of the day. A few persons came with just an hour to work before quitting time but got to help out. At the end of the day when the workers were leaving, they each got paid. To everyone's surprise, each worker got the same amount of money. They each got what the owner had said he'd pay them for a full day's work, regardless of how many hours they worked. Doesn't seem fair, does it?"

"God's mercy is like that. Some people find it easy to say yes to God. And other persons struggle because of disease or other circumstances that make it difficult for them to accept and live in ways we think they should. But that doesn't stop grace. Divine grace is always inviting. You know how much you love your mother and want her to have peace. How much more does God love her and long for her? God offers grace and peace and honors her freedom to embrace those gifts."

"So maybe it is like that with your mother. Maybe she is like the one worker who gets in just before quitting time. Whatever steps she had previously taken or not taken, maybe now she is realizing God's full offer and accepting. And God is granting her what is promised. She is being comforted and enjoying the peace of the kingdom."

"Can I still pray for her?"

"God never tires of hearing our prayers. Would you like to pray together now?"

"Please."

I extended my hands, and with her acceptance of the invitation, we held each other's hands. "God, giver of life as we know it and giver of eternal life as it remains hidden from us, we bring Mrs. Brown to you. You know she is at a crossroad in her journey. We ask that you continue to walk with her and grant her whatever her spirit needs. May she find peace in knowing you. May your Spirit comfort Deb as she seeks you in the midst of her sorrow. In Jesus' name, Amen."

We sat quietly. Deb's crying ceased. Then I asked about some of the good memories she had of her mother. She remembered the birthday party when she was eight years old and the cake her mother made. She told of a summer vacation to Lake Michigan, and the memory brought a smile to her face. I offered to talk with her again if she wished. We parted outside the chapel door, where her husband was waiting for her.

At the end of my shift, I reflected on my encounters. In which visits did I listen well? Which visits challenged me? What might I have said differently? Again, I prayed that the Spirit would help each person I had encountered hear and remember things that would draw them closer to God.

Each family's needs differ. With Mrs. Brown's family, I spent a lot of time. Although Mr. Brown was facing many issues, he chose not to address them. Doug was coping; his concern was with his sister. Thus, it was my conversation with Deb in the chapel that seemed the most significant to me. However, I trust and do not discount that other exchanges also conveyed comfort. I believe that God ministers in many ways that I am not aware of.

The chapel conversation with a family member raises a theological issue: the salvation of the patient. Especially when death is fast approaching, Christian family members may want to be assured of their loved one's salvation. They feel responsible yet are often unsettled about how to bring some resolution to the matter. They may look to the chaplain as an authority and one who can fix the situation. If the patient is coherent, this expectation presents a two-sided challenge, to provide support for the family and to the patient. To complicate matters, the family and patient may not be looking at the situation in the same way. While salvation may be the family's agenda, it may not be the patient's. Patients may not be interested in talking about their salvation, or may have found peace but without using the language that the family is looking for. As chaplains, we must always be aware of and sensitive to those differences and proceed with respect and caution.

Of course, the same respect and care are needed in cases where the patient is dying and unresponsive, as in the story of Mrs. Brown. The focus in that case, however, was more on the family and their concerns. The daughter was struggling with the question, Will my mother go to heaven? Because Mrs. Brown was not able to speak to me, I had no content from her to reflect on. Neither had I had any previous conversations with her from which I might have provided some comfort to the daughter. Therefore, I could not even begin to know this woman's inner relationship with God. I could not know, nor did I need to know. It was not mine to determine Mrs. Brown's spiritual status and destiny beyond death, even though the family was looking to me for answers.

As a clinical pastoral education student, when I first encountered this issue of a family wanting assurance from me about their dying loved one's salvation, I was uncomfortable. I did not want to give them a yes or no answer, and I wondered if I was avoiding a theological position. If I knew what I believed, should it not follow that I could give them a clear response? I do believe that one needs to confess Jesus as Lord and Savior. Knowing what I believe gives me security and a foundation from which to work. However, it does not give me the authority to decide if dying persons believe as I do. I will hope and pray for their peace, but it is not my responsibility to figure out their salvation. The idea of personal salvation is, on the surface, simple; however, it is actually extremely complex and mysterious. Maintaining the idea that salvation is a mystery brings me freedom from my own anxiety over not having a direct answer to give the family. I can minister out of the mystery and not be caught up in the family's anxiety about it. I can create a space to honor their concerns and offer comfort so they can trust and live within the mystery.

For Doug and Deb, I was able to accept their feelings and validate their anxiety and struggles without adding my agenda. Deb wanted her own religious beliefs to bring her comfort, but the opposite was happening, which concerned Doug. Reflecting with Deb and offering another perspective on the dying process seemed to lessen her fear and open the way for her inquiry about scripture. Taking that as a clue, I offered a story from scripture to emphasize the aspect of God's mercy in the mystery of salvation. I hoped she could once again use her faith as a resource to bring her comfort.

Deb deeply loved her mother, and her sorrow was great over the reality of losing her. She remembered the painful times of relating to her mother and the tension it caused in the family. She was trying to reconcile that image of her mother with what she thought a saved person should look like. Deb vacillated between feelings of responsibility and guilt for not making sure her mother was at peace with God, on the one hand, and, anger with her mother for not taking responsibility herself, on the other hand. Deb wondered if there was still hope for salvation even after her mother died. All these thoughts and feelings converged, and she was overwhelmed. She was seeking a resolution that would bring her comfort.

In order to offer comfort, I addressed the mystery. I shared my view that we do not understand how the inner self communicates with God. Dying is a process, and we do not know at what point the interaction changes from this life to the afterlife. Just because we see the physical body fading, we cannot be sure that the spirit is fading at the same rate. This view takes the responsibility off the family member and puts it back on the patient and God. In the end, the responsibility is not the daughter's. It is the patient's, and the process is between the patient and God. In recognizing this, Deb could trust that her mother and God were still significantly connected.

This perspective did not completely assure Deb, however. She seemed to need more assurance in order to trust. I sensed that the assurance of God's presence would help decrease her fear. I welcomed her spontaneous reference to scripture and took that as a clue as I sought to comfort her.

It was at that moment that the story from Matthew 20 came to me. I had not used that Bible story before to bring comfort in a dying situation. Where did that idea come from? I had not recently read that scripture or heard a sermon on it. Without further consideration, I began. At first, I felt a bit uncertain about how the story would unfold in that setting. I knew it would illustrate God's mercy beyond our human reasoning. However, was it the comfort Deb needed? I had always read this passage from the perspective of the worker who had worked all day long, and as a challenge to stop calculating the perceived unfairness of God's rewards. I soon realized that from the perspective of the worker who got in late, the parable was a great comfort. To be the recipient of God's extravagance was to enter a realm where grace and freedom reign. I believe that God's steadfast love and faithfulness are available to all of us.

I hoped that reflecting on the perspective of the last group of workers in the parable helped Deb release some fears, trust in God's grace, and find hope in the mystery of salvation. During the story, Deb was listening but did not respond in any other way. I could not tell how it was affecting her. She did not make any comments about the story at the end, but rather turned to the topic of prayer. Praying together seemed to still her struggling mind and soul, and freed her to remember positive things about her mother. As we concluded, she was no longer crying and appeared more relaxed.

The following day I met Doug in the stairway. I asked him how his mom was. "About the same," he said. "And thank you so much for comforting my sister. Deb really liked that story you told her. It turned her around. She's even repeating it to her friends. She is so much calmer about all this. I always knew that you guys helped out, but now I really understand."

"Oh, I am so glad. Thank you for telling me. My thoughts and prayers are with you and your family," I responded. "Take care."

"Thank you. See you later," said Doug.

As I started back up the stairs, I said a prayer for the family, and a prayer of thanksgiving for the grace that had inspired me to choose the vineyard story. I was also grateful to hear what had transpired with Deb, and that she was feeling more peaceful about her mother's salvation. Doug and Deb had learned that a chaplain comforts and points them to the Comforter. Here was evidence that grace is generously available for this stage—and every stage—of the journey.

Care in the face of perinatal loss

Trishia Penner

My pager went off at 9:30 a.m., summoning me to the labor and delivery area of the hospital. A family, almost at their due date, who had been expecting a healthy baby, heard the news, "There is no heartbeat. Your baby has died."

These heartbreaking words are spoken to pregnant women and couples more often than most people know. Perinatal loss, which is a pregnancy loss or the death of a fetus or baby either during pregnancy or soon after birth, occurs in 15 to 30 percent of known pregnancies.[1] While perinatal loss is common, often people choose to hold this experience silently. Many stories of pregnancy loss remain untold. While families have their own reasons for keeping the story to themselves, such silence about pregnancy loss prevents the public from being aware of its prevalence. Some have said that perinatal loss is one of our society's great unresolved griefs.[2]

Most people receiving care in the labor and delivery unit associate the place with the exhilaration of new beginnings, new life, and happiness. When a chaplain receives a call from this unit, it usually means that one family will be experiencing something very different. They will be experiencing a life change, but not the one that they had been anticipating for the past months. When I am called to this unit, it is nearly always because a child has died just before or after birth.

As a chaplain who works in the women and child program at a tertiary care hospital, I rarely know ahead of time what I will experience or what challenges and sadness my patients and their families will undergo. Some days are full of tragedies. As a chaplain, on those days I remove my sandals, metaphorically, because I walk in sacred space. The day can be unimaginably terrible for parents who are eagerly anticipating the arrival of their first child. It can be a day of extreme guilt for a mother who did not welcome the pregnancy and who wonders whether her negative thoughts caused the baby to die. It can be a day of complete bewilderment when an overwhelmed

Trishia Penner is a chaplain, Women and Child Program, St. Boniface General Hospital, Winnipeg, Manitoba.

[1] Adele Pillitteri, _Maternal and Child Health Nursing_, 2nd ed. (Philadelphia: J. B. Lippincott, 1995), 385.

[2] Joy Jonson, et al., _Miscarriage: A Book for Parents_ (Omaha: Centering Corporation, 1983), 3.

woman and her family find out that she is pregnant and at the same time that she is losing the pregnancy.

The role I play in these lives changes with the particular situation. Sometimes I am the confidante, the girlfriend who walks alongside the young woman going through this experience alone. At other times, I play the role of confessor, hearing the guilt people carry—for real and imagined sins against their unborn child. Sometimes my role is a priestly one, as when I am called in for ritual and blessing in order to formally recognize God's presence with this family and this child. Sometimes my role is to advocate for the patient, ensuring that health providers know of the patient's physical pain or medical questions. To other patients I bring resources and booklets, which become helpful as they move out of the fog of shock. The roles I play with each person and family depend on their needs, personalities, and comfort in receiving spiritual care.

Just as people's needs differ, how they perceive and go through this experience will also differ; grieving is an individual experience. Although some themes tend to come up often, individual response to such loss can range anywhere from relief to complete misery, to regret, guilt, or anger. People may feel several of these emotions at the same time.

For the family eagerly anticipating the addition of a child, pregnancy is a quintessential time in their lives: a time of new life and new hope that changes their lives and their future. Hopes and dreams that began when people were children themselves begin to come to fruition. When they experience pregnancy loss, hopes and dreams are thwarted. The future, which seemed exciting although perhaps daunting, now feels bleak.

For others, pregnancy can be an unexpected, unwelcome outcome of inadequate birth control. For these women and couples, pregnancy can be even more of a rollercoaster. Early pregnancy can be a time of deciding how and whether to accept this event. When pregnancy loss occurs, they may transfer their anxiety to the pregnancy loss, and feelings of guilt ensue. Whatever the feelings, positive or negative, surrounding the pregnancy, perinatal loss is an experience never forgotten.

When I walk into the room of a woman or family who has experienced a miscarriage, it is essential that I listen critically and read the signs of this experience's impact. People respond to miscarriage in diverse ways. A woman who miscarried at ten weeks' gestation told me that this loss was just as difficult and traumatic for her as if her two-year-old daughter had died, because she had bonded with this child in this short period. Another woman I met saw the death as an inevitable rite of passage, because her mother and sisters each experienced at least one miscarriage before they were able to carry a pregnancy to completion. Cues such as a patient's history with pregnancy, miscarriage, stillbirth, and therapeutic abortion inform my approach. Past events, however, do not tell me how families perceived those experiences and how they perceive their current situation. So while I may say to a family who has been crying, "I hear today is a terrible day," to most I try to offer as open an introduction as possible, in order to accommodate the woman's experience and that of her family.

Two vignettes

When I arrived on the labor and delivery unit, Jenna, the nurse, communicated with me about the situation and family with whom I would be working. Sarah and David came to the hospital for Sarah's checkup, just a week before her due date.[3] Nurses—first a junior nurse, then a senior nurse—could not find a heartbeat. When the nurses asked Sarah whether she had felt the baby move recently, she indicated that she was having a busy morning and could not remember anything recently but had felt the baby moving a lot during the night. The doctor did an emergency ultrasound, which confirmed what the nurses had begun to suspect: the baby had died. Although Sarah was partially dilated already, they chose not to wait for labor to happen naturally, and they began the induction process. This was Sarah's second child; she also had a ten-year-old son.

When I walked into the room, I found Sarah and David holding hands. Their eyes were red-rimmed from crying. I introduced myself to them, explained what spiritual care is, and began by commenting, "I hear that today is a terrible day."

They nodded, and together we sat in silence for a minute or two, until Sarah's next contraction finished. In the silence, the humming of the fluorescent lights seemed loud.

Sarah broke the silence. "I didn't even notice. I didn't even realize that the baby hadn't moved all morning," she said, and tears spilled from her eyes. "This is my baby. I should have known."

"This is my first child, although I love Nathan dearly," her husband indicated. "I have never been as excited about anything as I was about this. I can't quite believe that this is happening."

Through many tears, and some laughter, Sarah and David talked about moments from the pregnancy. They talked about the excitement of finding out about the pregnancy. They related the comical story of how they told their families. They talked openly about what their plans had been for the maternity leave Sarah was going to take, and how wonderful she had thought it would be to spend a year at home taking care of both of her children. As we talked, Sarah's contractions became more frequent, and I received another page. I informed the nurse and let the family know that I would be back later.

---

[3] Details have been changed in order to protect confidentiality.

Caring for Kimberly

My second page of the day was to see another woman who had also experienced a pregnancy loss. She was on the gynecology unit, the unit that cares for women with early pregnancy loss. Before I entered the room, I gathered my resources and asked the nurse whether there were any unusual circumstances that I should know about before entering the patient's room. The only thing the nurses were able to tell me was that this was the first time the patient had been pregnant.

When I walked into the room, I saw Kimberly in the room by herself, flipping through a book. I introduced myself to her and asked how it was going.

"Good. It's going okay." She said, polite smile on her face.

"I've read a couple of things by that author, too. What do you think of the book?"

"To tell you the truth, I have no idea. It's the first book that I've read by her, but I can't really concentrate today."

"Difficult day, hey?"

"Yeah. I've never been a hospital patient before, except for getting my tonsils out when I was a kid."

"This is a bit different." I smiled.

"I don't remember being so thirsty as a kid. I've been here since eight in the morning, and I thought I'd be ready to leave by now, but they haven't even taken me for the surgery yet. They didn't tell me that it would be such a wait."

"I guess there are a lot of unknowns in this whole experience."

"Yeah, I've been in and out of the emergency department for two days already, always praying and hoping that everything was still okay. When I started bleeding, I went in, and they said that everything still looked okay, but they wanted to make sure with an ultrasound. I guess it wasn't going well, though. When I went for my ultrasound, they said that the baby had already died. They think it might have been dead for a couple of weeks, because it looked very small for how far along I was in my pregnancy." Kimberly became quiet and seemed lost in thought.

Kimberly's verbal cues that her pregnancy was something for which she had hoped opened the door for me to acknowledge the loss she had experienced through miscarriage. After a moment, I commented, "It's amazing how a person can become so attached to a new life when it is still so very little."

Kimberly's tears started to flow.

"When my husband and I found out we were pregnant, we were so excited, and really, really scared. We had hoped to have a child, but when it happened, it was overwhelming to imagine how our lives would change, and how we'd be completely responsible for another person."

We continued talking about her hopes and dreams for this child. She talked about her experiences and memories of being pregnant, which I took as an opportunity to give her the resources the hospital had compiled. These resources include a booklet on miscarriage and a keepsake booklet to write down her thoughts, due date, and a name for the baby. I also gave her support group information and a written blessing, which I offered to do with her if she wanted me to. When I talked about how our hospital would respectfully cremate her baby's remains, and include them in a memorial service, Kimberly's tears began again.

"I wonder why this happened. I wonder what I did for this to happen. Before I knew that I was pregnant, I was playing volleyball. I was diving for the ball. I wonder if I hurt the baby. I can't think of anything else it could be. I did everything else right. I didn't do any of those things that they tell pregnant women not to do. I didn't drink. I didn't have long, hot baths. I've been on folic acid for almost a year. Playing volleyball was the only thing I could have done to hurt this baby." Tears poured down Kimberly's face, as guilt racked her body.

People understand the logic of cause and effect. When it comes to pregnancy loss, people look for cause and effect, wondering what may have precipitated this event. Differing existential worldviews can influence which "Why?" questions are asked. Kimberly's initial question sought the physical, scientific explanation for the death of her baby. Others choose a theological route, wondering why God allowed this loss to happen. Some question in a deistic humanist way, asking whether this happened because they are bad people. Regardless of which question they ask, people frequently wonder what they have done wrong to bring about miscarriage.

Many times, the "Why?" question will find an answer as the woman and her family heal from this experience. In providing spiritual care, my task is to support and guide them in finding their own answers. In their need to find answers, people sometimes blame the loss on themselves—on activities or choices that have nothing to do with the miscarriage itself. Part of facilitating the healing process involves dispelling myths. Often the things that people feel guilty about are not real but imagined sins against their unborn child.

"You know, Kimberly, you might want to ask your doctor about playing volleyball. I don't want you to blame yourself for something that you could do nothing to change. It sounds like you did everything right. I don't know why this happened, but I know that this happens even when people do everything right."

"We had everything planned so carefully. We bought a new house, and my husband just got a promotion, so I would have been able to stay at home to take care of the baby. It just doesn't seem fair. There are girls out there who are drinking and doing drugs, and they're able to have babies. I do everything right, and I lose it. I loved this baby so much. I don't understand why my baby didn't survive."

"Sometimes these things don't seem fair."

"They don't. But I will always remember about this baby. It will always be the first. You said earlier that you could do a blessing. What exactly is that?"

I explained to Kimberly the prayer I could offer, which combines scripture and spontaneous prayer. She asked for a blessing to be done for little Peanut—a nickname that they had used for the baby since the beginning of the pregnancy. I thanked God for welcoming this little baby into God's presence, just as Jesus welcomed the children, saying that the kingdom of heaven belongs to such as these. I also prayed for Kimberly and her partner, and for all the others who loved this little baby of theirs. After I offered the blessing, I squeezed Kimberly's hand, said goodbye, and left.

Miscarriage is sometimes thought of as an invisible loss. The woman and her family have no baby to hold and few things that acknowledge that this baby ever entered their life. For those who experience miscarriage, blessing is often important. It is a formal acknowledgement that this baby is a part of the family. The baby is called by name, establishing its personhood, acknowledging its existence. This little tiny baby also receives a blessing, one of the few gifts that could be given to him or her.

Caring for little David's family

After leaving Kimberly, I returned to Sarah and David. Their baby boy was stillborn, weighing 7 pounds, 4 ounces. He was 18 inches long. His umbilical cord had been wrapped around his body so tightly that it compromised his blood supply.

Before I entered the room, I met Sarah's ten-year-old son, Nathan, and her mother, Jane, standing outside the door. Nathan's face was wet with tears, as was Jane's. She had been trying to calm him after his experience of meeting his baby brother. Earlier he had stood on the far side of his mother's hospital room for only a minute or two before bolting out. He saw the baby brother from a distance. Nathan expressed strong reluctance to reenter the room.

Nathan's grief was deep, and his weeping brought the nurses in the area to tears. I floundered, having little experience with children and grief. After consulting with Jane, I asked Nathan if he would like to pick out clothes that he could give the baby.

Nathan walked with me to the cupboards containing baby clothing. I told him that he could choose anything he wanted from here for the baby, that he might be able to find a full outfit. Nathan quickly picked out a mint green sweater, smiling and saying that green was his favorite color. He found booties in aqua, which he thought looked good with the sweater. Finding a hat was a more difficult issue, because the selection was slim. While there were green hats, none was big enough for this baby. As we explored the cupboard together, Nathan spotted a hat that appeared to be big enough for his little baby brother. It was bright yellow. I wondered aloud whether the white hat that I had also found might go better with the other colors of the outfit, Nathan was insistent that his baby brother would like the yellow one better.

Nathan was so excited to show his parents the outfit he had chosen that he proudly walked straight into the hospital room. He showed his mom the clothes, explaining to her why his baby brother would like exactly this outfit that he had chosen. Together Nathan and Sarah dressed the baby, putting the sweater over the little white sleeper in which the baby was already dressed.

As this was happening, their pastor arrived at the hospital. Sarah and Nathan were admiring this little baby boy who was dressed in the beautiful but mismatched handknitted clothing that Nathan had picked out for him. Sarah was holding her baby, smiling with tears in her eyes. She invited their pastor to come close. "I think we're going to call him David, after his father," Sarah said. The tears had begun to fall down her cheeks again.

Jane led Nathan out of the room to allow the pastor to speak to Sarah and David.

Pastor John's hands were shaking. When I took a good look at him, I noticed that his whole body was shaking. "There will be another. There will come a day when you can have another child. We wonder why these things happen, but there is always a reason. One day you will know why this happened."

"Isn't he beautiful—my little David?" Sarah's eyes went up to meet Pastor John's. She held his glance for a few seconds. She looked so vulnerable, so willing to accept any guidance or direction that he would give her.

"Sarah, there will come a day when you will hold a beautiful crying baby in your arms. There will come a day when you have another child." Pastor John broke down in tears and left the room.

"He is so very beautiful, Sarah." I commented. "He looks a lot like Nathan to me, although I think that he has David's nose."

"I kinda thought so, too. I was hoping that he would have David's nose." Sarah giggled and cried at the same time. "I have a terrible nose. I prayed that this one would have his nose, especially if it was going to be a girl. Nathan had really been hoping to have a baby brother. They would have played so well together."

Sarah's tears became sobs. Her whole body rocked as tears of sadness overwhelmed her. David, who had been sitting withdrawn in the corner of the room, came over to her, put the baby back in the bassinette, and held her. I slipped out of the room.

What do we say?

It is difficult to know what to do for patients who are experiencing despair and suffering, and what to say to them. Pastor John did not choose the most helpful response. When he talked about future children, he was looking months or years into the future, while Sarah was looking only at her new baby boy who was not breathing but who looked perfect, with ten little fingers and ten little toes. She did not want another baby. She was not thinking about another baby. She wanted this baby. She had little David in her arms.

Given Sarah's situation, Pastor John's words might have been especially difficult for her. She was already in her late thirties. His words might only have served to remind her of her uncertainty about being able to have another child.

This pastor, who had the best of intentions, could not meet their need for acknowledgment of this child. We as clergy, family, and friends often do not know how to respond to pregnancy loss. In John's own pain and need to redeem the situation, he grasped at straws, trying to find something good in this situation. He wanted to make the situation better.

In a world that contains hurt and suffering, a very human response is to try to make things better. However, as spiritual care providers, friends, and family, we need to be aware that supporting a person who is suffering does not always mean cheering them up. For everything, there is a season. For this family, now was the time for sorrow and weeping. Now was the time to create memories that they would carry with them for the rest of their lives. They were not seeking to be moved out of that sorrow; time for that would come later. They only wanted to love and acknowledge this little baby of theirs in the few hours they had together.

Early pregnancy loss is often addressed just as awkwardly. Before a woman's body begins changing and growing, pregnancy may feel like an abstraction to those around a woman or couple. Yet the life of this woman and her partner begin to change from the moment of wondering whether she is pregnant. Many couples' lives begin to revolve around this pregnancy from the moment they suspect or know it exists. People struggling with infertility may love a baby even before it is conceived.

Kathie Mayo, a mother who experienced a stillbirth, expressed her responses to others' comments through a poem. While hers was a later pregnancy loss, people who experience pregnancy loss at any gestational stage may share the thoughts Kathie expresses about what words are hurtful and helpful.[4]

What do you say …

What do you say when a baby dies and someone says …
"At least you didn't bring it home."

---

[4] Kathie Mayo, "What do you say…?" in R. K. Limbo and S. R. Wheeler, *When a Baby Dies: A Handbook for Healing and Helping* (La Crosse, WI.: Lutheran Hospital–La Crosse, 1993), 72.

What do you say when a baby is stillborn
and someone says …
"At least it never lived."

What do you say when a mother of three says …
"Think of all the time you'll have."

What do you say when so many say …
"You can always have another …"
"At least you never knew it …"
"You have your whole life ahead of you …"
"You have an angel in heaven …"

What do you say when someone says …
Nothing?

What do you say when someone says …
"I'm sorry."

You say, with grateful tears and warm embrace,
"Thank you!"

We have no easy answers to give people; nothing we can do or say can change the outcome of this situation. In the quest to be helpful and supportive, we need to stay away from comments that minimize or justify this loss. Couples often hear "This happened for the best" or "There was something wrong with the baby anyway" or even "It was God's will." While couples may make these comments or come to these conclusions themselves, these are not answers for us to give them. No matter what our own experience is with loss, we can never say, "I know how you feel," because we do not share this same experience or the same interpretation of the experience.

There are no magic words to speak. When at a loss for words, however, supporters may offer certain comments and questions that some who have experienced a perinatal loss have found helpful or meaningful. People may appreciate: "I'm sad for you." "How are you doing with all this?" "Is there anything can I do for you?" "This must be hard for you." "I'm sorry." "I'm here, and want to listen." Sometimes the most honest comment is, "I don't really know what to say."

As spiritual care providers, we can make space for people to express themselves. We can listen and make room for silence, giving opportunity for grieving parents to express their story, feelings, and tears. We can discover their expectations, hopes, and fears. We can encourage them to be patient with themselves and not to expect too much. We can ask if they have any special requests or allow them the opportunity to create memories such as prayers or rituals to acknowledge the loss.

When I stepped out of Sarah and David's room, Pastor John was pacing the hall outside the door.

Clergy, like all who walk through the doors of a hospital, are potential recipients of spiritual care. Today was John's day to receive care.

"How are you?" I asked.

"How do you do it? How can you work in this area? I can't think of anything worse than seeing a child die."

"It's very sad when a baby dies. But I guess God gives each of us different gifts. I work here because I know that God has called me to help make this time as comfortable as it can be for the parents. We each have our callings."

Knowing that John would likely benefit from debriefing, I opened the possibility, saying, "The family looks like they might like some private time for the next few minutes. Would you like to get a cup of coffee with me?"

As a chaplain, I usually meet people in the vulnerable first moments, hours, or days of their loss. Although I keep in touch with a few families for whom I have particular concern, I leave most after a brief encounter, trusting that in the weeks, months, and years ahead, they will find some degree of peace, healing, and closure. While I may see them again briefly at the memorial service, I have hope that God will attend to them through other people from the community, such as their family, friends, and church. Each day that I work will present its own new crises. My choice is to leave these hurting people in the hands of God.

Caring for people with mental illness

Sherry Sawatzky-Dyck

The world of spiritual care in mental health bears little resemblance to Hollywood's "One Flew over the Cuckoo's Nest," with its large, sterile rooms filled with drooling, ranting and hospital-gown-clad patients. In the real world I work in, I turn my key in the lock of our adult psychiatric unit, and a small green light goes on, telling me I can push on the door and enter the unit. The floors are carpeted, and the walls are a warm taupe color. The staff are in street clothes, as are the patients. Patients know those on the health-care team by their first names, and the atmosphere is casual. I am one of the few staff on the unit who also work in other parts of the hospital. However, seeing patients here is a regular part of my week.

My spiritual care work is in a regional hospital that provides patient care for a region of more than 180,000 people living on the prairies of Canada. My job includes attending to the spiritual needs of three psychiatric populations: geriatric, adult, and youth. I also attend to the emergency ward, intensive-care unit, and the medical and surgical inpatient units. Similarly, I am on call for outpatient surgery, maternity, and a small children's ward.

An extremely enjoyable although taxing part of my work is in psychiatry. Some patients say being an inpatient in an adult psychiatric facility is what they imagine jail is like. On the other hand, I also hear that it is a comfort-able, homey, and caring community. Some people cannot wait to leave; others want to stay "forever."

Four vignettes

John

I walk into the unit and learn that a new patient has been referred by his psychiatrist. I look over John's file, talk to his psychiatric nurse, and confer with his psychiatrist. The doctor knows that John is suicidal but believes John when he says he will not kill himself because his religious beliefs forbid it. However, the doctor is wondering if the patient's devotion to his close religious community is getting in the way of his mental health.

It appears that John's religious community is blaming the devil for his auditory hallucinations and other psychotic behaviors. The doctor wants me

---

Sherry Sawatzky-Dyck is a chaplain, Brandon Regional Health Centre, Brandon, Manitoba.

to help in assessing the patient's willingness to try psychiatric medication as treatment. I confer with John, and it is evident that he believes God has abandoned him. He is certain that his mental health issues are a sign that God is punishing him for his unfaithfulness.

As John spends several weeks in the psychiatric hospital, his hallucinations decrease, but his depressive symptoms continue. He does not believe himself worthy of God's forgiveness or love, he tells me. He knows he needs to be discharged and to begin to live his life again, but he is afraid, he says. If he stays near the hospital, community rehabilitation services and outpatient mental health services are all available to him, as they would not be in his isolated rural community. He knows his home community understands that he needs help. They seem to be willing to support him for the time being. However, if he decides to live in the city and establish extended residency here, he believes his community could excommunicate and reject him. John acknowledges that he would feel both alone and free living in the city near resources and medical services. He also understands how comfortable but confining his home community has been for him. His family questions the value of secular treatment, and he begins to reevaluate his relationship with God and with them. He tells me he is becoming more assertive with them and more open about his struggles and questions about God's love.

John is unique in my work in spiritual care and mental health. Because of a shortage of chaplaincy staff in our facility, only those with specific spiritual, religious, or grief issues are referred to me. Unlike most of my patients, John is not currently involved in a grief process and is not in major distress about relational conflicts. A significant part of John's treatment must address the symptoms of his unstable psychiatric condition, but he also has theological needs and cultural needs, which are intensely spiritual.

Corey

Corey has been referred because of relationship struggles. He and his wife are going through a separation, and she tells him alcohol and violence have been major factors in the deterioration of their relationship. He thinks he can quit drinking anytime and initially does not believe he uses alcohol to cope. He claims his wife has restricted his visitation with his young children because of his angry outbursts. He is now being treated in the hospital for depression and suicidal ideation.

Corey has identified a huge spiritual gap in his life. He does not come from any church or religious background but says his hospitalization has brought him to a crossroads. He tells me he is looking for a place to belong and a sense that there is more to life than just being alive. Over the next week or so, he agrees to address his alcohol addiction. He starts looking for a faith community to attach himself to, and we talk about his beliefs, goals, dreams, and connections. He is learning to forgive himself for his failures, and he is learning to forgive others for the ways he believes they have failed him. He is learning to recognize and listen to his internal voice as the voice of God speaking to him. He will need to continue to find support and accountability as he struggles to find joy and peace in his life. However, he is hopeful about the journey.

Susan

Susan, a middle-aged woman with no prior history of a psychiatric admission, struggles with a chronic psychiatric condition. She has come to the hospital with severe depression and suicidal ideation. She was once employed in a high-stress professional career. Now she finds herself unable to work full time in any capacity. She came to the hospital with intense grief after the sudden death of a friend.

We talk, and it is evident that Susan's grief did not begin with the death of her friend. We discover that she has much unresolved trauma in her life, and this death has brought it to the surface, despite valiant efforts to store those feelings far away. She says her new job makes her feel trapped, and she yearns to find power and control in her life. Her family relationships are in turmoil, and she feels powerless to implement change.

Through much searching, Susan finds she is able to connect with God once more. She has been blaming God for her psychiatric symptoms, but she now sees them as a way to connect with people and a way to glorify God's strength and power in her life. Upon discharge from the hospital, she reconnects with a faith community. She has quit her job and started a business at home. She is learning to forgive herself for failing in what she perceives as her duties, and she is learning to forgive her family for not being perfect and for being unable to give her what she needs.

Susan continues to struggle with depression, but she has created for herself a network of support and connection, finding God in relationship and love.

Kathy

Kathy, like many patients in the psychiatric unit, has entered the hospital after experiencing a prenatal loss. Since her miscarriage, she finds herself unable to work and in the throes of a major depression. She has a history of chronic depression but finds this instance particularly difficult to manage.

A teacher by profession, Kathy is used to working with people and handling difficult situations. She says she is embarrassed about how this death has affected her, and she is eager yet fearful about getting back to work. She says her husband claims to be supportive, but she doubts that he really understands. Through many visits, I discover that her workplace has been very stressful. The miscarriage, it seems, was not the cause but a catalyst of her present situation. Kathy describes herself as a perfectionist who is hardest on herself. She also finds herself in the role of a caregiver for her family of origin, and she frequently attempts to rescue them from crises in their lives.

As Kathy learns to give up control of things she cannot change, such as the behaviors of members of her family, she also learns to take control of her own life and her own choices. Slowly she is learning to listen to the small voice inside her, which she believes is God directing her. Although she is afraid about where God might lead, she is beginning to trust, if ever so slightly. She continues to struggle as she slowly goes back to work and learns to communicate with her husband again. She is also learning to set appropriate boundaries with friends and family, so that she does not become the rescue team for all of them in their struggles.

Kathy is learning to find peace and joy in her life again but believes her biggest challenge is to find a sense of purpose and meaning in her quest. Church participation is not the answer for Kathy at this point in her life, and relationships continue to be difficult for her. As she is able to get her depression under control, she finds herself alone in the work of establishing boundaries and healthy relationships. As difficult as this long process has been for her, and as tempting as it is to fall into old patterns, Kathy is finding that she is nurturing her soul, and this makes the journey worth the effort.

Issues faced by spiritual caregivers

Unique features of mental illness

As research shows, the auditory and visual hallucinations, obsessive-compulsive or suicidal thoughts, and deeply depressive symptoms are very real for our patients. For some, mental illness is a disease process not yet fully understood, and for others, their illness is a series of traumas and coping mechanisms that have accumulated to result in mental health symptoms. For most, it is a combination. Most who suffer from mental illness do so in silence. The stigma around mental illness still exists for our patients. Many factors contribute to the persistence of the stigma.

My work is in acute care as well as in mental health. In acute care, I have often been called to the bedside of someone who has just received the bad news of a chronic or terminal physical illness. The symptoms of the illness are clear, and tests show a definitive diagnosis with a clear disease process. In most cases, treatments exist to provide some symptomatic relief, and in some cases, treatment aims at a cure. Patients with cancer or heart disease, for example, receive literature about managing their disease, and surgery or medical procedures offer possible solutions. Rehabilitation and support groups also offer help, and often our patients know of at least one other person with the same or a similar diagnosis.

We all know someone who has suffered from cancer or heart disease, and most people are not afraid to speak openly about their disease. Even breast cancer, cervical cancer, and prostate cancer, which were taboo subjects for previous generations, are now spoken of openly. Television and radio offer early detection strategies and lifestyle changes for prevention.

Mental health patients often do not have an evident disease process. Diagnostic tests are of limited value, considering the difficulty of recognizing mental illness for what it is. Patients often feel guilty for "allowing" their mental health issues to interfere with their lives. Families become frustrated and embarrassed by their loved one's behavior and inability to cope. Marriage breakup is common, and social isolation is a huge problem.

If more than one doctor diagnoses and treats a particular adult patient, often the second doctor will give the patient a different diagnosis than the first. Perhaps the second treating doctor has new demographic or anecdotal information not available to the first treating professional, or perhaps new symptoms have presented themselves. Similarly, new medications may be available, or the patient may interact with a medication in an unusual way for various reasons, and the doctor must work creatively to provide relief. These changes create a sense of uncertainty as mental health patients struggle to find their place in the world.

Patients and faith communities

Those who are admitted to our mental health facility fall into two major groups: those who come from a faith community and those who do not. Many of those for whom a faith community is part of their history gain strength in their faith and derive hope from God's presence as they struggle. Some blame God (or the absence of God) for their mental health symptoms, believing either that God is punishing them or that God has abandoned them. Others believe this journey is a means of testing or strengthening their faith and their ability to witness.

For many others coming from a faith community, help arrives late in the process. Many hear from their pastors and communities that mental health issues are the product of lack of faith, that if they would just live a righteous life and pray harder, they would not be having this experience. For these folks, admission to a psychiatric hospital is very difficult, and many do not stay long.

For patients who do not come from a faith community, struggling with mental health issues has much the same effect. It leads some to search for meaning and a relationship with the Wholly Other. For others, it confirms that God is dead, because a loving God would never subject his children to such pain and anguish.

Guidelines for Christian caregivers

Richard Wheatcroft suggests that the social world of first-century Palestine in Jesus's time was organized around the contrasts or polarities of pure and impure, clean and unclean. "The effect of the purity system," he adds, "was to create a world with sharp social boundaries ... what Walter Wink has called a Domination Society."[1] The isolation and abandonment experienced by mental health patients today is similar to the ostracism of those considered unclean in first-century Palestine. North American Christians of the twenty-first century believe we live in an era of tolerance and understanding. However, that understanding falls short in relation to mental illness; often those from faith communities suffer the most. Such persons feel judged, abandoned, and alone. To find themselves excluded, misunderstood, and (unofficially) declared impure only compounds their suffering. They often hear that their breakdown is a failure of faith.

To understand why a society believes as it does, Walter Wink suggests that we must understand its worldview. Our worldview, he adds, largely determines what we can believe about life, faith, and the world around us. If we are not aware of the worldview we gravitate toward, it will continue to determine our behavior without our even being aware of it. Worldviews, he suggests, "are not just the presuppositions by which we think, but the very foundation of thought itself."[2] Wink cautions that people who have difficulty believing in prayer, spiritual healing, the life of the spirit, or God can be seen as dealing far more with a worldview issue than with a theological problem.

A worldview provides a picture of the nature of things: where is heaven, where is earth, what is visible, what is invisible, what is real, what is unreal. Wink suggests that the first-century Christian worldview could be called the Traditional Worldview or Ancient Worldview. In this view, everything earthly has its heavenly counterpart, and everything heavenly has its earthly counterpart. Every event on earth has its parallel event in heaven; every event or circumstance has its visible (earthly) and its invisible (heavenly) aspect. Originally, this worldview held an understanding of the world as flat and heaven as just above the sky. The "up" of heaven sends answers to prayer "down" to earth.

The worldview of modern Christians has perhaps changed little since Jesus's day. Because we know that the world is not flat, our concept of the "up" of heaven has changed. However, the view that events come "down" from heaven either to afflict us for sin (or lack of faith), or to reward our intercessory prayer, remains common.

Stanley Hauerwas explains that as the early Christians listened to Paul extol the virtues of suffering, they believed suffering to be an opportunity to live in a way more faithful to the new age they believed had begun. "Their suffering did not make them question their belief in God, much less God's goodness.... Suffering, even their suffering from evil and injustice, did not

---

[1] G. Richard Wheatcroft, *Bible Study: Building Community with Our Differences*, Presentation at 1997 Annual Forum of The Center for Progressive Christianity (Gig Harbor, WA: The Center for Progressive Christianity, 1997), 1.

[2] Walter Wink, "The Next Worldview: Spirit at the Core of Everything," *Fellowship* 69 (May/June 2003): 1.

create a metaphysical problem needing solution; rather, it was a practical challenge requiring a communal response."[3]

The church in the U.S. and Canada today often struggles with the concept of suffering, particularly as it pertains to mental illness. Suffering as a result of religious persecution is not a metaphysical issue for the church, and suffering as a result of physical illness or calamity tends to bring people and powers together. However, suffering associated with mental illness has not historically motivated the church to action. Where there has been communal response, it has often been unhelpful. It appears that society in general—and the church in particular—makes a distinction between those who suffer from physical illness or calamity and those who suffer from a mental or emotional illness (even though mental illness is increasingly understood in terms of physiologic processes in the brain).

Certainly, the pastoral care response is different. Patients with mental illnesses are afraid not so much for their lives or their physical mobility as for their sanity. They are afraid for their relationships (present and future)—with loved ones, employers, God—and worry about their independence. They are afraid they will never be "normal" and that no one will notice or care. Our patients are afraid they will never be able to go back to university or get married. They fear they will never be employable or loved as they desire to be by their families. They are not afraid that their disease will ravage their body, as a cancer patient would be. However, they are afraid that manic outbursts or suicidal attempts will alienate family and friends and leave them even more alone. What is more, many of those struggling with mental health conditions are not afraid that their disease will kill them, but instead, that they will have to live in their own hell until a ripe old age.

The question, then, is whether we do in effect treat those with mental illness as impure or demon possessed, as in the time of the Bible, and thus still subscribe to the worldview that was commonplace in the time of Christ. If this is the case, are we not contributing to the predicament of those afflicted by mental illness? With the exception of sexually transmitted diseases such as HIV/AIDS,[4] or other conditions associated with behavior judged reckless or immoral, physical illness does not appear to have the negative stigma it once did. For bodily illness, the unofficial impure label is no longer common. The medical community understands the causes of some types of disease, such as lung cancer or Type 2 diabetes, and the media encourages us to make preventative lifestyle changes.

In my pastoral care experience, shame is rarely ascribed to most forms of physical illness. Although patients do ask, Why me? when they have been diagnosed with a seemingly random illness, a lack of faithfulness is not usually

---

[3] Stanley Hauerwas, *God, Medicine, and Suffering* (Grand Rapids, MI: Eerdmans, 1990), 84–85.

[4] This spiritual care issue is worth discussing in its own right.

offered as a cause of the disease. Similarly, these patients are not cautioned against seeking medical help or told that their health is an issue of faith—as is the case for some mental health patients. We do not easily link body and soul, but it appears we are slowly moving away from blaming the "up" of heaven for the "down" of physical illness.

Wink suggests that a healthier worldview is what he calls the Integral Worldview, which is seen in modern schools of thought throughout many disciplines. This worldview sees the spirit at the core of everything, with heaven and earth being two dimensions of the same reality. This worldview sees heaven not as up but as within. It believes not that everything is God, but that everything is in God and God is in everything.[5]

According to this worldview, mental illness, like physical illness, is one result of a fallen world. God is with those who suffer from depression just as God is with those who have cancer, and God works within these people to the same degree. The power of prayer has no physical limitations or boundaries; however, care needs to be taken with prayer, as too often it has been used in destructive ways (for instance in the case of misguided exorcism). "Because we are already related, and we are one body in God, God's healing power is already there ... and our prayer is simply a matter of opening the situation to God," Wink affirms.[6]

Seeing our patients not as impure but as children of God afflicted with illness and difficult circumstances will inevitably affect how we treat them. We have been called not to judge but to offer compassion, understanding, and care as we assist those in need.

Caregivers must become acquainted with the unique struggles faced by those who suffer with mental illness, and minister to them accordingly. Their struggles are complicated and often deeply spiritual. Many of those who suffer say that companionship and connection are what helps most. Our task is to assist with what Glen Horst calls soul work.[7] We need to listen and engage. We need to hear their stories, for it is in hearing their stories that we begin to uncover what those affected need in order to begin the healing process. We are aiming for health, not cure. For many, mental illness, health, and wholeness will be a lifelong journey. To hear the stories is to touch a person's spirit as he or she begins that journey.

Soul care for the caregiver

Spiritual caregivers must grapple with the issues discussed above, just as the church must. Our patients come to see us, looking for answers. However, they often feel judged by the very group of people called to offer love

---

[5] Wink, "The Next Worldview," 6.

[6] Ibid.

[7] Glen Horst is coordinator and educator of spiritual care at Riverview Health Centre, Winnipeg, MB.

unconditionally. Spiritual caregivers must be aware of their own worldview and understand their own stories and perspectives on suffering and mental health. It is difficult to listen to people's stories and help them sort out how to begin the healing process when we are stuck in our own stories and our own suffering.

The impact of mental health work on the spiritual caregiver is significant but no greater than the impact of other caregiving challenges. Whenever the essence of giving care is soul work, one must establish the trust required for others to open up their stories. Trust requires relationship, and relationship requires time and patience. Within a relationship, both parties need to give of themselves; the spiritual caregiver is no exception. Spiritual caregivers, whether working in mental health or any other part of healthcare, must be diligent about their own soul care.

Personal soul care requires the acquisition of tools for self-care. Research tells us, for example, that religious beliefs and practices are helpful resources for coping with illness and stress.[8] However, participation in the practices of a faith community does not necessarily equate with intentional soul care. As spiritual caregivers, we may be good at religious care and may attend our worship centers regularly. However, we must be careful that we do not use religion as a substitute for soul care but as a resource for it. We must admit that we also struggle and have stories that need to be told. We need to be intentional about telling these stories in appropriate ways to appropriate people.[9]

Many mental health spiritual caregivers work in isolation and expend so much effort in assisting others with soul care that we neglect our own well-being. We forget that we also need to experience being cared for. Depending on the size of the facility where we work, spiritual caregivers are often a small minority in a large pool of medical practitioners. Often, to be seen as a credible and valuable professional requires so much from us that it depletes our intellectual energy. Further, we expend our emotional energy in the care of others and tend to neglect our spiritual selves. We must attend to our own soul care so that we are at our best when assisting the soul care of others.

Conclusion

A blueprint for the spiritual care of those with mental health conditions does not exist. No two patients are alike, so no two interventions will be the same. However, unconditional compassion is consistently needed by all. People want human connection and relationship; we are social beings and

---

[8] See, for example, William R. Miller, ed. *Integrating Spirituality into Treatment* (Washington, DC: American Psychological Association, 1999).

[9] On the question of sensitivity to and skill for listening to personal story for the sake of soul care, see Jean Stairs, *Listening for the Soul: Pastoral Care and Spiritual Direction* (Minneapolis: Fortress, 2000).

crave contact with others. We can realize this connection through compassionate care. We must not fear those with mental illness or treat them as impure. The locks on the doors of our inpatient unit are there to keep those who are confused or self-destructive in a safe environment, not to keep us as spiritual caregivers out.

People with chronic mental illness suffer from isolation that is physical, emotional, and spiritual. It is the job of spiritual caregivers to give them a voice. We must help them tell their stories and accompany them in a healing process within a destructive and unpredictable illness. Their disease does not ravage heart or lungs but the sense of self and of wholeness. The work of ministry is immense, and in many cases, the faces of mental illness are unseen or hidden behind addictions, crime, and violence. However, we must venture forward with courage and with confidence that the Spirit is at the core of everything. If we hold the worldview that God is present regardless of whether that presence is visible, we can begin to assist by listening to the stories of mental illness. As these stories emerge and our patients experience the compassion they deserve, a healing process may somehow unfold.

Building therapeutic community

The chaplain as caregiver for staff

Robin Weldon Walton

Hospitals are places of human drama. Hospitals are also workplaces of those who come to serve people in need. The crises that regularly surround hospital workers can challenge their ability to deal with the events of their own lives. The pastoral caregiver has a unique opportunity to bring meaning, stability, and hope in the midst of the ever-presenting human drama of the hospital setting.

I begin this essay by discussing the role of the chaplain working amid hospital realities that make staff care essential. Two stories illustrate the chaplain's unique opportunity to care for staff. Next, I consider the complex dynamics of care for staff in the face of medical mistakes. I conclude with a survey of the broad range of contributions made by chaplains in caring for the staff and institution of the hospital.

Realities that make staff care essential

The life-altering events that patients endure rock the sense of fairness, justice, and dignity of those who care for them, often evoking existential crises. Those who work in hospitals expose themselves to the reality that they and their fellow human beings experience unbelievable trauma, insidious disease, and tragic death. At times, only a thin line separates the caregivers' reality from the patients' experience. Sensitive caregivers will be aware of the struggles that other staff undergo and help them find ways to talk with coworkers about the hospital's human drama, ameliorating its impact. Such support may involve speaking quietly with the pharmacist who has tears running down his face when he learns that a four year old has just been diagnosed with a terminal disease. It may involve examining the fears of the nurse who is caring for a dying elderly woman in the last stages of Alzheimer's, shortly after this nurse has watched her mother go through a similar process. It may include debriefing with an intern who, in the last months of her training, experiences personally the impact of a tragic death, after watching many such deaths with little emotion.

Robin Weldon Walton is manager of pastoral care, Doctors Hospital, Columbus, Ohio.

If these staff members are going to function, if they are going to continue to open their hearts to the people they serve, and if they are going to look with hope toward the years of a career before them, then someone must journey with them in the moments of doubt and strain that threaten to shift them off course. Is anyone else in the hospital better able to meet these needs than the spiritual caregiver?

The astute and caring chaplain can support employees in doing their jobs well, lessening the impact of the trauma of this work. The chaplain can also illumine, in the stresses of this work, a sense of calling and meaning for staff members, which can invigorate them for the duty at hand, encourage their compassion, inspire them to grow in their dedication to their profession, and thus to find hope for the future. This is holy work.

Societal pressures

Hospitals are a microcosm of society. Within our walls, we frequently face the underbelly of society. Our patients present to us the effects of abuse, addiction, criminality, and poverty. Sometimes they themselves are the victims of these societal ills; sometimes they are responsible for them. Staff are tempted to a variety of reactions, even perplexing responses, ranging from anger toward the victim to sympathy for the perpetrators. These reactions may be rooted in personal experience, or they may reflect political or cultural biases.

The hospital chaplain has a responsibility to caregivers, patients, and families. It is impossible without deep conversation (which at times may be warranted but is not always feasible or advisable) to understand the origins of a staff member's reactions to patients and situations. Understanding would help uncover the reasons for the staff member's actions or reactions, but in reality, this understanding is of limited value in the dynamic work environment. If the chaplain uncovers political or cultural biases, what then would the chaplain perceive as his or her role?

The chaplain's energy I believe is best directed toward encouraging the hospital worker to be the best caregiver possible in a challenging situation. Caregivers benefit from the reminder that their job is to provide competent care to all, that the dignity of individuals stems not from the decisions they have made or the experiences that have come to define them but simply from their humanity. It will prove counterproductive to discuss the ills of society in this moment. Such a conversation could lead to polarization of staff, further castigation of the patient, or a loss of credibility for the pastoral caregiver. A sympathetic conversation with the caregiver to discuss what exactly is making this experience so hard for him or her, and a redirection toward the tasks at hand in the context of duty to the patient and the values of the institution for which they work, will be more beneficial and efficient than a political or cultural debate. Later, as the chaplain's relationship with that caregiver grows, opportunities to delve further into the attitudes that made patient care difficult in that situation may prove beneficial.

Human condition

The Catholic Health Association has identified ten causes of death directly linked to people's spirituality: loneliness, depression, lack of self-esteem, psychic abuse, ill-managed stress, loss of self-worth, lack of social support, sense of abandonment, little meaning or purpose, and lack of authority.[1] I would add lack of hope to this list. With this list in mind, walk down the hallway of any hospital, look into each room, glance at the face, the body language, the personal effects of each patient, and see if one of these attributes doesn't jump out at you. This list has convinced me that these underlying emotional conditions, with clearly spiritual implications, are at work in many of the sick patients in our hospitals. This list alone gives sufficient reason for hospitals to employ chaplains, a good number of chaplains, whose sole purpose is to promote healing for patients in the midst of these conditions. Spiritual caregiving can contribute to emotional resilience and lessen the likelihood that people fall ill as frequently or as severely. However, this essay focuses not on spiritual care for patients, but for those who serve these patients.

How does the reality that our patients come to us with emotional as well as physical ills affect the staff? How can chaplains help staff in the face of this emotional landscape? The emotional states listed above are rarely the presenting diagnosis for hospitalization. In fact, they are usually not overtly identified; you might think of them as background noise. Though seldom recognized outright, they are a powerful force within and surrounding the patient. The reverberations of these conditions may touch places deep within caregivers, perhaps at a subconscious level. For this and many other reasons, patients affect caregivers in different ways. We as caregivers may be confused and surprised by our reaction to patients. We usually see ourselves as static and self-understood entities, so we place the responsibility for the varying reaction on the patient and not on ourselves. Thus in a sense, we tend to blame patients for the ways we react to them. The vigorous pace of hospital work does not encourage reflection or self-examination. We assume that we are fine, yet our reactions distance us from the patient.

Chaplains need an ability to stand back from the situation and view the players broadly with no malicious intent. Caregivers may distance themselves from their patients—pained individuals—whose very emotional makeup may well threaten the caregivers' emotional balance. If no one addresses this situation, a few destructive things may happen. The patient will not receive the full compassionate care that they need, thus reinforcing the deprivation of their emotional state. Caregivers may view themselves in a negative light, thinking, perhaps, that there are certain patients they cannot care for well, or that they are becoming cynical and hard-hearted. Their self-identity thus changes for the worse. If these attitudes continue unchecked for the patient or the caregiver, they will compromise healing.

---

[1] Photocopy, Catholic Health Association (St. Louis, Missouri).

Chaplains can intervene when they sense such tensions arising. Offering an insightful word of reflection, such as, "She [the patient] strikes me as such a lonely individual," might change the assumptions that caregivers have made about their patients or themselves. Chaplains, in visiting patients, may uncover interests or other coincidental similarities that patients and caregivers share (pets are often a subject of great appeal). Patients in emotional or spiritual distress usually lack a sense of control over their own lives. Many caregivers also have chaotic lives and find stability and solace in the time they spend at work. Helping patients find parts of their lives where they can feel safely and successfully in control will be a positive step in their healing. Caregivers who are able to rediscover their competency for the care of challenging patients will find renewed hope in their own lives.

Folks troubled with any of the above emotional burdens often have disruptive family relationships. This circumstance poses quite a problem in the hospital. Anytime chaplains can calm, coach, or reassure demanding or openly dysfunctional family members, or even set limits to define behavior that is acceptable in the hospital, they are freeing medical caregivers from the need to be as deeply involved in the family dynamics. This is a huge gift that chaplains can give to the staff and a worthy function they can provide, making them a valuable part of the healthcare team.

Systemic pressures

As healthcare costs in the United States rise, physician reimbursements dwindle, leaving physicians disenfranchised by the system. As the numbers of uninsured and underinsured patients increase, the stresses on our healthcare delivery system seem insurmountable. Many of the problems are typical of hospitals all over the country, yet we have to figure out how to deal with them locally. Healthcare systems are so fragmented that virtually every patient falls through the cracks at one point or another, without always being aware of it.

Disenfranchisement, fragmentation, and financial stress create an unhealthy environment for the practice of healthcare. Unhealthy or not, this is the environment in which we work. Chaplains must not see these issues as beyond their influence, or view the effort to address them as too toxic an endeavor. Chaplains may be among the few who clearly see how such stressors affect hospital staff.

Chaplains can be a prophetic influence in the face of these systemic pressures. At times, we need to work to make the hospital financially viable, which may begin with proper administration of our own department and representing good stewardship to our peers in other departments. We can try to lessen the stress of hospital stays and help close gaps we notice that may be delaying discharge. Sometimes patients or families are responsible for delays in discharge, because they have not come to accept their current situation. We can certainly play a helpful role by staying on top of our caseload and spending time in ways that help with stewardship of the hospital's resources. We can help our institutions draft sound policies for charity care and collection of bills. We can name injustices that we encounter and use our ethics committees effectively as they begin to shift their focus from end-of-life decision making to dealing with economic and other justice issues.[2]

Caring for caregivers: Two stories

Praying for a dying coworker

A nurse on the mental health unit was diagnosed with brain cancer. Her symptoms were already debilitating, and she never returned to work. She died a year later. Her husband never accepted the diagnosis of terminal illness. The seasons of her illness and treatment brought devastating times, alternating with peaceful and somewhat hopeful ones, but she never again drove her car or was able to go out of the house without assistance.

The pastoral care staff is close to this unit. We have supported staff in official capacities and played significant roles in their lives. We regularly see patients there and conduct a weekly spirituality group with the patients.

When the staff member, who had worked on the unit for many years, became ill, chaplains were immediately made aware of her illness. Our ministry toward the patient and family was minor. The patient was never admitted to our hospital, and the family had their own clergy to look after them. Rather, our ministry was to the staff of that unit. We were asked to visit the staff once a week to pray with them. The first meeting was very structured, including breath prayer, guided imagery, and petitions for the ill staff member. About twenty people gathered. Subsequent meetings were smaller, though a regular group gathered. At first, we prayed only and specifically for the staff member. Over time, however, our focus evolved.

Looking back, the chaplain came to be seen as a professional who could do the following:

- discuss of the meaning of illness
- identify the differences in how people in the group viewed prayer; because no one else wanted to pray aloud, they asked me to continue to lead the prayer
- accompany the staff as they struggled to walk with their former coworker over the long haul (help them identify ways that they could meaningfully stay in touch, contribute to the family's needs, learn to talk to her husband, be a sounding board for the patient who needed people to hear her fears)

---

[2] Our ethics committee has recently developed a subcommittee to discuss access to care. We are looking at issues that involve how the poor are treated and how we can leverage our assets and the assets of other hospitals in our community, and the assets of community itself, to work toward a local system that assures the same care for the poor that those who have adequate insurance receive.

- deal with the staff's realism, which conflicted with the husband's hopefulness
- facilitate talk about how to display and experience this work group's compassion
- deal with guilt when the intervals between direct contact with the coworker were long
- talk about reactions to visiting her
- pray in other ways, sometimes for other sick people they knew, for the unit's patients, about the ways society treats these patients; lamenting the broken medical system, holding onto hope despite its failures, and lifting up to God the "spirit" of the unit

When their colleague died, many of the staff attended the services. As a group, we ritualized her passing. We realized that we had journeyed with her spiritually (she was gratefully aware of our weekly prayer times), and the journey was significant for all of us.

After the death, I continued to keep our appointments, but folks had less and less time to meet. I recognized with them that this season was over, and we suspended meeting together. However, the relationship of chaplains with that unit was strengthened, our ministry to their patients enhanced, and the morale of the unit continued to be evident in their attentiveness.

A tragic death

It was five o'clock on a Friday evening. Pleased that I was already on my way home, I could not help but become uneasy when I saw a message from the chief medical officer on the duty pager. Not on-call myself, I continued on my way home, but the page was repeated, once, twice. I realized I had better get out of traffic and call in. I telephoned to find a very upset physician, beside himself that one of the medical residents could not be found. The physician told me there was nothing I could do right now but asked if I would talk to the resident's parents the next time they called in.

Before the evening was out, we all learned that he had been found dead in a motel room three states away, apparently of an overdose. Little by little, the pieces of the story came together: A pharmacist had questioned a prescription that the medical resident had tried to fill. The resident realized that he had been videotaped trying to fill the bogus prescription. He retreated, then got in his car, packed a few things, and left town without calling anyone. A couple of days passed before his body was found. His parents had been notified. No one had known about his drug abuse.

Thus began a pastoral care response that I can now succinctly organize in three stages: initial response, intermediate response, and prevention. In no way did our response feel ordered at the time. As it turned out, this death became the first of three resident deaths over the next few years. The scenarios differed greatly, yet our response to this first one became a prototype for the others.

During the *initial response* to this crisis, chaplains fielded questions from the various people affected. The young man's fellow residents and the staff that had worked with him asked questions such as, "Why didn't he tell me?" "How did I not know?" "Why wasn't I able to help?" Faculty members asked, "How is it that our supervision of him did not prevent this?" "How could we have intervened successfully?" "What will happen to the rest of the class, and how do we help them?" Family members of the resident wondered, "How do we talk about this tragedy?" "How can we help the other young doctors not go down this path?" "How do we survive?" Many asked, "Was it suicide?" "An accidental overdose?" "When will we know?" "Does it matter?"

These questions were raised by many individuals, in many conversations, over many days. As our first response, we chaplains spent time with one another, asking these questions among ourselves, practicing our answers for one another. This kind of support for the pastoral caregiver cannot be overemphasized. When new challenges presented themselves throughout the ordeal, we regrouped and repeated the process.

We sat with the resident's coworkers, fellow residents, and close attending physicians as they debriefed about his death and their last encounters with him. A mental health professional assured them of the normalcy of their reactions and assisted them to focus on helpful ways to cope. This led to many one-on-one conversations with us as chaplains. There were many tears, fears, questions, and prayers. Many expressed self-doubt.

We sat with the faculty as they yearned for a healthy path through this tragedy. We talked about the stresses, the lessons, the questions. We considered which questions were relevant and how to memorialize the young man's life meaningfully. We worked on plans for a memorial service. A local psychologist and poet was commissioned to write a poem, which we framed and hung where the residents would see it.

We spoke with the resident's family, trying to bring comfort in the midst of their uncertainty and pain, as well as helping them express themselves to the residents and faculty, whom they wanted to comfort and reassure. The family decided to come to the memorial service, so their needs were part of our planning.

All of our efforts were brought together in a memorial service designed to honor the resident and respond to the needs of his family, fellow students and coworkers, faculty, and the general hospital community. At the time, this felt like a culmination of the situation, but we soon recognized that what we had done was only the beginning of the response we were sensing would be needed.

Our *intermediate response* to this event began with the installation of a plaque. Spiritual care personnel continued to walk with staff in the midst of their lingering questions, impressions, and learning. Professional counselors were also available, yet the chaplains who walked with these folks on a daily basis played a significant role in the ongoing care. Meetings with faculty and medical education staff attempted to discern the lessons to be learned.

As a result of our intermediate response, steps for the *prevention* of such tragedies were identified. These steps have become part of the education program for subsequent residents. These include a reminder to students that they are not alone, along with encouragement to build community, build and maintain relationships, find mentors, and learn from the unwise choices of others. Acknowledging that the study of medicine is not everything, we now emphasize to residents the importance of maintaining hobbies, exercising, and having fun. We recognize frankly that residency is often a stressful time and that residents might find themselves coping in unhealthy ways. We urge residents, especially in such times, to seek the guidance of spiritual caregivers who are competent and trustworthy. Chaplains are available to help identify stressors and assist them to deal with these issues in constructive ways, thereby minimizing the threat to their careers if residents do not confront unhealthy patterns until superiors do so.

The chaplaincy staff takes the opportunity to communicate these thoughts during intern and resident orientation every June. Most of these young people have just graduated from medical school; some have spent a year in intern-ship elsewhere but are new to this hospital. Besides the above information, which relates to their role as faculty and staff of the hospital, I strongly make the point that chaplains are people in the hospital who support the interns' and residents' growth and well-being. We stand with them to help make the most of the professional development they will experience in this phase of their training. We want to inspire them to offer patient-centered care and to develop holistically, personally, and professionally with an ethical and moral component. We emphasize that we have things to teach, we are safe people to discuss difficult things with, and we always desire the best for them.

The conclusion of our presentation is a powerful moment. These young people appreciate knowing that we will provide a safe haven. They want to do well. They are relieved to know that someone wants to inspire them, because they recognize that so many forces in the workplace breed cynicism and contempt.

Dealing with medical mistakes

One of the most disturbing events that can happen in a hospital is a medical mistake that results in injury or death of the patient. Stories of this sort appear in newspapers with frequency. Besides the needs of the patient and family, the chaplain must be aware of the toll this event takes on staff—those who may be responsible, and those caring for the patient.

The first thing to consider about potential medical errors is the hospital atmosphere. The pastoral care department can become involved in influenc-ing this atmosphere prior to any event. Since National Patient Safety Stan-dards are now a major focus of the Joint Commission for the Accreditation of

Health Care Organizations in the U.S., it is inconceivable that any accredited hospital would not have a patient safety committee. While chaplains may not be involved in this committee's clinical planning to improve processes for the prevention of mistakes, each chaplain needs to be aware of this focus, encourage compliance, and prepare the institution to respond honorably in the event of such a mistake.

It is clear from the literature that full disclosure to the patient and family—quickly, competently, and compassionately—is the best way to handle the aftermath of a medical mistake or any significant unexpected outcome.[3] This makes sense on a variety of fronts: the medical needs of the patient can be recognized and treated aggressively rather than shrouded in secrecy, the staff involved can be identified, and the blame game may be put to rest. A "post-mortem" on the event is required so that the places where processes broke down can be identified and corrected, so that retraining of staff can be designed, and in a few cases, so that discipline of careless and negligent staff can be assured.

Full disclosure to the patient and family ought to involve the assistance of the pastoral care staff. In best practice, staff will have already referred this patient and family to the chaplain for support, because an unexpected negative event has taken place. When disclosure is anticipated, a planning meeting needs to involve those who are going to do the disclosing, most often the attending physician and possibly another physician who was involved in the actual event. If a person from another discipline made the mistake, it is still the responsibility of the attending physician to make the disclosure to the family.

The planning meeting would normally include the attending physician, a representative from risk management or hospital legal counsel, a representative of medical staff leadership, the vice president of nursing, and the director of pastoral care. The situation should be fully but succinctly presented and the condition of the patient and prognosis for survival delineated. The chaplain can share about the state of mind of the family, the extent of their current understanding of the event (if any), and any other pertinent observations, to prepare the physician for what the family will likely bring to the meeting. The attending physician communicates to the group the wording of the disclosure. All parties may participate in honing the physician's message.

The meeting with the patient or family should be attended by appropriate family members and held in a private and comfortable location. The setting is something that the chaplain can help arrange. The number of representatives from the medical team should be kept to a minimum in the family meeting. It is undesirable to overwhelm the family with a large group of important-looking people. Medical team participants are therefore selected

---

[3] See an interesting account of the program called "Sorry Works: Can Apology, Honesty Stem the Med-Mal Tide?" *Medical Ethics Advisor* 21, no. 3 (March 2005): 25–36.

in advance to include the attending physician, the chaplain, and one other representative of the hospital or medical staff.

In the meeting with the family, the physician should state briefly what happened, without mentioning names of caregivers. It is not appropriate to air before the family any turf battles that may be raging behind the scenes. It is not important to go into every detail of the situation, because family members likely will not be able to absorb it all at this point. If the family wants that kind of detail, they can request it later. Answer the questions they ask. It is important to share all information they need in order to make informed decisions about their loved one's future healthcare. The goal of the conversation must be very clear, and disclosure of the event kept in simple and broad terms. All information necessary to inform the decision makers must be provided. As always, when this meeting ends, the patient and family need to know how to reach those in attendance if they have more questions, and when to expect another meeting. At this point, it may be wise to supply them with the phone numbers of the president of the hospital, the vice presidents of medical affairs and nursing, and the chaplain (assuming that all of these have received a briefing on the situation and the status of the disclosure).

When the meeting concludes, the chaplain needs to stay behind with the family at first as quiet support. The chaplain, by now, is well educated in the particulars of the event and can clarify what was said in the meeting without adding any new medical information. The chaplain can assist the family in setting up subsequent meetings to review the situation, clarify information, and make further plans for the patient's care. Support of the family will continue in the normal fashion and may differ little from other unexpected changes of status. Chaplains encounter patients and families mired in anger and distrust of the medical team on a regular basis and must be able to handle those dynamics if they enter this situation.

I have alluded to turf battles and finger pointing that may be going on behind the scenes. In actuality, the planning meeting prior to the family disclosure may alleviate some of these dynamics. Dwelling on blame often short-circuits or delays clear admission of responsibility as well as the possibility of resolution. Chaplains know that confession is good for the soul. When someone who feels responsible in this event is identified, if this person's supervisor is battling with other disciplines to point blame in other directions, the blame hinders the process whereby the ones in need of confession, absolution, and resolution may receive the assistance they need. I had a personal experience with such a medical mistake in which a nurse was implicated in an event that was life threatening to a patient. The president of the hospital called me and asked me to minister to the nurse. When I called the nurse's supervisor, however, she thanked but rebuffed me and would not give me the name of the nurse. The supervisor did not want her nurse feeling or taking responsibility for an event that the supervisor was convinced was the fault of the physician.

Because I was not involved in a root cause analysis of the event, I am unsure to this day if, in the end, the nurse was implicated. I never learned who she was, so I was unable to minister to her. However, she was given my name and number. I heard that she was going to see her own clergy. I hope that proved helpful. I know, however, that the remnants of this kind of experience can lead to burnout, traumatic response, an overwhelming fear of making another mistake, and even the shortening of a career or depression. I believe the assistance of a healthcare chaplain could have benefited this nurse; however, I needed to honor her right to privacy. Chaplains have the opportunity to be a pastoral presence in work groups for other crises. It may be that I (or one of the other chaplains) have indeed ministered to her by words or actions in other situations. What we say and do as chaplains will be taken in by a variety of people and applied in a variety of ways never known to us.

The shape and breadth of staff care

The chaplain is the hospital professional who is responsible for addressing questions of meaning. Most people in the midst of a troubling situation are caught up in their own reaction to it. It takes time, distance, and refreshed perspective to bring calm and relief. Time is a luxury in short supply in a hospital. Things happen quickly. Usually too few people are available to do too much work, and the effects of many situations may accumulate in negative ways.

Chaplains are the only professionals in the hospital system who are trained to have, in the midst of complicated turmoil, a sure recognition of their own reactions as well as a detached broader view. As caregivers for hospital staff, competent chaplains display a unique perspective that
- sees the situation more clearly
- discerns the points of stress for those involved
- sees the places where our human need is threatened by the situation
- has navigated similar waters before and therefore has confidence
- is willing to be fully present
- has courage to step into the unknown as a knowing guide
- has faith that God's presence can be experienced
- has found peace with the fact that not all societal pressures can be met with conclusive action, but exhibits patience and satisfaction with doing what we can to have a positive impact on the situation in the moment
- is free from the need to fill silence with meaningless words and platitudes

- can accompany people pastorally over time
- can bring ritual and facilitate closure

The chaplain's contribution to the health of the institution

The chaplain (the pastoral care department as a whole) has the opportunity to bring a prophetic voice to the culture of the hospital setting. The chaplain functions as the pastor of the institution. The chaplain meets the pain of the people and elicits the hope that we can go on in the midst of encounters with suffering. The chaplain needs to take all opportunities afforded to expand spiritual care influence by becoming a respected member of the institution, together with the clinical team, the operations team, and the medical staff.

The chaplain's prophetic voice speaks of health in holistic ways. This voice speaks the truth in love to individuals, speaks truth to the power structures, and represents morality. It cries out for justice and advocates for patients, families, employees, the poor, and those otherwise disenfranchised. Further, it contributes to preventing harm and encouraging growth by helping to design teaching opportunities that will address life crises, promote healthy coping, foster a sense of community and a culture of humanity, and invite a yearning for the divine.

Settings for the prophetic contribution might include prayers of invocation, lectures for medical and nursing staff, presentations and workshops for special groups, writing for hospital publications such as *Pastoral Care Reflections*,[4] participation in community events, and work on ethics and compliance committees and various other committee opportunities within the hospital framework, including regular unit meetings.

Chaplains need to assess and use the tools at hand in a given hospital setting. On September 11, 2001, in response to the terrorist attacks, we held impromptu observances of prayer in work areas. We announced a gathering for noon in the lobby; many people came. Recognizing that our common purpose with the rescuers and medical responders knit us to the national crisis, I put out an "All Staff" e-mail in the afternoon to help ameliorate some of the impact and maintain a highly functioning workforce. We suggested to patients that they not spend all day watching the coverage. Nevertheless, preoccupation with the disaster slowed healing times. Much conversation was needed for reassurance and renewing of hope.

Chaplains need to be bold about standing firm in our position within the institution, bringing comfort and hope to people in situations that evoke discouragement and inertia. We stand with individuals and speak to the health of the institution by optimizing its function in the community.

In sum, healthcare chaplains have a unique opportunity for ministry in the dynamic environment of a hospital. The scope of our influence is practi-

---

[4] In our hospital, this newsletter comes in the form of a weekly e-mail to all staff.

cally limitless. Therefore, we need to discern what our institutions need and what spiritual resources can do to meet those needs. We need to represent ourselves as agents of growth, change, and morality, as well as faith. This takes considerable and deliberate effort. Surely one of our most important missions is to support those who have dedicated their lives to the care of the sick and dying.

Part 3
Special concerns in chaplaincy ministry

16

The chaplain as reflective practitioner and pastoral theologian

Leah Dawn Bueckert and Daniel S. Schipani

Competence in spiritual caregiving in the hospital setting includes the commitment to learn from ministry experiences and to bring that learning to bear on our interactions with patients, families, and staff. Such reflection and application are the particular focus of this essay. Using a vignette involving a chaplain, a nurse, and a patient, we will illustrate the kind of systematic analysis that characterizes chaplains as reflective practitioners and pastoral theologians.

Because this essay stems from our collegial conversations, we hope that it will demonstrate the value of collaboration in the reflective process. The vignette below relates a spiritual care encounter that took place when the authors of this essay were chaplain (Leah Dawn Bueckert) and supervisor (Daniel S. Schipani). The portions told in first person singular reflect Leah Dawn's narration of this chaplaincy experience. The reflections on the experience, in the first person plural, reflect our partnership in research and writing as it has extended beyond the initial chaplain-supervisor relationship.

In this essay, we use the term *reflective practitioner* as Donald A. Schön has developed the concept.[1] A pastoral theologian is one who reflects critically and constructively on the ministry of care, broadly viewed, to contribute theoretical understandings and practical guidelines.[2] Practical theology, the

Leah Dawn Bueckert is a chaplain resident at Lutheran Hospital in Fort Wayne, Indiana; Daniel S. Schipani is professor of pastoral care and counseling at Associated Mennonite Biblical Seminary in Elkhart, Indiana.

[1] *The Reflective Practitioner: How Professionals Think in Action* (New York: Basic Books, 1983). Schön's discussion of the creative process involved in "reflection-in-action" and "therapeutic knowledge-in-practice" is especially helpful (3–69, 105–27). His notions of professional knowing and knowledge enhance the understanding and practice of clinical learning such as CPE training.

[2] This is the Protestant understanding of the term in the U.S. and Canada. In Roman Catholic circles, *pastoral theology* is a broader concept (sometimes a synonym for practical theology)

larger discipline to which pastoral theology belongs, reflects critically and constructively on the life and ministry of the church in its socio-historical context, in the light of the normative biblical vision of *shalom*, God's reign as the commonwealth of peace, justice, and well-being for all people. Both pastoral theology and practical theology focus special attention on formation and transformation.[3]

In the first part of the essay, I (Leah Dawn) relate a particular instance of spiritual caregiving in the hospital, in which I—as chaplain—had an opportunity to function as mediator and messenger. In order to highlight the benefits of critical and constructive reflection on ministry, our (Leah Dawn and Daniel's) interpretive comments about interpersonal dynamics and the process of communication are inserted at several points in the narrative.

The practical-theological model of transformational logic proposed by James E. Loder serves as the main conceptual framework in our discussion.[4] In the second part, we present an example of constructive appropriation of psychological tools and a discussion of biblical and theological themes that informed my ministry in the caregiving event presented in the first section.

The chaplain as mediator and messenger

"I have a job for you, if you want to do it," Myra told me. She was an experienced nurse on the post-surgical unit of the hospital where I was working as a chaplain. She told me that Verna, a patient of hers, was refusing to eat or drink and was saying that she was going to die and really did not care.[5] A seventy-two-year-old woman, Verna had pyelonephritis, an inflammation of the kidneys stemming from a urinary tract infection.

This care-giving opportunity set in motion a potentially transformational process. In the following pages, we illustrate the recognizable, interconnected steps of this process, using the model of transformation outlined by James Loder. These steps are (1) conflict in a context of rapport, (2) interlude

---

that includes the theology, education, and practices of ordained priests working in parishes; its subject matter includes sacraments, liturgy, preaching, teaching, and counseling.

[3] James N. Poling, "Pastoral Theology," in *The New Dictionary of Pastoral Studies*, ed. Wesley Clark (Grand Rapids: Eerdmans, 2002), 258–59.

[4] James E. Loder, *The Transforming Moment*, 2nd ed. (Colorado Springs: Helmers & Howard, 1989), 35–64. For further study of Loder´s contribution to interdisciplinary studies and practical theology, see James E. Loder, *The Logic of the Spirit: Human Development in Theological Perspective* (San Francisco: Jossey-Bass, 1998); James E. Loder and Jim Neidhardt, *The Knight's Move: The Relational Logic of the Spirit in Theology and Science* (Colorado Springs: Helmers & Howard, 1992); and Dana R. Wright and John D. Kuentzel, eds., *Redemptive Transformation in Practical Theology: Essays in Honor of James E. Loder, Jr.* (Grand Rapids: Eerdmans, 2004).

[5] Names have been changed to protect privacy and ensure confidentiality.

for scanning, (3) constructive act of the imagination (moment of insight), (4) release of energy, and (5) interpretation and verification.[6]

Conflict in a context of rapport

> Myra told me that medically Verna was doing well—well enough to go home in the near future. But Verna's condition would soon deteriorate if she continued to refuse food and drink, and if her sense of hopelessness continued to consume her. Myra was considering placing a pic-line[7] for intravenous nourishment. She also suggested the possibility that Verna, in voicing her sense of impending death, did care about living.

> Myra asked if I could pay a visit to Verna. She suggested that there might be emotional dynamics beneath the surface that it would be helpful to know about. I agreed to talk with Verna.

Reflecting on the above interchange, we notice first that the purpose of spiritual caregiving in this case was twofold: the chaplain sought to be helpful to the nurse and to the patient simultaneously. The chaplain became a mediator as she was triangled in good faith by the experienced nurse. We use *triangling* here to mean a deliberate, conscious, and agreed-on process, set in motion with shared understandings on the part of both nurse and chaplain. Further, this triangling is nonmanipulative, explicitly focused on the care and well-being of the patient. In the triangling process, the chaplain became a messenger, or angel.[8]

Awareness of a conflict is the first step in the pattern Loder calls a "knowing event." The nurse's need to know how to care for Verna elicited a conflict. When she told the chaplain about her dilemma, the conflict became a "baffled struggle in a context of rapport."[9] Loder's phrase implies that for significant change—transformational learning, personal growth, and healing—to happen, the situation of challenge characterized by a sense of lack or tension (felt by both Myra and Verna) must be processed within a holding environment. This emotional-social space is a place of support and guidance conducive to appropriate resolution. In the event described, significant rapport existed between chaplain and nurse. In the context of their relationship of mutual trust, respect, and collaboration, the chaplain readily agreed to undertake the visit requested by the nurse.

---

[6] Loder, *Transforming Moment*, 35–44.

[7] A pic-line is a percutaneous intravenous catheter.

[8] The word *angel* comes from the Greek *angelos*, which means messenger.

[9] Ibid., 37.

> I entered Verna's room and stopped to talk briefly with the woman in the first bed. Then I commented that I would like to say hello to her neighbor. I looked around the curtain to see Verna opening her eyes. I introduced myself and, after making sure that it was a good time to talk, inquired about her experience of surgery. She answered my questions and told me that she was feeling increasingly better. All the while, she regarded me with a mildly alarmed and defensive expression. When I asked if her family had been there to see her, she said they had.

The chaplain needed to keep in mind the patient's physical, emotional, and spiritual situation, as well as the opportunity to collaborate with the nurse. Despite the fact that another patient was in the room, she created a place of comfort. The chaplain had been specifically referred to this patient, and she wanted to communicate to Verna that she was there to help, and that hospital staff was hearing the patient and working together to address her needs. Eventually the chaplain would say to her, "I understand that you have some concerns. Would you like to talk with me about them?"

Interlude for scanning

> Verna's food tray with broth and beverages was set up in front of her. I asked if I was interrupting her lunch. She responded with disgust, at some length: "The combination of stuff they give you here is toxic! I won't drink that stuff—so we fight." I expressed hope that she would soon feel better and be able to eat something more substantial. She responded that she would be returning home in a couple of days. Surprised by her words—in light of Myra's report that Verna had been saying she was going to die—I asked, "That's the plan?" She affirmed that going home was the plan.

An interlude for scanning is the second step of Loder's model of transformational logic. It includes subconscious and conscious efforts to understand the nature of the initial problem or conflict, and seeking possible solutions. In other words, scanning happens as caregivers and care-receivers try to find out what is really going on (as reflected in the behavior of the patient, for example) and how to address the challenges as constructively as possibly.

In this interchange, scanning was taking place. The chaplain's questions were meant to lead Verna to come to voice and to help her (and the caregiver) seek clarity about her situation.[10]

> Somewhat bewildered, and wondering where to go next with the conversation, I commented about the bouquet of flowers standing on her shelf. Verna replied that the bouquet would have been very different if the sender had known what the florist would put together. Apparently, the sender of the flowers would not have been impressed with the final product, nor was Verna, although Verna's daughter had nonetheless politely phoned to thank the sender.
>
> As we returned to the subject of Verna's surgery, a physician entered the room and began a conversation with the woman in the next bed. I asked Verna if, apart from her concern with the food, she felt that she was recovering. She said she was. I asked what she found helpful to focus on while spending time in the hospital. She replied, "I focus on getting myself healed up and out of here"—another surprising comment, given what Myra had told me. Verna added that medical staff had identified medical problems that she had initially been unaware of. I asked if she had any anxiety or concerns about those things, and she answered that she did not. Again, she commented that she planned to be home in a couple of days.
>
> The conversation on the other side of the curtain was getting loud and distracting, and I was having trouble hearing what Verna was saying. Although I wanted to continue the conversation, I decided to ask Verna if she'd like me to stop in again later to talk more.[11] Before I left, I asked her if she found prayer helpful. She replied, "Sometimes, but not

---

[10] The notions of "coming to voice" and "seeking clarity" come from Christie Cozad Neuger, *Counseling Women: A Narrative, Pastoral Approach* (Minneapolis: Fortress Press, 2001), chapters 3 and 5.

[11] Loss of privacy is an unpleasant fact for hospital patients. Chaplains need to keep three things in mind when conducting private conversations with patients in a shared room. First, it is important to distinguish between our discomfort as caregivers who have access to more privacy, and any discomfort the patient may be experiencing from lack of privacy. It is essential not to confuse our needs and urgencies with the needs and urgencies of the people we serve. Second, caregivers should always check with the patients or otherwise determine their level of comfort or discomfort under the circumstances. Third, sometimes our caregiving work focused on one of the patients in the room will positively affect a roommate, either by the manner and the spirit of the care offered, or in spoken prayer, words of encouragement, Bible reading, and so on.

a lot. I do believe in the Lord though." I suggested again
that I would return later and expressed my hope that her
recovery would go well. She thanked me, and I left.

For those giving care to Verna, three sets of goals were at work: those of the
chaplain (spiritual care for Verna and collaboration with Myra), those of
the patient (comfort and recovery), and those of other hospital staff—Myra,
in particular (care for Verna). It is helpful to keep in mind the distinction
between, and the convergence within, these sets of goals.

A little while later, I told Myra about my conversation
with Verna. When I mentioned that Verna had talked
about going home in a couple of days, Myra said, "She's
totally the opposite now, isn't she? I just went in there a
little while ago, and she was up and laughing. The same
thing happened yesterday. In the morning she was crying,
and in the afternoon she was laughing. Maybe she's not a
morning person. Maybe she gets ticked off, and we need
to leave her alone until after lunch."

This sequence illustrates the step of interlude for scanning, played out in
relation to the nurse. Myra reiterated her earlier sense of being at a loss about
how to understand and care for her patient. In the listening presence of the
chaplain, Myra (or both caregivers) scanned for an answer.

About two hours later, I returned to Verna's room. She said
she was feeling bloated and nauseated. The curtain was no
longer dividing the room between her and her roommate.
I thought I might not stay long, because of her physical
discomfort, but she responded freely and at length in our
conversation, so I stayed for about fifteen minutes. I did
not detect the defensiveness in her eyes that I had noticed
during our first meeting.

By reading Verna's body language, the chaplain confirmed that she had established rapport. The chaplain had become an ally to Verna while remaining
her nurse's ally.

Verna stated, "The eating thing is not that big a deal." She
added that even if she did not eat in the hospital, she would
not have trouble eating when she got home. The medical
staff would probably send her home even if she did not eat;
in fact, they had tried to send her home that day. I returned
to the theme of prayer that we had begun to address just
before I left the first time. She indicated that she did not
have a religious community but that some of her friends

were Christians. They were praying for her—"which has helped immensely," she said.

Insight or intuition, and release of energy

Because it was the day before Thanksgiving, I asked Verna whether her family had plans for the holiday. "It's the first time I won't have anything to do with it," she said, "but that doesn't matter." She added that the holiday was not a big deal for her anymore, although her grandchildren still got excited about it. This year, her daughter, son-in-law, and grandkids were going to be traveling to New York for an event with her son-in-law's family. She commented, "If I get out of here, I don't know where I'll go."

"You live alone?" I asked.

"Yes."

"So you'd feel uncomfortable being at home by yourself while you're recovering."

"Yes."

At this point in the conversation, the chaplain experienced a moment of insight, characteristic of the third step of Loder's model. It reflects the constructive work of the imagination by which an insight, intuition, or vision emerges—often with convicting force—and supplies the key to the resolution being sought. Verna revealed to the chaplain the heart of her sense of threat and anxiety: she was afraid of being at home alone while she was recovering. For the pastoral caregiver, Verna's apparently inconsistent behavior, which had baffled her nurse, now made sense. Verna's disclosure elicited clarity and relief for both chaplain and nurse.

"Would there be anyone who could spend some time with you or pop in on you once in awhile?" I asked.

"I wish that someone could stay with me."

Not knowing quite how to respond, I said, "I hope that by the time you leave here, you will be well enough to feel comfortable staying at home."

The chaplain was alluding to hoped-for improvement in Verna's physical and medical condition. Her comment may have suggested that she did not attach the same significance to Verna's emotional, relational, and spiritual longings that she attached to Verna's physical well-being. Verna seemed to fear that she would suffer loneliness. Other possible responses would have been, "Would you need someone to stay all day with you?" "If you could have someone there, whom would you like to have stay with you at home?"

> Before I left, I asked if Verna would be open to having me pray with her. She said she would, and I prayed.

Verna's comment that the prayers of some of her Christian friends had helped her immensely implied that she would have a favorable disposition toward prayer for herself in this context. It was still wise for the chaplain to ask her whether she wanted such prayer; in this way, prayer became her choice.

> When I had finished praying, Verna thanked me. Her roommate, who had been a silent listener to the whole conversation, made appreciative comments.

The reference to Verna's roommate illustrates an instance in which pastoral care ministry in the hospital setting benefited a person who witnessed caregiving.

> Again, I went to talk with Myra. When I explained Verna's anxiety about going home to an empty house for Thanksgiving, Myra said that made everything a lot clearer.

The insight felt by the nurse with intuitive force was followed by a release of energy. The fourth step in the unfolding process of transformation is the release of the energy bound up in sustaining the original conflict situation. This release is a subconscious response to the resolution and serves as evidence that the personal investment in the situation has reached a conclusion and the conflict is over. Myra welcomed resolution to the dilemma that she had been confronting. The sense of resolution resulted when the chaplain effectively fulfilled a mediating role while acting as a messenger.

Interpretation and verification

> Myra commented about how hard it is to be alone over the holidays. She affirmed that hospital staff could find a way to have Verna stay through the weekend. She also said that she would speak to the doctor, because he determined that Verna would go home that afternoon.

Interpretation of the imaginative solution is the fifth and final step of transformation and is both retrospective and prospective. Retrospectively, we need to ascertain if the resolution found fits the original conflict (because sometimes our intuitions and insights are actually misleading). Prospectively, we must be accountable for our intuitions and insights by sharing them with other people also involved in the situation (in this case, with Verna's nurse and doctor).

Interpretation and verification made possible decisive forward movement in provision of care for Verna. Myra could care for Verna holistically. The interactions with Verna and Myra were also helpful to the spiritual caregiver, who was personally and vocationally affirmed through being entrusted to help find out (diagnose or "know with another") what was happening with Verna. Eventually even the physician, who had been insisting that the patient go home, learned the source of Verna's reluctance. The transformational process was complete, because the nurse was finally able to resolve the dilemma.

The chaplain's contribution

What was the chaplain's contribution as mediator and messenger? Care for Verna was enhanced when staff arranged for her to stay in the hospital until her daughter and son-in-law returned. The nurse, at first exasperated with the patient's inconsistent behavior, gained greater understanding of the reason behind it. This understanding equipped her to respond more help-fully. Verna's physician gained insight that informed his medical judgment and his treatment recommendations. The episode demonstrated the value of the chaplain's contribution to the healthcare team. And the incident strengthened the collaborative relationship between chaplain and nurse. All those involved—including Verna's roommate—acknowledged the chaplain's caregiving ministry.

Psychological and theological reflection

Lawrence E. Holst observes that chaplains practice spiritual caregiving at the intersection of two worlds, the world of the hospital and medicine, and the world of the church and religious faith. He argues that the tensions chaplains experience as they navigate between these two worlds fall into four categories of inherent "in-betweenness": (1) the context of the hospital, (2) the chaplain's specialized training, (3) the strong influence of psychology in the chaplain's ministry, and (4) the conflicting perspectives of medicine and religion.[12]

Holst highlights medicine's and religion's conflicting perspectives on suffering and emphasizes that the chaplain's role is not to explain, cure, or eliminate disease. Rather, the chaplain seeks to engage the sufferer, while harboring no illusions about the banishment of suffering. Quoting Eugene Peterson, Holst suggests that pastoral care has a different purpose: "'The task of pastoral care is to join the sufferer, to enter the pain, to engage the absurdity,

---

[12] Lawrence E. Holst, "The Hospital Chaplain: Between Worlds," in *Hospital Ministry: The Role of the Chaplain Today*, ed. Lawrence E. Holst (New York: Crossroad, 1985), 12–27.

to descend into hell … not to minimize or to mitigate the suffering,' but to help the sufferer to put the suffering into perspective."[13]

In our vignette, the chaplain needed certain information in order to care effectively. She needed to know Verna's medical condition (diagnosed as pyelonephritis), the treatment Verna was receiving, and the overall prognosis. Thanks to the chaplain's work, the nurse was able to persuade Verna's doctor—the medical expert in the caregiving team—that it would be best for his patient to stay in the hospital during the holiday weekend. In this instance, the nurse and the chaplain were able to provide holistic care and healing by addressing emotional and spiritual needs of the patient that those providing medical treatment had not recognized. The chaplain fulfilled a pivotal role in the situation as a pastoral and spiritual caregiver.

Integrating psychological insights

As reflective practitioners and practical theologians, chaplains must be able to integrate psychological concepts and tools into their spiritual caregiving ministry. Like other spiritual caregivers, such as pastoral counselors, chaplains can apply concepts from human science in order to understand a situation better and then act in accordance with those understandings. We can use these tools to analyze systemically the power dynamics of transactions that took place in caring for Verna.

The chaplain was part of a caring team that included the nurse, the medical doctor, and other supportive staff. We can visualize two sets of triangular relationships including, on the one hand, the patient (a woman), the nurse (a woman), and the medical doctor (a man); on the other hand, the patient (Verna), the nurse, and the chaplain (a woman). If we include Verna's neighbor (Patient 2, a woman) we can construct the following diagram:

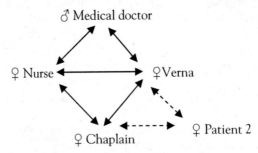

Here is our interpretation of the power dynamics in this situation. The chaplain became an effective messenger and mediator while the patient was coping with her anxieties and fear the best she could. Using power cat-

---

[13] Ibid., 25; citing Peterson, *Five Smooth Stones for Pastoral Work* (Atlanta: John Knox, 1980), 101.

egories developed by Rollo May,[14] we suggest that by the time Myra asked the chaplain to intervene, Verna was expressing herself with "manipulative power" (power *over*). Such use of power, paradoxically, is often observable in marginalized or oppressed people, who use it as a defense mechanism. This strategy is a way of resisting, by demanding attention through displaying apparently dysfunctional behavior.

The nurse and the physician typically had been caring for the patient with "nutrient power" (power *for*). The chaplain was eventually able to mediate resolution, because she employed "integrative power" (that is, power *with*). The situation included potential for either the nurse or the doctor to exercise "competitive power" (power *against*), because they needed to make a decision about the length of the patient's stay at the hospital.

A brief examination of the professional role and gender dynamics in these relationships reveals that the two women care providers collaborated with each other and with the female patient, apart from the male physician. The women were able to find a deeper meaning in the behavior of the patient, which led to resolution of a difficult situation.

Biblical-theological themes

As noted in our introduction to this book, Lawrence Holst asserts that the primary role of hospital chaplains, expressed through diverse functions, is "to help others experience as fully as possible the reality of God's presence and love"[15] The chaplain who cared for Verna fulfilled this primary role by effectively functioning as a mediator and messenger. She became a bearer of good news, and her caregiving work helped the patient experience a measure of divine grace. As the chaplain reflected on the ministry situation with a colleague, biblical images and theological themes emerged as meaningful foundations of her practice.

The chaplain embodied good news, first, by showing compassionate care in the presence of Verna's anxieties, concerns, complaints, and expressed wishes. This care entailed communicating respect for the patient. She took Verna seriously and sought to understand her on her own terms. Simultaneously, she was seeking to elicit in Verna hope that her needs would be adequately addressed during the hospital stay and beyond. Psalm 71:9 provides a biblical message that links the plight of the patient to the chaplain's responsibility for compassionate and respectful caregiving: "Do not cast me off in the time of old age; do not forsake me when my strength is spent."

By providing a listening ear, the chaplain became aware that Verna was anxious about being sent home without adequate support. She anticipated that—in the absence of her daughter and family—she would feel increased

---

[14] Rollo May, "The Meaning of Power," in *Power and Innocence: A Search for the Sources of Violence* (New York: Norton, 1972), 99–119.

[15] Holst, "The Hospital Chaplain," 52.

vulnerability, mingled with loneliness, during the holiday. These feelings were exacerbated by the natural anxieties connected with hospitalization and recovery.

The patient's predicament can be further understood by applying James Loder's analysis of "the fourfold knowing event."[16] Loder describes such an event in terms of the four epistemological dimensions of the lived world, the self, the void, and the Holy. Elaborating on these dimensions, Loder writes, "Being human entails environment, selfhood, the possibility of non-being, and the possibility of new being. All four dimensions are essential, and none of them can be ignored without decisive loss to our understanding of what is essentially human."[17] Loder's perspective helps us avoid the reductionistic approach of the human sciences, which normally operate in a bi-dimensional epistemological framework—self-world—rather than a four-dimensional framework. Reductionism happens whenever we fail to take into account the existential-spiritual issues of "being more" (for example, the personal experience of redemptive transformation associated with forgiveness) and "non-being," (for example, the threat of death and evil underneath when we face illness alone).

Verna's way of dealing with her anxieties bi-dimensionally included certain coping mechanisms ("unconscious ego defenses," psychoanalytically speaking) aimed at manipulating the hospital environment. These defenses were only partially and temporarily effective in neutralizing the patient's anxieties, even as they held potential to alienate her caregivers. But the mediating work of the chaplain made it possible to transform the self-world dynamic by reminding the patient of the larger reality of the Spirit. Verna's "void" could thus be confronted directly, so that she could experience new hope and strength.

The chaplain, therefore, became a bearer of good news analogous to the good news of salvation. Salvation in this caregiving encounter involved, in Loder's terms, "transformational negation," that is, the negation of the negation. Viewed in this light, for Verna and her caregivers, the transforming process included (1) confronting the void (especially in the form of anxiety related to being weak and alone during a holiday), (2) becoming more human (neutralizing certain coping mechanisms that exasperated the nurse, regaining freedom to choose and to trust God and the caregiving staff, etc.), and (3) being more open to the reality of the Holy.

Verna had indicated that she was not participating in a faith community, and she did not seem to be an actively religious person. But she had also said that the prayers of her friends had meaning for her. In light of Verna's affirmation of the value of intercessory prayer, the chaplain offered to pray with and for her. Even though the patient was not directly connected with the church,

---

[16] James E. Loder, *Transforming Moment*, 67–91.

[17] Ibid., 69.

she was open to receiving pastoral care given by the chaplain as a trustworthy ministering person and as a reliable representative of a Christian faith community. Prayer was meaningful because, on the horizontal (bi-dimensional) level, it was a supportive and encouraging resource for Verna.

For a theological perspective, we draw from Mennonite theologian James Reimer's writing about prayer. Reimer suggests that prayer, rightly viewed and practiced, is not a technical act of self-indulgence, superstition, or manipulation of God. Rather, prayer is communion with God in God's threefoldness:

1. In praying we contemplate the divine mystery, that which is beyond ourselves.
2. We meditate on this mystery as revealed to us in the Christ-event.
3. We open ourselves up to the present power of this divine reality as God's Spirit meets our spirit. This mystery transcends us, yet is closer to us than we are to ourselves. It is our very ground and center. Prayer is to find our own ground in God and to open ourselves to what God is already doing in the world.[18]

Using Reimer's words, we might say that Verna could experience prayer as a way of searching for the wisdom and the knowledge of God.[19]

In retrospect, the exchanges with Verna evoke a realization that, once again, a chaplain has fulfilled the primary role of helping someone encounter the reality of divine presence and love. The words from Isaiah 52:7 fittingly affirm the blessing of such an encounter: "How beautiful upon the mountain are the feet of the messenger who announces peace, who brings good news, who announces salvation."

---

[18] A. James Reimer, *The Dogmatic Imagination: The Dynamics of Christian Belief* (Waterloo, ON: Herald Press, 2003), 63.

[19] Ibid., 62.

Holistic care as a moral imperative

Insights from women's experiences of hysterectomy and mastectomy

Leah Dawn Bueckert

"Am I not more than the sum of my parts?" a woman asks. "Of course," comes the commonplace reply, which assumes that one's identity remains intact even if the physical body is altered in some way. Yet Western culture's obsessive preoccupation with the perfect body, and a medical system that tends to treat people by focusing exclusively on the parts, send a subtle (or not so subtle) message that human worth lies in the aggregate of parts and not in the person as a whole. Rarely do women sense this message more keenly than in the experience of hysterectomy or mastectomy. Against this prevailing cultural trend, I argue that healing grows out of being cared for as a whole person. Caring well (that is, holistically), therefore, is a moral issue involving care of self, the care of one's partner[1] or significant other(s), medical care, and the care of the Christian community.

What follows is an exploration of this thesis according to the four tasks of practical theology identified by Richard R. Osmer and Friedrich L. Schweitzer.[2] In the first section below, "Listening to women's voices," three narratives introduce the *descriptive-empirical* task. These include stories of two women who had hysterectomy surgery, and an account of one woman's experience with bilateral mastectomy.[3] Second, "Interpreting women's experience" explores the *interpretive* task by identifying significant issues and

---

Leah Dawn Bueckert is a chaplain resident at Lutheran Hospital in Fort Wayne, Indiana.

[1] I use *partner* throughout the essay as the term that best recognizes that both married and un-married couples wrestle with experiences of illness, surgery, and recovery. Although I discuss heterosexual partners, studying the process of illness and healing among lesbian couples is likewise important.

[2] Richard R. Osmer and Friedrich L. Schweitzer, eds., *Developing a Public Faith: New Directions in Practical Theology: Essays in Honor of James W. Fowler* (St. Louis: Chalice Press, 2003), 1–11.

[3] For an illuminating presentation of the prejudices and traumas surrounding the experience of many women who undergo hysterectomy, see Lise Cloutier-Steele, *Misinformed Consent: 13 Women Share Their Stories about Unnecessary Hysterectomy* (Toronto: Stoddart, 2002). In addition to the accounts of personal experience, including the author's, the book includes advice

questions rising out of the women's experiences. Third, "Identifying norms for holistic caregiving" focuses on the *normative* task by examining and revising the ethical and theological norms that are reflected in the issues and questions. Finally, "Reshaping the practices" considers the *pragmatic-strategic* task of developing guidelines for women and their caregivers.[4]

Listening to women's voices

Rachel's story of hysterectomy

Rachel,[5] a forty-year-old single woman, went to her doctor for a physical examination, expecting to have a routine check-up. She was shocked when he told her that she had ovarian cancer. The cancer was discovered on a Thursday, and on the following Monday, Rachel had a hysterectomy. Because of the seriousness of her condition, Rachel did not have the luxury of preparing mentally and emotionally for the surgery. It was a life-saving procedure but a sudden loss nevertheless. In addition to anxiety produced by the presence of cancer and the shock of the unexpected and invasive surgery, Rachel also came face to face with the fact that the option of bearing children was no longer available to her. For Rachel as a single woman, the loss of reproductive organs was devastating. Another reason for the shock of the experience was the rarity of ovarian cancer among women her age. Rachel's treatment following surgery involved six months of chemotherapy. She speaks of being "out of commission" for a year. Some of the fears she faced going into surgery included fear of death, fear that the cancer would be inoperable, and anxiety about the hospital setting.

Rachel's doctor was a Christian whom she trusted. Her family and friends were as supportive and encouraging as they could be under the circumstances, offering sympathy and assurances that she would be all right. Sometimes they acknowledged being at a loss for words and sat silently with her. Rachel especially valued the opportunity to speak with women who could identify with her experience. Occasionally, humor had a healing effect. However, depression and mood swings were part of her experience of hospitalization and recovery, and while humor was helpful on some days, it was hurtful and destructive on others.

Rachel's faith was a support to her throughout the experience. In the years that followed her surgery, she shared about her experience in the context of her faith story in various Christian settings. Most of the reflection Rachel did in relation to her experience was a matter of conversation between herself and

---

on alternative treatments, a medical terminology section, a list of questions women should ask their doctors before agreeing to the surgery, and a list of resources.

[4] Some of these reflections stem from conversations with Daniel Schipani, in the context of our collaborative work on spiritual caregiving.

[5] The names of the women in the first two narratives have been changed to protect their privacy.

God. Her pastor communicated with her only indirectly through her mother, never addressing Rachel directly. Eventually Rachel came to the point where she did not need to dwell on the ordeal but could move ahead with life.

Helen's story of hysterectomy

Helen was fifty years old when her struggle with uterine fibroids brought her to the point of choosing to have a hysterectomy. Because she worked as a full-time nurse, the bleeding and low energy caused by the fibroids were problematic. In Helen's words, "If I wanted to continue as a working woman, I pretty much had to have the hysterectomy." As she proceeded with the hysterectomy, she consented to have her ovaries removed at the same time.

Looking back now, she said, she might have opted for a less radical surgery. At the time, her gut feeling was that she was too young to have her ovaries removed. However, both of the female professionals she consulted recommended their removal. Helen commented that the whole process was very business-like and that she would have valued a more sympathetic approach. As it was, Helen started wearing a hormone patch as soon as she had the surgery, which was a good thing, she said. However, as of a year or two ago she had discontinued it. Her physician had recommended hormone therapy to reduce the risk of osteoporosis and heart disease, but recent studies, she said, deny the extent of such benefits and indicate that, in fact, hormone therapy increases the risk of cancer and other illnesses.

Pat's story of bilateral mastectomy

Pat Fallis's great grandmother died of breast cancer in her seventies. Pat's grandmother died of the same illness at age sixty-seven.[6] Her mother was fifty-eight when she, too, died of breast cancer. With this ominous history in her family, Pat, in her late thirties, decided to be proactive and have a bilateral mastectomy before any cancer began. She was especially concerned because the tumor found in her mother's breast was only the size of the tip of a pencil by the time it had spread to several lymph nodes.

Reflecting on her mother's dying process, Pat writes, "When I think about some of the decisions that were made during this time, I realize how little input my mother had. She lived in a generation when doctors were gods, and whatever they said went. Mom's doctor started to 'hit' her with all kinds of treatments when it was too late. I was with her when he prescribed her first dose of chemo. He was not straight with her about her condition, and I realize now that he did not allow her to be part of the decision-making process around the treatment and the progression of her disease."

Pat thought about having elective surgery. Before her mother died, she said to Pat, "You better be very careful, 'cause this thing seems to be happening about ten years earlier with each generation." A year after her mom's death,

---

[6] Pat has given permission to use her real name in this essay.

Pat went to see her gynecologist about the possibility of having an elective bilateral mastectomy. She gathered opinions from a number of doctors. The decision-making process began with collecting information. She met with her surgeon "every six months to talk about the surgery procedure, problems, reconstruction options, and the fact that not all of the breast tissue can be taken out." She gathered information from friends and relatives. Pat also became more aware of "how society views breasts and the dominant place they have in our culture and psyche." One of the doctors had informed her that her risk for getting breast cancer was forty percent, so Pat "started watching the weather for the chance of rain. It often rains when they say there is a forty percent chance of precipitation!"

Pat's closest family members and friends responded in a variety of ways. Unfortunately, her husband was not emotionally supportive during her decision-making process. "My husband's only comment was, 'Well, can you buy new ones in any size!'" Before her surgery, he would not talk about it, until she told him one day that she needed to know what he thought. He replied, "It doesn't matter. It's your body."

She recalls that her daughter made the comment, "Well Mom, if they're going to kill you, I think you could live without them." Her best friend was a major support. Together they created several ways of preparing for and marking the significance of Pat's surgery, including making a cast of her naked torso.

Pat engaged intentionally in several methods of decision making and preparation. She kept a journal and was attentive to her dreams. She prayed. She went to see a counselor for several months, had professional photographs taken of herself nude from the waist up, and visited and counseled with her minister. She did private sessions in visualization and self-directed art therapy. Throughout this process, Pat came to understand that "my breasts were not me, and I am me without any number of my body parts.... Once I got to this point, it was clear that I was going to have the surgery."

"The surgery went very well. I recovered very quickly. I was fully prepared after the surgery to go through a grieving process and was prepared with several ideas of things to do to help the grief, but I didn't need to. I didn't grieve. I was only relieved. I have never regretted it and know it was the right decision for me." Pat affirms that this process was also a spiritual journey. It involved discerning God's call for her life. She had the sense that the Holy Spirit guided the whole experience, and she felt carried along through it. Looking back, she sees it as one of three major transforming events in her life, alongside giving birth and the death of her parents.

Pat was satisfied with the work of her (female) surgeon. Among the signals of sensitivity for which Pat was grateful were the neat stitches that her surgeon made, leaving only the faintest of scars on her chest. Pat also appreciated the clear bandages that covered the stitches, so that she could see the results of the surgery immediately. After her surgery, Pat noticed that people were awkward and uncomfortable around her, until they realized that she was still the same person. Pat has prosthetics but rarely uses them, because she feels comfortable without them.

Interpreting women's experiences

Many women's stories, such as those recounted above, portray the kind of care that facilitates healing, as well as painful instances in which needed care was lacking, thereby hampering the process. The present section addresses several issues and questions rising out of the stories. In so doing, it highlights issues such as access to information, availability of resources for discernment in light of the information, and availability of emotional support in each of the four dimensions of holistic care outlined in the introduction: self-care, the care received from one's partner or significant other(s), medical care, and the care of the Christian community. Although pain and conflict are undeniably part of the experience of loss, drawing attention to problematic dimensions may reveal areas in which care might be improved and so facilitate the journey through pain rather than exacerbate suffering.

Care of self is a crucial stepping-stone to healing. Rachel's surgery happened so quickly after the diagnosis of ovarian cancer (and fortunately so) that she really did not have time to prepare for the loss. Much of the task of self-care, therefore, happened during recovery and beyond. In Helen's case, self-care included evaluating her desires and responsibilities in relation to her career. Helen concluded that to continue with a full-time nursing career required a hysterectomy. Career involvements were for her a factor in the decision making.

Adjusting to and embracing one's changed body after surgery, and coming to terms with what these changes mean, are challenges for all who undertake such surgery. The process is one of deep struggle for many, but it is a necessary journey nevertheless. After her hysterectomy, Rachel needed to mourn the loss of the possibility of bearing children. Because hysterectomy or mastectomy is so personal and invasive, many women are silent about their experiences, or have been silenced by others. This silence greatly reduces the potential for healing. After a mastectomy, some women prefer to have sexual intercourse only in the dark.[7] Accepting one's changed body after surgery can be very difficult.

Responses of significant others at the prospect of a woman's surgery are important. Responses vary, depending on the particular situation (the nature of the relationship, the seriousness of the illness precipitating the surgery, the length of time between diagnosis and surgery, the ages of those involved).

---

[7] Nancy Fugate Woods, *Human Sexuality in Health and Illness* (St. Louis: C.V. Mosby Company, 1984), 347.

Such illnesses and surgical procedures can be threatening for the woman involved and can threaten her relationship with significant others.

Rachel spoke about her family and friends being as shocked as she was by the gravity and suddenness of her diagnosis of ovarian cancer. Her family members and friends struggled to find words. Rachel sometimes found humor helpful during her hospitalization and recovery. However, she also experienced depression and mood swings and felt hurt when visitors were not sensitive to her frame of mind or emotions, cracking jokes that would have been more appropriate in another place and time. Too many offers of help and superficial words of consolation were irritating. Rachel preferred having someone close acknowledge the lack of appropriate words and instead simply be present with her.

Pat recounts the pain and disappointment of living with a spouse who would not involve himself in her decision or experience. His refusal to talk about it with her was discouraging, as were his responses of inappropriate humor and apparent indifference. The anguish of having a nonsupportive significant other is a serious impediment to the process of healing. With both hysterectomy and mastectomy, the question of sexual intimacy after surgery is an issue. In the case of hysterectomy surgery, physiological changes may bring alterations in sexual function. On the other hand, research finds that, for some, "mutilating" surgeries become an occasion for the deepening of a relationship, including its sexual dimensions.[8]

In addition to self-care and care received from significant others, holistic care encompasses the interactions of women with medical professionals, interactions that do not always make a woman's well-being top priority. A consistent theme in women's stories about hysterectomy and mastectomy is experiencing the medical procedure from beginning to end as very business-like, impersonal, and matter-of-fact. Busy schedules and an emphasis on competence and professionalism have taken their toll on the ability and responsibility of medical practitioners to engage with their patients as whole human beings. It was perhaps for these reasons that Rachel regarded the hospital setting with anxiety.

A second issue arising from interaction with medical professionals is inclusion of women in decision making about their own health. As recounted tragically in Pat's story, no one had adequately informed her mother about her own condition, nor was she empowered to make decisions about her treatment. When Pat began to explore the possibility of a bilateral mastectomy, she received extensive information from medical practitioners but little guidance regarding next steps. Her surgeon, with whom she met every six months to talk about what would be involved, was a fortunate exception to this pattern.

---

[8] Sheila Kitzinger, *Woman's Experience of Sex* (New York: G. P. Putnam's Sons, 1983), 297–309.

Reflecting on her own experience, Helen remembers her gut feeling that she did not want to have her ovaries removed along with the hysterectomy. However, both of the female physicians she sought out for opinions encouraged her to have them removed without consulting her feelings about the matter. Helen acknowledges that she does not know what problems the procedure may have prevented, yet she thinks she might choose differently if she were to do it over again. Perhaps the physicians she talked to did indeed offer Helen good advice; nevertheless, she wonders if their recommendations would have been different had they considered Helen's own feelings and thoughts.

Pat was satisfied with the work of her surgeon in that the scars after her mastectomy were hardly noticeable. Pat spoke of being saddened and angered by the messy scars some women have, that indicate hasty and poorly done surgery. Her observations point out that an aesthetic as well as an ethical dimension exists for taking women's perspectives into account during the preparation for and experience of surgery.

Christian communities have the potential to be sources of guidance and support for women going through the experience of hysterectomy or mastectomy. Realizing this potential requires that these communities make room for women to verbalize such experiences and share in a variety of ways, yet such sharing does not always happen. In many churches, women do not feel comfortable talking about their surgeries, for a variety of reasons. In Rachel's case, her minister kept updated on Rachel's condition by speaking with her mother. That he never engaged with Rachel directly suggests his discomfort with the matter. Pat met occasionally with the minister of her church, a woman whom Pat usually appreciated and found helpful. Yet the pastor's matter-of-fact approach, while liberating in some ways, had the effect of minimizing some of Pat's emotions and ambivalence.

Identifying norms for holistic caregiving

In my introduction, I asserted that healing grows out of being cared for as a whole person and that caring well is a moral responsibility. It is clear that certain dimensions of care, for one reason or another, have been absent in many women's experiences of hysterectomy or mastectomy. By reflecting on the instances in which lack of care is apparent, one can correct or revise the ethical and theological norms evident in those instances and advocate for the implementation of norms that promote greater wholeness and healing.

The choice to care well for oneself is a moral imperative. It is contingent on theological norms about caring for the self. For example, the view that regards self-care as self-centeredness diminishes not only the woman's capacity to respect herself and mobilize her own healing resources but also her capacity to give and receive love and care. Depending on the seriousness of the illness, the age of the woman, the success of the surgery, and the nature of her relationship network, the methods of self-care (and the freedom to engage in them) will vary from woman to woman. While stating that self-care is a woman's moral responsibility, we must be mindful of the degree of disempowerment some women experience.

To her credit, Pat was intentional about taking on the responsibility to care for herself. From her first consideration of having the bilateral mastectomy, to actual surgery, recovery, and beyond, Pat found ways to gather necessary information and guidance, express her thoughts and feelings, and honor her whole being—body, mind, and soul. Shortly before surgery, she wrote a poem expressing her gratitude for the gift of her breasts and her courageous and intentional release of them.[9]

> I thank the Goddess for the gift of my body
> For the gift—this greatest gift
> handed down to me through my parents
> It is a miracle to have
> the greatest gift we hold
> I thank you for these breasts
> which have been a part of me since the beginning
> a part of me I have mostly taken for granted
> These breasts which enticed a lover
> and nourished my children
> I thank you for these breasts
> which are a part of me
> but are not me
> I am who I am
> regardless of my body parts
> I am who I am
> I thank you for my breasts
> but I do not need these breasts to be me
> I am who I am without them
> When they are gone
> I will mourn their loss and celebrate my life
> and fulfill the plan intended for me
> Lost gifts remain close to the heart
> I give them back to the Goddess
> with thanks

This exercise allowed Pat to acknowledge the reality of her pain but move on to celebrate life. In Rachel's case, part of self-restoration after hysterectomy took the form of investing care in the lives of orphan children in Jamaica with whom she had previously established relationships. This service, freely given, in turn strengthened her personal and vocational identity. She also

---

[9] Reprinted by permission of the author.

continued to cultivate her relationship with God and shared about her experience in various Christian contexts.

Loss of the uterus, ovaries, or breasts—which represent life-giving and nurturing capacities uniquely present in women—involves a grieving process. Honoring that grief is an essential component of self-care. In relation to hysterectomy and mastectomy, care for self builds on the knowledge that, while losing part of one's body, one continues to be not only fully human but also fully woman.

The stories of Rachel and Pat offer several insights related to care from significant others. Rachel spoke about the hurt caused by comments from family members and friends that were not sensitive to her changing frame of mind. A crucial aspect of caring well as a significant other is, in Rachel's words, to "take cues from the patient," and to "let the patient call the shots." In other words, a significant other communicates care by being attentive to and following the lead of the recipient of care.

A partner's attitude toward the relationship and the surgery is crucial in the healing process. Women whose partners are accepting, yet who do not pretend that the surgery does not make a difference, are better equipped to make the transition into recovery smoothly. The best possible scenario is to invite the partner also into a grieving process.[10] When Pat's spouse said, "It doesn't matter. It's your body," he minimized Pat's experience and likely betrayed his own discomfort about and avoidance of the issue. Part of his silence may have involved a fear of hurting her with the truth of his own sense of sexual loss. By privatizing her body rather than accepting it in the context of intimate relationship, his comment communicated lack of care for her sense of self and body.

Experiences of mastectomy and hysterectomy affect sexual intimacy. With mastectomy, the visible loss of a part of the body that is so glorified and eroticized in Western culture requires adjustment on the part of the couple as well as affirmations of beauty, both physical and relational. In the case of hysterectomy, the loss of the uterus (and sometimes ovaries) may affect sexual function. Women may have either an increase or decrease in sexual pleasure, depending on their surgery.[11] Rebekah Miles, in *The Pastor as Moral Guide*, writes about the difference between marriage involving obligation and marriage directed primarily toward self-fulfillment. She notes that "recent shifts in American culture and Christian pastoral theology make self-fulfillment a primary norm for marriage, trumping other norms and even undercutting enduring obligations."[12] When the sexual relationship involves care for the

---

[10] Mary James Dean and Mary Louise Cullen, "Woman's Body: Spiritual Needs and Theological Presence," in *A New Pastoral Care: Women in Travail and Transition*, ed. Maxine Glaz and Jeanne Stevenson Moessner (Minneapolis: Fortress Press, 1991), 99.

[11] Kitzinger, *Women's Experience of Sex*, 300.

[12] Rebekah L. Miles, *The Pastor as Moral Guide* (Minneapolis: Fortress Press, 1999), 87.

well-being of the other, mastectomy and hysterectomy surgery may also provide a special opportunity for deepening expressions of love.

It is helpful for partners to be involved in preparing for and adjusting to life after the surgery. The effect of hysterectomy (and to some degree, mastectomy) on family planning and desire for childbearing varies, depending on the age and life stage of the woman and her partner. Some women are relieved to be free of the burden of birth control, yet others, such as Rachel, are devastated by the fact that they have lost the possibility of becoming pregnant.

Pat was fortunate to have a best friend who supported her throughout her experience of surgery. Together they celebrated Pat's body, mind, and soul and held creative rituals to mark the significant loss and transition. Her friend's care is an expression of the moral responsibility to care for significant others, be they spouses or other loved ones. This friend, a significant other to Pat, concretely practices an ethic of care. In my essay, "Glimpses of the Heart of Caring: A Chaplain's Story," I have demonstrated the essential role for an ethic of care in spiritual caregiving. Such an ethic includes a commitment to do what is compassionate, caring, and just in a given situation; to build relationships and community; and to become accountable, especially to the care-receiver, for caring well.[13]

Some medical practitioners are highly skilled in treating their patients as whole persons. However, many women report that treatment by their physician or surgeon leaves no room to acknowledge the loss or grieving process. An expectation for empathy and sensitivity from professional caregivers does not imply that these women are overly emotional and needy. Rather, it reflects the need they have to be honored as whole human beings who inevitably face the existential task of integrating loss and significant change into their lives. The professionalization of healthcare has resulted in compartmentalizing, in which some care providers keep boundaries around emotion in a way that limits the possibility of empathizing with patients.[14] On one hand, care providers need to develop and maintain appropriate emotional boundaries. On the other hand, each care-receiver needs to be honored in the uniqueness of her context. Russell B. Connors and Chris A. Franke support the need for such respect. "We propose that competent caregivers are not only technically adequate," they suggest, "but are also able to be present to their patients throughout all the stages of treatment. We stress the importance of viewing healing as a response to the holistic needs of those who suffer."[15]

---

[13] Leah Dawn Bueckert, "Glimpses of the Heart of Caring: A Chaplain's Story," in *Mennonite Perspectives in Pastoral Care and Counseling,* ed. Daniel Schipani (Elkhart: Institute of Mennonite Studies, 2006), forthcoming. For further discussion of the ethic of care, see chapter 18 in this volume, "The Ethic of Care in Spiritual Caregiving."

[14] Russell B. Connors and Chris A. Franke, "God and an Ethic of Care: On Being Immanuel," in *Medicine and the Ethics of Care,* ed. Diane Fritz Cates and Paul Lauritzer (Washington, DC: Georgetown University Press, 2001), 229.

[15] Ibid., 208.

In the same article, Franke draws on insights from her own experience of surgery. "One of the most important factors in the healing process was my encounter with the surgeon who did the mastectomy.... He was interested in knowing what I knew about my condition, answered our many questions, and explained (and re-explained) what could be done, and how and why. His manner was one of complete attentiveness to the two people with whom he sat."[16]

Part of caring for the whole person involves the manner in which information about the surgery is provided. Like Franke, Pat had a surgeon who was committed to caring for the whole person. Attentiveness to a woman's questions and concerns, and focus on the human being over and above her body parts, communicate a commitment to the ethic of care.

I have made the case that caring well (that is, holistically) through experiences such as hysterectomy and mastectomy is the responsibility of several parties: the woman herself, significant others committed to her well-being, and the medical practitioners involved in treatment. The church, too, by claiming to be a community that addresses whole persons, has a significant role in the work of healing. Both Rachel and Pat indicated connections with their church communities that were positive and helpful. Rachel valued opportunities to share in Christian settings about her experience within the context of her larger story of faith. Pat found conversations with her minister a valuable resource. She also articulated the transformative influence of the mastectomy experience on her life as being deeply rooted in the spiritual.

Caring for the whole person involves a shift from the focus on cure to a focus on care. With such an emphasis on care, the church can be a community of healing and hope. It can be a community where struggles, sorrows, and joys can be shared, where wisdom and discernment can be sought, and prayers are offered. Perhaps one of the most important tasks of the church is to express explicit and consistent messages about body image, gender identity, relationships, self-care, and sacrificial love. It is crucial to realize that these messages include not only those that the church claims to believe and teach (that is, the explicit curriculum). Rather, the implicit messages conveyed in the use of language, attitudes, preferences, or priorities (that is, the hidden curriculum) are often more powerful forces in moral and character formation. In fact, liberation from some of the oppressive messages about issues such as gender and body image has come primarily through developments outside the church (for example, the work of feminists toward equality between women and men). However, with humility, the church also has a prophetic voice in a culture that dehumanizes people in many ways.

The church can also be a place of support and nurture for medical professionals. At its best, the church is a community that embodies and inspires the commitment to care holistically for people. It can provide opportunities

---

[16] Ibid., 230.

for medical practitioners to share and evaluate their occupational insights, experiences, and struggles, through Sunday school series, preaching, and small group meetings, to name a few avenues. Medical practitioners have valuable contributions for the Christian community, and vice versa.

Above all, care and healing in the church are about the ministry of accompaniment—partnering, for example, with women throughout their journey of illness, surgery, and recovery. When the church engages in the ministry of accompaniment, whether or not cure and recovery happen, the church acknowledges the difficult experience of illness and values persons as whole human beings in the context of community. In this way, the church incarnates divine love. Connors and Franke write, "In our view, the most important thing that we can say about God is that God is the one who is with us; God is Immanuel. When we become aware of God's caring presence in the midst of difficulty and suffering, the experience can be transformative.... [Such] caring and transformative presence can be glimpsed in the caring presence of our fellow human beings."[17] Pat identified her experience of surgery as one of three major significant events in her life. The church community, as it carries out the ministry of accompaniment, can be a catalyst for and witness to resilience and transformation.

Reshaping the practices

This final section focuses on specific, practical guidelines for extending care to women experiencing hysterectomy or mastectomy. These guidelines grow primarily out of experiences of women but also out of examination and revision of ethical and theological norms that are foundational for holistic caregiving as a moral imperative. For the sake of clarity, I group the guidelines below according to the four dimensions of care.

Guidelines for self-care

- Be proactive in searching out necessary information, consulting a variety of sources.
- Seek out trusted individuals or groups who can help with discernment in light of the information.
- Pay attention to gut feelings, and welcome new insights about body, healing, and relationships.
- Find ways to express feelings and thoughts (journal, write poetry, sculpt, paint, sketch, listen to or make music).
- Find one or a few people you trust, with whom to share struggles, pain, hopes, and joys.
- Care for the body: pay attention to nutrition, rest, exercise, and necessary medications/treatment.
- Mark the transition in a tangible, creative way.

---

[17] Ibid, 232.

- Affirm the inherent beauty and sacredness of the body, of womanhood (that is, the unique experience of being a woman) and personhood (that is, the experience of being human).
- Practice spiritual disciplines you are comfortable with (prayer, meditation, study of scripture), and draw from the resources of your faith tradition.
- Celebrate life!

Guidelines for significant others such as partners, friends, and relatives

- Walk alongside the woman throughout the journey, communicate openly, accompany her on visits to doctor or surgeon.
- Communicate acceptance and love by presence, word, and deed.
- Be willing to participate in a grieving process.
- If you are her sexual partner, be prepared to embrace altered sexual experience in creative ways.
- Acknowledge the significant transition in a tangible way (a special ritual, for example).
- Affirm the inherent beauty and sacredness of the body and of her womanhood and personhood.
- Be available to offer timely emotional and spiritual support and encouragement.
- Be willing (and become competent) to be a partner in discernment and accountability (that is, support her commitment to remain true to herself and the healing process).

Guidelines for medical care providers

- Be attentive to the person in the context of her relationships, address her questions and concerns, and encourage her to tap into emotional and spiritual resources.
- Provide full information as much as possible.
- Discuss options and procedures and their benefits and drawbacks.
- Encourage the person to gather several informed opinions.
- Acknowledge to the person that the experience of hysterectomy or mastectomy will involve a grieving process.
- Be mindful of the whole human being and communicate this mindfulness throughout the whole healing process: preparation, surgery, and recovery.
- Make sure that all members of the caregiving team are fully on board regarding the medical and moral imperative of holistic care.
- Take advantage of available resources that spiritual caregivers, such as chaplains and other ministering persons, can offer.

Guidelines for the care of the Christian community

- Teach consistently the values of holistic care.

- Practice a ministry of accompaniment, especially through pastoral care and counseling for women, couples, and others.
- Provide a place where there is freedom to share about and name the pain, struggles, and triumphs of women going through illness and surgery.
- Be explicit and empowering about messages to children and youth about body image, beauty, gender identity, self-care, and relationships.
- Provide support groups for women dealing with experiences of hysterectomy and mastectomy.
- Offer clearness meetings in which several members of the community meet with the person to assist in discernment about treatment options, or focus groups consisting of a few people with whom the person meets for a specified length of time.
- Offer rituals: (1) in small group settings to mark the experience of specific women; or (2) in the wider congregation, to provide space for marking experiences of loss in general.
- Consider providing a pastoral presence on the board of a health-care institution.
- Become a prophetic voice partnering with other institutions in society to promote holistic care as an alternative to the dominant values and practices.

In conclusion, if we believe that healing is the best of all journeys, and that healing happens in the context of being cared for as a whole human being, then holistic care is a moral imperative. Many women who have gone through the experience of hysterectomy or mastectomy, like Rachel, Helen, and Pat, have encountered unfortunate situations in which such care was absent. Lack of care may relate to difficulties with self-care, unsupportive loved ones, dehumanizing medical interactions, and inhospitality on the part of Christian communities. By reexamining the ethical and theological norms at the foundation of care, revisions may make possible fruitful and holistic care. Affirming new norms involves celebrating the inherent beauty and sacredness of body and womanhood, the possibility of greater love growing out of a commitment to the well-being of a significant other, the ability of medical professionals to be attentive to the broader context of the person, and the place of the church as a healing community. In other words, such comprehensive, multidimensional caregiving realizes the moral imperative of honoring women's experiences of loss, grief, healing, and transformation.

The ethic of care in spiritual caregiving

Leah Dawn Bueckert and Daniel S. Schipani

Excellence in spiritual caregiving requires an ongoing commitment to minister competently out of an *ethic of care*. This ethic involves a disposition to care empathetically and critically for people on various levels—interpersonal, institutional, social, and political. The ethic of care is normative for all who seek the redemptive transformation of individuals and communities.

Spiritual caregiving in the hospital is a setting in which the ethic of care is foundational. Our colleagues have vividly documented diverse manifestations of the ethic of care in parts 1 and 2 of this book, even though we did not ask them to make explicit reference to this ethic. In this essay, we use chaplaincy in the hospital to illustrate the ethic of care in practice. We start by presenting an overall understanding of this new moral theory, including origins, characterization, and critique. Second, we present biblical and theological grounding for the ethic of care from the perspective of our Mennonite faith tradition. Finally, we illustrate application of the ethic of care using stories from the hospital setting and chaplaincy ministry.

Understanding the ethic of care

Origins

Research psychologist Carol Gilligan first introduced the concept *ethic of care* in her book, *In a Different Voice*.[1] In this work, Gilligan presented an alternative view of moral development in response to psychologist Lawrence Kohlberg's theory of moral reasoning. Kohlberg had based his view of moral development on the virtue of justice, defined in terms of individual rights and fairness. He suggested that his model, established on the basis of empirical research with boys, was universally applicable. In contrast, Gilligan focused on the development of virtues of responsibility and relationships, rather than justice, because in her observations of girls and women, she had

Leah Dawn Bueckert is a chaplain resident at Lutheran Hospital, Fort Wayne, Indiana; Daniel S. Schipani is professor of pastoral care and counseling, Associated Mennonite Biblical Seminary, Elkhart, Indiana.

[1] Carol Gilligan, *In a Different Voice: Psychological Theory and Women's Development* (Cambridge, MA: Harvard University Press, 1982).

noticed the importance of these virtues. Gilligan asserted not that justice is the standard for males and relationships the standard for females but rather that responsibility within relationships and a sense of justice are aspects of moral development in both genders (although perhaps differently expressed in each). In addition to questioning the universal applicability of Kohlberg's theory, Gilligan challenged the dominant Western conception of the self and morality. The conception she challenged proposes individuation, impartiality, and impersonal and universal principles as key to moral maturity, rather than emphasizing the contextual and relational nature of the self.

Gilligan initially proposed the term *ethic of care* to emphasize relationship commitments as contrasted with individual rights and fairness; however, her intention was to hold in balance the importance of both elements. Gilligan did not go beyond naming the concept to begin delineating the content of an ethic of care. Her work, nonetheless, stands as a significant contribution to moral development theory from a feminist perspective. In the twenty-five years since the publication of her book, an increasing number of feminist and other ethicists, especially in the field of biomedical ethics, have begun to define the ethic of care and to explore its implications as an alternative moral theory.

Characterization

A clear-cut, widely held definition of the ethic of care is not easily found because the concept is still in an early stage of development. However, a sampling of voices reveals the provisional components of a holistic moral theory. Nel Noddings, in *Caring: A Feminine Approach to Ethics and Moral Education*, asserts that we care because we have been cared for. We are selves fundamentally in relationship and it is the need and desire to maintain relationships that motivates the practice of care. At the same time, Noddings distinguishes between *natural* caring (the spontaneous desire to act for the welfare of the other) and *ethical* caring (the deliberate choice to act for the welfare of the other, based on the paradigm of natural caring and rising out of the "I must" within). Therefore, while ethical caring involves effort to care for the other as one would care for oneself, such care is, nevertheless, based on the memory of the experience of having been cared for and having reached out in care.[2]

These preliminary definitions point to the need for cautions, questions, nuances, clarifications, and qualifications, some of which we explore below. For the purposes of this essay, we focus on prominent themes and limitations of the ethic of care, in order to elucidate its role in the task and privilege of bearing good news.

---

[2] Nel Noddings, *Caring: A Feminine Approach to Ethics and Moral Education* (Berkeley: University of California Press, 1984), 79–90.

Tom L. Beauchamp and James F. Childress, in *Principles of Biomedical Ethics*, emphasize that the ethic of care focuses on mutual interdependence, emotional responsiveness, and openness to the needs of the other as the other sees those needs. Beauchamp and Childress point out that the ethic leads to partiality and non-neutrality, not simply as morally permissible, but as expectation, especially in the case of caregiving professional practice. It does so by focusing on moral experience characterized by compassion, kindness, empathy-sympathy, a sense of friendship, and actual caring behavior.[3]

In their essay, "God and an Ethic of Care: On Being Immanuel," Russell B. Connors Jr. and Chris A. Franke gather themes from Nel Noddings, Milton Mayeroff, and other proponents of the ethic of care. Drawing on these sources, Connors and Franke posit five characteristic dimensions.[4]

- Caring assumes being-with as a moral possibility. Even though all experiences are unique, human solidarity and the ability to recognize others' experiences with attentiveness and empathy are possible. Availability, presence, and awareness (including social awareness) are necessary dimensions of caring.
- The caring relationship involves mutuality. Paradoxically, the caregiver commits to the well-being of the other while remaining committed to her or his own growth and well-being. Even if the relationship is asymmetrical (as in the practice of ministry), an element of reciprocity remains.
- Feeling plays an important role in caring. One communicates care and empathy to the extent that one is open to another's reality and experiences.
- Caring is not passive or "wimpy." It is not primarily about being nice or liking someone. Rather, it involves a commitment to act in behalf of those who are suffering or oppressed. This may involve strong, decisive moves to guide others to a new place in their life journey.
- Caring is a life pattern. Caring is not only a virtue but also a comprehensive way of ordering one's life. It has to do with character and vocation.

According to the ethic of care Connors and Franke describe, obligations within relationships are the primary reference point for ethical decision making, action, and reflection. The ethic of care focuses on mutual interdependence in relationships, which calls for attached attentiveness to others' needs, especially needs of sick and otherwise vulnerable people. The ethic prefers responsibility and responsible caring over detached respect for rights.

---

[3] Tom L. Beauchamp and James F. Childress, *Principles of Biomedical Ethics*, 5th ed. (Oxford: Oxford University Press, 2001), 376.

[4] Russell B. Connors Jr. and Chris A. Franke, "God and an Ethic of Care: On Being Emmanuel," in *Medicine and the Ethics of Care*, ed. Diana Fritz Cates and Paul Lauritzen (Washington, DC: Georgetown University Press, 2001), 212–13.

Further, this ethic highlights the moral role of affect (emotion, feelings).[5] The ethic of care is critical of liberal moral theories that value impartiality, detached fairness, and universal, abstract principles, unless those principles allow room for discretionary and contextual discernment and judgment in specific situations.[6]

To Connors and Franke's characterization we add the following observations. First, a direct connection exists between the development of the concept *ethic of care* and a feminist approach in the disciplines of psychology and ethics. Second, by interest and design, feminist psychological and ethical concerns are oriented not only to personal and interpersonal (micro) levels of human experience but also to institutional and to social (macro) levels.[7] Third, the ethic of care is now considered to have come of age as one kind of moral reflection among the families of moral theory that point to action-guides (that is, principles or dependable guides to practice) and virtues on the part of the practitioner.[8] Fourth, even though Gilligan and others originally made sharp distinctions between the ethic of justice and the ethic of care, agreement is now widespread on the need to (a) integrate justice as a dimension of care, and (b) view the ethic of care not only as personal and interpersonal but also as social ethic.[9]

Critique

Having thus identified the contours of the ethic of care, we now highlight key points of criticism. Four observations are noteworthy. First, judging by standard criteria of theory construction,[10] the ethic of care is still underdeveloped because it lacks "a developed and integrated body of reflections to supply the concepts and connections needed to satisfy [such] criteria."[11] Second, some proponents of the ethic of care must reflect critically on issues such as their tendency to deemphasize justice, principles, impartial judgment, and rights and obligations. Third, those advancing the ethic of care must consider the potential problem of sacrificial caring and, especially, the connection between

---

[5] Ibid.

[6] Beauchamp and Childress, *Principles,* 371, 374.

[7] A case in point is the significant influence of feminist ethics and ethics of care in the field of biomedical ethics, as documented in Diana Fritz Cates and Paul Lauritzen, eds., *Medicine and the Ethics of Care* (Washington, DC: Georgetown University Press, 2001).

[8] For a clear presentation and critical evaluation of moral theories relevant for biomedical ethics, see Beauchamp and Childress, *Principles,* 337–83.

[9] Kathryn Tanner discusses the move toward integration (that is, beyond a moral dualism between an ethic of care and an ethic of justice) and greater complexity in feminist ethics; "The Care That Does Justice," *Journal of Religious Ethics,* 24, no. 1 (Spring 1996): 171–91.

[10] Standard criteria of theory construction, the conditions of adequacy for an ethical theory, include clarity, coherence, completeness and comprehensiveness, simplicity, explanatory power, output power, and practicability; Beauchamp and Childress, *Principles,* 337–83.

[11] Ibid., 374.

women's experiences as self-sacrificing (or self-denying) care providers and their subordinate status. Therefore, a theory of the ethic of care must build in safeguards and correctives so as not to reinforce patterns of subordination and oppression. Fourth, the ethic of care needs consideration and application within a broad framework that includes much more than the private sphere of interpersonal relationships.

Regarding the ethic of care in the public sphere of life, ethicists Kathryn Tanner, Joan C. Tronto, and Nel Noddings offer valuable perspectives. Tanner writes, "Following the feminist adage that the personal is the political, feminist ethicists are reconceiving the values, forms of reasoning, and nature of relationships highlighted in an ethic of care by subjecting them to a more overtly political analysis."[12] She recounts the work of ethicist Susan Okin who casts the relationships of the immediate family in terms of power relations, the structures of which she closely relates to the political realm of business and government. On a different note, Tronto reflects, "It is easy to imagine that there will be some people or concerns about which we do not care. However, we might ask if our lack of care frees us from moral responsibility."[13] Tronto further suggests that a danger of the ethic of care is that it can become a justification for caring solely about those with whom one is most intimate. While this is an important warning, Noddings guards against this possible pitfall with her distinction between natural and ethical caring.[14] She notes that people naturally care more for those who are closer but suggests an ethical responsibility to care for anyone, in a way reminiscent of natural caring. Our ability to care is, of course, not limitless; hence Noddings' stress on self-care of the caregiver.[15]

In spite of its limitations, the ethic of care as a moral theory holds the promise of significant further development. The ongoing contribution of spiritual caregivers as reflective practitioners and practical theologians may be a source for that development. Another source may be the systematic exploration of related moral theories, such as H. Richard Niebuhr's vision of the responsible self,[16] within the field of Christian ethics.

Biblical and theological grounding for the ethic of care

The ethic of care undergirds all forms of bearing good news. While the ethic of care is not originally or exclusively a Christian ethic, to recognize

---

[12] Tanner, "The Care That Does Justice," 174.

[13] Joan C. Tronto, "Beyond Gender Difference to a Theory of Care," in *An Ethic of Care: Feminist and Interdisciplinary Perspectives*, ed. Mary Jeanne Larrabee (New York: Routledge, 1993), 249.

[14] See the section on characterization, above.

[15] Noddings, *Caring*, 79.

[16] H. Richard Niebuhr, *The Responsible Self: An Essay in Christian Moral Philosophy* (New York: Harper & Row, 1963).

the theological import of the ethic of care is indispensable for a Christian understanding and practice of life and ministry.

To the extent that the ethic of care illumines and informs Mennonite social ethics, the biblical paradigm of shalom has potential as a Mennonite contribution to an enhanced view of the ethic of care. Shalom as a biblical motif points to the optimal integration of peace and justice and to holistic well-being, toward which the ethic of care strives for all. The psalmist points towards this vision: "Love and faithfulness meet together; righteousness [or, justice] and peace kiss each other."[17] Well-being diminishes if we neglect either justice or peace. Striving for justice at the expense of harmonious relationships undermines the possibility of shalom as much as does preserving peace at the expense of "rightness" in relationships. Justice is not complete without peace, and peace is not complete without justice. To speak of shalom is to name the interconnection of the two. Shalom, therefore, is the goal of any ethic of care, and such an ethic is grounded in previous experience of shalom (however incomplete or fleeting).

One of the great biblical accounts of shalom is the Exodus story. In Deuteronomy 6, the Israelites are called to keep the covenant with Yahweh and the laws, in grateful response to their deliverance from Egypt."[18] It is the memory of the mercy Yahweh extended in liberating the Israelites from slavery in Egypt that animates their devotion to Yahweh as well as their care for one another and for strangers in their midst. They are called to care because they have been cared for. The biblical strategy of evoking the memory of care received in order to motivate extending care to others may suggest to us that if anything obscures or distorts the memory of care received, the ability to extend care will greatly diminish. The ethic of care, according to Noddings, involves a decision to care for the well-being of others based on the experience of care received and the responsibility to respond with care. "This memory of our own best moments of caring and being cared for sweeps over us as a feeling—as an 'I must'—in response to the plight of the other and our conflicting desire to serve our own interests."[19]

Jesus, in his interactions with Pharisees, challenged the observance of law when done at the expense of merciful relationships. For example, in Luke, Jesus makes this very point when accused of eating grain and healing a man's hand on the Sabbath.[20] In Mark, he challenges the Pharisees' preoccupation with rules, rights, purity, and appearances, by asking, "Which is lawful on the Sabbath: to do good or to do evil, to save life or to destroy it?"[21] As a teacher of an alternative wisdom, Jesus appealed to an ethic of care, compassion, and

---

[17] Psalm 85:10.
[18] Deuteronomy 6:4-25.
[19] Noddings, *Caring*, 80.
[20] Luke 6:1-11.
[21] Mark 3:4.

mercy, not abolishing the law but fulfilling it in creative and redemptive ways. This value threatened those upholding the status quo, who began plotting to harm Jesus.[22] As Connors and Franke assert, an ethic of care is not "wimpy." It is radical and courageous in challenging injustice, while speaking and acting out of concern for the well-being of those perpetrating the injustice.

The ethic of care is based on relationships. It is easy to demonize those with whom one has no direct contact. When one meets at the level of friendship a person who is a member of a group toward which one hold prejudice, it commonly happens that the encounter exposes unfair judgments, which soon begin to fall away. One begins to put oneself in the shoes of the other and to see his or her humanity. One realizes that the person is not so different from oneself. The other becomes neighbor. With the dissolution of prejudice, the propensity toward violence decreases significantly, and the responsibility to respect the other becomes prominent. The ethic of care proposes that such relationships of respect are the basis for moral decision making. This ethic expresses the desire to make enemies into friends, a challenge to which many Mennonites strive to respond. Jesus poses this same challenge with his words, "Love your enemies, and pray for those who persecute you."[23] Reconciliation becomes possible when one decides to care for a person one would just as soon not care for. In cases of abuse of various kinds (physical, sexual, emotional), however, the ethic of care must incorporate safeguards to equalize power and cautions against premature forgiveness and reconciliation, so as not to further victimize the victim.

Finally, Jesus's statements in the Beatitudes provide further illumination of the unity of mercy and justice. In the center of the Beatitudes, the verses appear, "Blessed are those who hunger and thirst for righteousness, for they will be filled. Blessed are the merciful, for they will be shown mercy."[24] Perhaps it is not simply chance that these two sayings stand side by side in the core of the Beatitudes. Here is more reinforcement of the indispensable connection between mercy and righteousness. Shalom, the context in which human wholeness is possible, is at the center of good news. Those who bear good news and minister from the ethic of care within specific institutional and social contexts become agents of transformation who realize Jesus' vision of healing and wholeness.

The ethic of care in spiritual caregiving

Of the many possibilities that might illustrate application of the ethic of care, we focus on spiritual caregiving in the hospital as a way to illustrate

---

[22] For an illuminating discussion of Jesus's ethics (and politics) of care and compassion as an alternative to the purity system, see Marcus J. Borg, *Meeting Jesus Again for the First Time* (San Francisco: Harper, 1994), 46–68. Borg subsequently presents Jesus as a teacher of an alternative wisdom (69–95).

[23] Matthew 5:44.

[24] Matthew 5:6, 7.

through specific examples the contribution of this ethic for broader society.[25] We discuss the chaplain's role within the medical system, followed by three stories: a response to medical errors, a woman's experience of mastectomy, and a final vignette about patient privacy. The purpose of these illustrations is to demonstrate ways the ethic of care may guide a sense of moral responsibility.

Chaplains in a hospital setting in North America work within the Western biomedical healthcare delivery system. In many ways, ideology, technology, and economics severely compromise the current system. The goals of healing, wholeness, and shalom diminish significantly in light of practices that tend to separate the person from the treatment and emphasize a narrow view of cure, to the detriment of quality of life. The chaplain must be aware of the system's brokenness. The ethic of care requires that the chaplain be a prophetic voice in the hospital, an advocate for treatment of each person as a whole human being. As an agent of hope and a representative of a faith community that proposes an alternative to depersonalization, the chaplain calls for and nurtures shalom that is often lacking in the modern biomedical healthcare context.

Responses to medical error

According to *Hopkins Medicine*, 98,000 fatal medical mistakes occur every year in the United States healthcare system.[26] Spiritual care providers in these situations have the opportunity to work with families and staff in ways that encourage accountability and reconciliation. Lawsuits become a search for justice in response to medical error. The practice of an ethic of care on all sides goes beyond litigation and moves toward acceptance of responsibility on the part of medical care providers. Such an ethic seeks to motivate openness, in those suffering the consequences of an error, to receive explanations, apologies, and efforts to make what amends are possible.

In a recent article in *The Mennonite*, Joe Kotva and Timothy Jost speak about "mediation over litigation." Addressing medical negligence and malpractice, they suggest that "patients rarely sue physicians with whom they have an ongoing relationship of trust and respect or who honestly apologize

---

[25] Two powerful examples of the ethic of care operating outside the hospital context are Christian Peacemaker Teams and the Victim Offender Reconciliation Program (VORP). In these programs, "righteousness and peace kiss each other." Christian Peacemaker Teams are specially trained groups of people sponsored by the historic peace churches. These teams position themselves in the midst of volatile situations (for example, Palestine or Iraq), seeking to prevent violent confrontation. VORP is an organization independent of the criminal justice system that nevertheless works in cooperation with it. The VORP mediation process seeks just reconciliation between offenders and victims. See Howard Zehr, *Changing Lenses: A New Focus for Crime and Justice* (Scottdale: Herald Press, 1990), 158–74.

[26] Mary Ann Ayd, "A Remedy of Errors," *Hopkins Medicine* (Spring/Summer 2004), http://www.hopkinsmedicine.org/hmn/S04/feature1.cfm.

for mistakes."[27] Kotva and Jost speak about the responsibility of patients and physicians alike to treat each other with respect and to seek to maintain a relationship. Such responsibility requires patients who have been harmed to seek out the physician and receive an explanation for the mistake. The physician must explain what happened, listen empathically to the patient's experience, and acknowledge the injury. The willingness of both parties to maintain a relationship through accountability and honesty reflects the spirit of an ethic of care. The following story of Josie King recounts a powerful example of such a process.[28]

Josie King was an eighteen-month-old girl who contracted second and third-degree burns from climbing into a hot bath. She received treatment at Johns Hopkins Pediatric Hospital where she was recovering well. However, two days before she was to go home, Josie died of severe dehydration and misused narcotics. Sorrell King, Josie's mother, having noticed a decline in Josie's well-being, had raised concerns prior to her daughter's death, but hospital staff disregarded the concerns. During the family's initial shock, confusion, devastation, and rage, the hospital selected George Dover, a pediatric hematologist who was not Josie's doctor, to serve as the line of communication between hospital administration and the King family. *Hopkins Medicine* describes Dover's first encounter with the Kings:

> When he arrived that winter day at the Kings' suburban Baltimore home, Dover knew he had a lot of listening to do. When he did speak, he said the one thing, perhaps the only thing, that mattered.
>
> "We knew what had happened," says Sorrell King. "We wanted someone to tell us why—why didn't they listen to us when we said something was wrong with Josie, why didn't they give her something to drink? We were involved with our lawyer then. We were going for it. If George had said, 'We're not sure what happened,' we would have thrown him out. But he totally did the right thing, at least from our perspective. He said, 'I am so sorry. This happened on my watch, at my hospital. I will help you get to the bottom of it.'"
>
> To physicians who've seen their malpractice insurance premiums skyrocket in recent years, Dover's promise could

---

[27] Joe Kotva and Timothy Jost, "Mediation over litigation," *The Mennonite* (October 4, 2005), 30.

[28] Peter Pronovost, *Josie's Story* (Baltimore: Johns Hopkins, 2002), VHS recording.

seem tantamount to handing the Kings' attorney his case on a plate. Dover didn't view it that way.[29]

Sorrell King eventually spoke to Hopkins medical professionals and, together with Peter Pronovost, Director of Patient Safety, launched the Josie King Patient Safety Program in 2002. The Kings received a monetary settlement from the hospital, a portion of which they decided to donate to the new program.[30]

This story illustrates a mother's choice to maintain a relationship with the professionals responsible for her daughter's death, to channel her anger and grief into working collaboratively with the staff at Johns Hopkins—holding them accountable, encouraging better interdisciplinary communication, and involving herself in programs geared toward prevention of these tragedies. From the perspective of an ethic of care, we recognize courageous commitment to peace and justice within relationships that helped remedy systemic neglect of the well-being of persons and their families. As advocates of holistic care, spiritual caregivers likewise are a voice for peace and justice within the hospital setting, facilitating the possibilities of such reconciliation.

Psychotherapist William J. Doherty speaks of the need for a competent caregiver to have not only knowledge and skill but also a caring disposition. We cannot truly help someone we do not care for. The caring bond between caregiver and care-receiver is at the heart of the healing process; it is the main vehicle for the effectiveness of the caregivers.[31] It is not only what the caregiver does that matters, but also how he or she carries out particular actions.[32]

Experiences of mastectomy

The previous chapter presented Pat's story of bilateral mastectomy. Pat's great-grandmother was diagnosed with breast cancer at seventy years of age, her grandmother was diagnosed at age sixty, and her mother at fifty. When Pat was in her thirties, she elected, with her family history in mind, to have a radical bilateral mastectomy as a preventive measure. Healing from such an intrusive surgery as mastectomy, as with many kinds of surgery, requires the practice of an ethic of care on at least four levels. First, the woman's

---

[29] Ayd, "A Remedy of Errors."

[30] Ibid.

[31] William J. Doherty, *Soul Searching: Why Psychotherapy Must Promote Moral Responsibility* (New York: Basic Books, 1995), 115–37. Doherty's discussion of the moral character of the therapist is especially pertinent to the ethic of care. He argues that to become a good therapist takes much more than knowledge and skill. It requires certain qualities of character or virtues, in the sense of predispositions to do what is good and right in a given situation. Caring, Doherty believes, is the cornerstone virtue and the essential moral prerequisite for therapists.

[32] Beauchamp and Childress, *Principles*, 370.

commitment to self-care plays a key role in the healing process. Pat gave herself time to consider her plan, gathering information and speaking with specific people about her options. Pat processed her experiences before and after surgery through art, journaling, and talking with friends. Self-care is an integral component of the ethic of care. In the words of Noddings, "If caring is to be maintained, clearly, the one-caring must be maintained. She must be strong, courageous, and capable of joy."[33] The chaplain plays a significant role in assisting care-receivers to mobilize their resources for self-care.

Second, an ethic of care is evident in the positive accompaniment of significant others in the woman's life. By participating empathically in the process of surgery and recovery, from a stance of natural caring, these people embody the foundation on which ethical caring is based. Unfortunately, Pat's husband refused to be a conversation partner with her throughout this experience. The spiritual caregiver in such an instance might help to facilitate communication between husband and wife.

Third, according to an ethic of care, the medical professionals involved in the surgery commit themselves to being attentive to the concerns and particular context of each woman undergoing mastectomy. Pat's surgeon was open to meeting regularly with her before the operation to talk about the procedure. She also did an expert job of stitching up the wounds on Pat's chest, leaving the faintest scars possible. Pat was fortunate. Many women go through the trauma of having too little information or preparation before surgery. Some are left with messy scars because of careless operating procedures. The chaplain can play an educational role for staff regarding the integration of competence and caring. The chaplain can also be a liaison between patients and professionals, promoting harmonious and just relations.

Fourth, the church community guided by an ethic of care commits itself to supporting these women in their midst according to an ethic of care. The faith community supports women who have undergone mastectomy by providing opportunities for them to share about their experiences of surgery and loss, as well as by providing clear and empowering messages regarding body image, sexuality, and gender roles. Pat found a helpful conversation partner in her pastor. Such a community of faith can be a place of hope, healing, and shalom. Spiritual caregivers in the hospital encourage care-receivers who are part of a religious community to draw on that resource for support.

Patient privacy

A hospital chaplain planned to make a follow-up visit to a patient and family she had seen a few days earlier. In order to make this visit, the chaplain needed to inquire at the nurse's station for the room number. She spoke with a nurse (whom she had not met before) and posed her inquiry. As it turned out, because the chaplain did not know the last name of the patient, the

---

[33] Noddings, *Caring*, 100.

nurse (for patient privacy and confidentiality reasons) could not provide her with the room number.

In this scenario, both the nurse and the chaplain were caring for the patient. The chaplain was operating primarily from an ethic of care, focusing on the needs of the patient. The nurse was operating primarily from an ethic of patient rights and due process including, of course, attention to the legal responsibility of the hospital. Given the concerns about liability that currently hover in hospital air like perpetual black clouds, it is understandable that nursing and medical staff are poised to enforce laws regarding confidentiality and patient privacy. Speaking in terms of an ethic of care, the chaplain had a relationship with the family such that a visit would have been beneficial and warranted. She also had relationships with staff members in the hospital who could vouch for the validity of her role as a spiritual caregiver. However, the chaplain did not have a relationship with that particular nurse.

While the ethic of care does not diminish the importance of protecting patient privacy, it does seek to hold rights and due process in balance with the particular context and needs of the care-receiver. This balance is challenging to maintain within a system that tends to treat people in a fragmentary way. The chaplain's role in such a system includes addressing the care-receiver holistically and bringing the holistic perspective to the rest of the treatment team.

Conclusion

The ethic of care is a new and developing moral theory that holds much promise. A contribution from feminist thought and experience, the ethic is a reminder that mutual interdependence in relationships is the foundation and goal of moral decision making and responsibility. Concerns for both peace and justice are integral to an ethic of care, especially when these concerns are grounded biblically and theologically. These concerns closely mirror peacemaking efforts such as mediation in conflict situations.[34] The quest for harmonious relationships within the broader vision of shalom is guided by an ethic of care, which itself grows out of the experience of having been cared for. Advocating for the holistic treatment of people, calling for accountability while facilitating reconciliation, encouraging empathy in balance with competence, and placing needs in balance with rights are ways spiritual caregivers model an ethic of care applicable within the hospital setting and beyond.

---

[34] Consider, for instance, Mennonite Conciliation Service's approach to mediation in Carolyn Schrock-Shenk, ed., *Mediation and Facilitation Training Manual*, 4th ed. (Akron, PA: Mennonite Conciliation Service, 2000).

Interfaith spiritual caregiving

The case for language care

Leah Dawn Bueckert and Daniel S. Schipani

"The tongue of the wise brings healing ... and a word in season, how good it is!"[1] These words from the wisdom tradition of the Bible are especially fitting when applied to the challenges and possibilities of interfaith spiritual caregiving. Communicating with people whose faith and culture differ from our own requires special attention to our use of language. Such language care demonstrates a stewardship of language that caregivers need to develop for the fruitful practice of their ministry.

In light of their training and unique role in the hospital, chaplains have the responsibility to practice language care in order to engage effectively in the interfaith and intercultural communication that is essential to their spiritual caregiving ministry. Further, chaplains have a daily opportunity to minister at the intersection of the hospital culture and the culture(s) of patients and their relatives. In so doing, they foster interfaith communication, a special kind of intercultural communication.

By hospital culture we mean the ways hospitals organize themselves and function as institutions and healthcare systems. Thus, a hospital's culture includes roles, norms, symbols, regulations, patterns of operation, specialized language, and so on. Chaplains play a significant role as catalysts of communication between this culture and that of patients and their relatives. For example, the chaplain often serves as mediator between the healthcare team and patients or relatives, and she or he interprets meanings and practices to patients and families as an active member of the healthcare team.

In our increasingly multicultural and religiously pluralistic social context, we find it essential to understand interfaith communication as a special type of intercultural communication, bringing the insights of intercultural communication to bear on interfaith communication. Certain skills and

Leah Dawn Bueckert is a chaplain resident at Lutheran Hospital, Fort Wayne, Indiana; Daniel Schipani is professor of pastoral care and counseling at Associated Mennonite Biblical Seminary, Elkhart, Indiana.

[1] Prov. 12:18b, 15:23b.

attitudes have been identified as indispensable for effective intercultural communication. These include awareness of ethnocentrism and one's own assumptions, adjustment of expectations, placing understanding before judgment, maintaining personal integrity, the significance of learning another's language, acknowledgment of spiritual integrity present in different religious cultures, the relationship between language and worldview, the significance of nonverbal communication, and the need to develop a communication ethic. These very skills and attitudes are also essential for the practice of interfaith communication in spiritual caregiving.[2]

Language care involves both caring deeply *for* language itself and communicating care *through* diverse forms of language. This process involves the choice and use of language for the sake of communicating and collaborating. Therefore, language care is not simply a matter of cultural or political correctness. It is more than lip service to communicating respect; the language of care requires an unfailing commitment to minister well. It involves the effort and skill to communicate with care-receivers in such a way that they feel heard, understood, and encouraged to participate, in their own terms and to the extent of their abilities, in the therapeutic communication process. It stems from an ethic of care (see previous chapter), care for the sake of healing, and the responsibility to the care-receiver for caring well.

The first part of this chapter presents two stories that introduce the discussion of language care in spiritual caregiving. The stories illustrate the kinds of hospital situations that make interfaith communication indispensable. The second part of the chapter includes descriptive, interpretive, and evaluative considerations of the forms of language employed by care-receivers and caregivers and of the quality of the communication process. The third and final part of the chapter focuses on guidelines and requirements for the effective practice of language care, related to the person of the caregiver and to professional competencies and practices. All of these reflections stem from our conviction that, for spiritual caregivers, language care is not an option; it is a therapeutic requirement and moral obligation.

Interfaith communication in chaplaincy ministry: Two stories

The following stories demonstrate the need, place, and nature of interfaith communication. The first story recounts interactions with Sunny, a Christian woman on the post-surgical unit. The second scenario tells the story of Steve, a man dying of lung cancer, who volunteered that he was an existentialist. We follow the two scenarios with our assessment of the forms of language used in each interaction.

---

[2] Recent research in psychotherapy and counseling connects issues of cross-cultural communication and spirituality, as documented, for example, in Mary A. Fukuyama and Todd D. Sevig, *Integrating Spirituality into Multicultural Counseling* (Thousand Oaks, CA: Sage, 1999).

Sunny[3]

Sunny, a forty-nine-year-old woman, was recovering from open-heart surgery when I met her. During our initial conversation, Sunny volunteered that she believes in God and that she prays and reads the Bible, although she does not attend church. Near the end of this visit, I offered to pray with her, but she verbalized her preference that I not do so. Over the next month, I met with Sunny several times a week, until she returned home. During this time, she had two further surgeries to remedy a problematic chest incision. After the first of these two surgeries, she requested that I pray with her, and I did so.

As we got better acquainted, Sunny confided that she had been skeptical in the beginning about my intentions as a chaplain—first, because I was a woman, and second, because she was not in the mood to be "preached at." In her experience, women were expected to be silent in the context of the church. Yet she came to value my involvement with her as a female chaplain, saying, "If God is calling you to be a chaplain, that's great." Sunny also affirmed my approach to caregiving. She spoke with appreciation of my ministry of listening and conversation instead of preaching. When I responded, "I believe that the presence of God is known better through the sharing of conversation than in dispensing moral platitudes," she replied, "Well, he sure spoke through you."

Our meetings included discussing Sunny's hopes to work toward the restoration of broken relationships with her sisters. Before her final surgery, I met several members of her family. At the request of Sunny and one of her sisters, I led the group in a prayer for Sunny's well-being, for the healing work of the medical staff, and for the upbuilding of the family as a whole. During the recovery process that followed, Sunny and I had the opportunity to reflect theologically together on the presence of God in the midst of suffering. Sunny initiated reflections on this subject, saying that in her understanding, human beings—not God—are the cause of much of the suffering in the world. As her discharge date drew near, she spoke with me about her desire to reconnect with a Christian community. She confided that through the experience of surgery she had come to believe "God is number one for me." I received her comment as an indication that she had discovered greater hope and trust.

Steve[4]

Steve was a sixty-year-old man with terminal lung cancer. When I introduced myself as a chaplain, he told me that religion was not really a part of his

---

[3] Sunny generously gave me (LDB) permission to write her story based on my experience of our interactions. I have altered all personal identifying information, including her name, to protect her privacy. For a fuller discussion of this story, including a systematic analysis of the dynamics involved, see Leah Dawn Bueckert, "Glimpses of the Heart of Caring: A Chaplain's Story," in *Mennonite Perspectives on Pastoral Care and Counseling*, ed. Daniel S. Schipani, (Elkhart, IN.: Institute of Mennonite Studies, 2006), chapter 9, forthcoming.

[4] The story of Steve is a composite of my interactions with several different patients (LDB).

life. He seemed dubious at first about conversing with me. I suggested that I would tell him about my role as a chaplain and he could then decide if he was interested in continuing the conversation. I told Steve that I was interested to know how the hospital team might best support him during his stay and I wanted to inquire about personal sources of support which for some people include a religious community and for others do not. Steve nodded and proceeded to describe his philosophy of life, stating that he considered himself an existentialist. According to Steve, human existence and experience are authoritative; "God" is not part of the picture. Human beings are free agents, and there is no source of absolute truth or definitive code of morality. Steve also shared a vibrant interest in, and deep respect for, the varieties of religious expression in the world, expressing appreciation for the different paths in the human quest for meaning. I articulated a similar admiration and respect for the many different religious traditions.

Steve told me about his prior experiences in the Christian church and about the way its exclusivism had turned him off; he was angry about the church's arrogance in presuming to determine who is acceptable to God and who is not. He told me about extended family members who continue to pray for him in their anxiety about his destination in the afterlife. I asked Steve about what sustained him now during his struggle with lung cancer. He told me about significant relationships with family and friends and spoke about the experiences that had brought him great joy in life, such as traveling. Reflecting further on the illness, he elaborated by saying, "I don't believe there is anything after this life. But that's okay. I've had my kick at the can. My kids are grown and married and have good jobs. They'll be fine."

Near the end of the visit, I asked Steve if I could pray with him. He answered affirmatively and so, in prayer, I expressed gratitude for our meeting and the sources of support that Steve had named. I voiced the desire that Steve would continue to experience care during his hospitalization. Afterwards I indicated that I would return in a couple of days to say hello, if that was all right with him. He replied that he would welcome my visit, and then we said goodbye.

Context of interfaith communication

Patients come to the hospital from many different cultural and religious contexts. Some people are closely affiliated with a particular religious tradition or community, and others have no such affiliations. The chaplain works with the care-receiver in discovering the different kinds of resources the person may have to draw on (spiritual and otherwise) that might facilitate the healing process. In addition to the care-receiver's sources of support, the healthcare team has resources to offer, including the services of spiritual caregivers. In each encounter between care-receiver and caregiver, the parties express issues of life and ultimate concern using a certain language. In this essay, we explore several *forms* of language used by both care-receiver and caregiver.

Before continuing immediately with that task, however, a few comments about the insights of Carley H. Dodd will serve to enhance our discussion. Many models address the process of intercultural and interfaith communication. Dodd's is one such model, illustrated in *Dynamics of Intercultural Communication*. Dodd explains the process by which two people from different cultures meet and communicate effectively. In sum, Dodd's model calls for participants to suspend judgment and bias while they engage in a third culture created by the intercultural participants, in order to explore mutual goals and common concerns. In other words, out of a perception of dissimilarity, participants A and B can carve out a third culture between them, a culture of similarity.[5]

Dodd suggests that intercultural communication is a creative process taking place between two people who perceive differences in each other. Rather than building walls, on the one hand, or, attempting to completely collapse their two cultures (an impossible goal), on the other, the two parties carve out a new reality between them in which they find common ground. Dodd's model is helpful in that it demonstrates the caregiver's purpose in establishing common ground with a care-receiver: so that the caregiver might collaborate with the care-receiver toward the shared goal of healing and wholeness.

At the same time, however, Dodd's model assumes a symmetrical relationship between person A and person B. In the case of spiritual caregiving in the hospital, as we mentioned above, the chaplain remains aware of the inherent asymmetry in the interpersonal encounter with patients and their families and normally does not expect the care-receiver(s) to assume the same degree of awareness of, and responsibility for, using language care. It is to the uses of language on the part of care-receivers and caregivers that we now return.

The care-receiver's use of language

Volunteering information: Telling the story

Expectations of the chaplain's role vary among patients and families. Generally the chaplain is regarded as a representative of a church or faith tradition and perhaps of God. Because of this understanding, a patient may voluntarily report information about religious involvements or make comments about the fact that she or he has no connection with a religious community. This happened in the initial conversation with Sunny. Soon after our introductions, she explained that while she does not attend church, she does believe in God, pray, and read the Bible. Steve in his own way also followed the pattern. He commented in a matter-of-fact but almost apologetic manner that involvement in a faith community was not part of his life (perhaps implying that my visit would be fruitless in light of our potentially divergent viewpoints).

---

[5] Carley H. Dodd, *Dynamics of Intercultural Communication*, 5th ed. (Boston: McGraw Hill, 1998), 6.

In encounters with other people, introducing oneself as a chaplain may elicit sheepishness and guilt on the part of the care-receiver, or it may elicit vehement antagonism and disdain. In yet other situations, a care-receiver may warmly welcome the chaplain. Regardless of the patient's particular affiliation or lack of affiliation with a religious tradition, the caregiver must always communicate respect and unconditional acceptance.

Every person is spiritual[6] regardless of religious context, yet patients express differently the language of their ultimate concerns—their quest for meaning, healing, wholeness, and hope. The expressions of the care-receiver may or may not involve explicitly religious language, depending on the context of the patient. As a caregiver, one seeks to participate as fully as possible in the preferred conceptual-linguistic framework of the care-receiver, while maintaining personal and spiritual integrity.

For any of a variety of reasons, the care-receiver may decline further conversation. In the culture of the hospital, patients are relatively powerless to control much of what happens to them during hospitalization. The chaplain, however, is one care provider a patient can refuse without facing an argument from the healthcare team. Respecting the personal integrity and preferences of care-receivers, an essential part of the chaplain's role, requires the use of language care.

Prayer and requests for prayer

Prayer and requests for prayer are other forms of language that reflect the unique spirituality of patients and their families. Prayer is a form of language that crosses cultures and religious traditions. It is one way people define and give expression to their deepest longings and greatest hopes—for healing, wholeness, reconciliation—and is a means by which they communicate a sense of trust in the mystery of life to sustain them and their loved ones.

Sunny indicated that prayer was something she found meaningful. At first, however, she declined my offer to pray with her. While making available the resources one brings, a spiritual caregiver who seeks to be attentive to the person's context takes cues from the care-receiver about what is welcome or not welcome. I continued to visit Sunny and eventually did pray with her regularly—initially at her request and subsequently by offering to do so. In other instances, a patient's or family's request for prayer may follow almost immediately after introductions have been exchanged. In still other scenarios, as with Steve, care-receivers themselves may not engage in traditional forms of prayer at all. Prayer with patients or families from a religious tradition other than one's own requires sensitivity. The chaplain may, in these situations, facilitate connections with a spiritual representative from that tradition or offer words of encouragement and support in the form of a blessing.

---

[6] We describe our understanding of the term *spiritual* in this book's introduction.

Expression of personal convictions and theology

Making sense and meaning out of illness, accidents, and losses necessitates an integration process in which people ponder such an experience in light of their worldview. Many patients will articulate this worldview in the language of their faith or religious tradition, which may include a range of images for the Divine or God. Frequently the care-receiver invites the chaplain to participate verbally in this integration process. Our use of the term *theology* to describe such reflection points to our observation that patients normally engage in "faith seeking understanding" (Anselm's classic definition of theology). Moreover, the reflective wisdom we observe in the patients we work with is often at a personal, practical, and down-to-earth level.

Near the end of Sunny's time at the hospital, she stated her conviction that "God is number one." In addition, Sunny's verbal reflections in my presence about the causes of suffering in the world indicated her perspective on the ways the human and the divine intersect and affect each other. Steve's expressions of personal conviction included his identification as an existentialist and his belief that there is no life after death. His elaboration on this philosophy and his interest in different forms of religious expression indicated a similar longing to understand the meaning of life, the nature of the transcendent, and the experience of being human.

In summary, the language of care-receivers—as they volunteer information about religious connections or spiritual perspectives, ask for prayer, express theological reflections or personal convictions, and so on—becomes the focus of the chaplain's careful listening. Listening well is the primary task in the chaplain's practice of language care. The chaplain remains aware of the inherent asymmetry in the interpersonal encounter with patients and their families, namely, the care-receivers' compromised position and the chaplain's relative position of power or advantage. Therefore, the spiritual caregiver never expects the care-receiver to assume the same degree of awareness of, and responsibility for, using language care in order to preserve the integrity of the interpersonal, intercultural, and interfaith communication process.

The caregiver's use of language

Probing questions: Gathering the story

Speaking with patients about their spiritual well-being is one of the primary roles of the chaplain. Interestingly enough, others often perceive this role in a narrow sense—that the chaplain is concerned only with the spiritual dimension, to the exclusion of physical, psychological, and social well-being. On the contrary, the chaplain's training and competence lie in the ability and responsibility to care for people as whole human beings.[7] Therefore, rather

---

[7] For a helpful discussion of both the narrow and broad definitions of spirituality, see Paul B. Pederson, et al., *Counseling across Cultures*, 5th ed. (Thousand Oaks, CA: Sage Publications, 2002), 277, 278.

than starting with questions geared specifically toward religious affiliations, an invitation to conversation about the person's immediate experience in the hospital communicates care for the person within her or his unique context. In fact, a premature focus on faith matters is at best a distraction and at worst a hindrance.

Of course, in the process of hearing a person's story and picking up cues about support systems already in place (or lacking), the chaplain may ask questions related to faith tradition, church affiliation, or religious experience. Questions that are nonjudgmental, such as, "Do you find prayer helpful?" or "What has helped you through past experiences of illness or loss?" may be invitations to further conversation about that which provides the patient with a sense of meaning and fulfillment. These and other questions serve to gather the information necessary to assess how the spiritual caregiver might be helpful to the care-receiver.

During this process of orientation and rapport-building, the caregiver needs to decide whether or how to engage in explicitly religious language, based on the care-receiver's expressed concerns, needs, and preferred uses of language. The choice to move forward with a particular kind of language may involve internal translation on the part of the caregiver. By translation, we mean the ways the chaplain interprets and communicates meaning and hope through the conceptual-linguistic framework of the care-receiver (which may differ markedly from that of the caregiver) and likewise interprets the latter's ways of communicating. Such translation must reflect the ethic of care and respect that sustains and guides the caregiver's commitment to care well under all kinds of circumstances.

Whenever the language chosen by the patient is not the preferred language of the caregiver, the caregiver is responsible to honor the patient's concerns and to make available the resources of spiritual care by using the kind of language that is fitting to the patient, while maintaining personal and professional integrity. Religious and cultural differences are real and not to be minimized, and much can be lost in translation. Familiarity with the culture of care-receivers facilitates effective translation. Pederson et al. recommend, "It is reasonable to expect that the more a counselor knows about the whys and wherefores of other cultures, the more effective he or she will be, both professionally and interpersonally."[8] Yet the languages of hope, love, meaning making, and transformation rise out of longings and questions that are fundamental to being human.[9] These concerns are the core of holistic well-being and holistic care, regardless of one's specific religious context.

---

[8] Pedersen, et al., xiv.

[9] For a discussion of universal effectiveness and culturally specific components in the psychotherapeutic context, see: Juris G. Draguns, "Universal and Cultural Aspects of Counseling and Psychotherapy," in Pederson et al., 29–50.

Chaplains may encounter situations in which the preferred religious language and framework of the care-receiver appear to be barriers to healing. In such circumstances, chaplains have the opportunity to engage sensitively in critical caring. We adopt the notion of critical caring from Valerie DeMarinis, who intends the term *critical* to imply both "careful judgment" and "crucial intervention," and interprets the term *caring* as "appropriate concern." Critical caring is thus "the ability for careful judgment and appropriate concern to work together for crucial intervention."[10] While engaged in such caring, the chaplain seeks to interpret the behavior of the care-receiver in ways that are acceptable by the patient and that neutralize anxiety. In instances where there is a serious ideological clash between care-receiver and caregiver, the latter may conclude, for instance, that the rigidity of the care-receiver's conviction seriously undermines the healing process. This may occur when interacting with patients who ground fatalistic views of their health conditions on certain biblical interpretations related to sinful behavior and punishment. In such cases, therapeutic communication is particularly challenging. Caregivers must be sufficiently self-aware to recognize the existence of their own blind spots and prejudices—a competence that will be discussed in more detail below.

Spoken prayer

Chaplains frequently pray with patients and families, and they sometimes read aloud from religious sources, such as the Bible. When Sunny was preparing for her final surgery, several of her family members had gathered to be with her. I read Psalm 121 and offered a prayer. A chaplain might pray in various ways, sometimes using standard form prayers and sometimes praying spontaneously, weaving together the expressed concerns of the patient or relative(s) with the explicit or implicit hopes and longings for healing, wholeness, justice, reconciliation, and so on. The more fittingly such spontaneous prayers reflect the care-receiver's expressed concerns and hopes, the more welcome and potentially healing they are.

Although Steve said that he was not affiliated with a religious tradition, and although he expressed annoyance with the anxious prayers of some of his relatives, the chaplain decided to offer to pray with him. Caregivers take cues from the patient about whether offering to pray will be welcomed or appropriate. Steve accepted the offer of prayer. The chaplain hoped that such prayer could affirm Steve's articulated wishes as well as provide a counter-example to the prayers focused primarily on whether he held right beliefs and would be "saved." In addition to spoken prayer in the presence of care-receivers, chaplains also may engage in private prayer in behalf of patients, families, staff, and themselves.

---

[10] Valerie M. DeMarinis, *Critical Caring: A Feminist Model for Pastoral Psychology* (Louisville: Westminster John Knox Press, 1993), 17.

Theological conversation

Theology involves reflection on the nature of God and the relationship between human beings, the universe, and the divine. Spiritual caregiving entails diverse uses of language, including some kinds of theological discussion and reflection. From time to time, chaplains engage in theological dialogue with patients, families, and colleagues. It is important that chaplains base these interactions in the care-receiver's experience and not in theoretical or doctrinal abstractions.

A measure of theological discussion is most appropriate, and potentially most meaningful and fruitful, when care-receivers initiate such reflections themselves. Examples may include having a conversation about the biblical book of Job with a patient who is clinically depressed and physically ill, or responding to a patient, upset about visitors, who quotes 1 Corinthians 10:13: "No testing has overtaken you that is not common to everyone. God is faithful and he will not let you be tested beyond your strength."

The images of God that we hold have a bearing on our responses to experiences of illness and loss. For this reason, conversations with patients about their images of God are significant. Such considerations can provide encouragement or bring to awareness perceptions that either enhance or hinder the healing process.

Embodying

Even if no explicit theological conversation occurs, an observer may detect theological dynamics implicit in visits with people who are hospitalized. The chaplain makes choices about what to make explicit and what to leave unspoken. Even when caregivers do not use traditional Christian terms, they are conscious of the fact that they inevitably express embodied or nonverbal language through the way they look at people and through facial expressions, body posture, tone of voice, gestures, and so on. When the words of our faith express love, truth, peace, hope, joy, freedom, humanization, community building, healing, and transformation, we must somehow reflect these values and virtues in the way we are bodily present to care-receivers. Embodying the good news of grace (as love) and wisdom (as truth) is for us the key to spiritual caregiving. This realization we deem essential in order for effective, truthful, and life-giving interfaith communication to take place.

Spiritual caregiving in the hospital, as in other settings, is about communicating hope, grace, and love in the midst of suffering and loss. Through word and deed, it communicates and elicits that which sustains. In many cases, the ministry of presence is a chaplain's gift to patients and their families and to the hospital staff. We can think, in biblical terms, of a ministry of presence at its best as the Word that becomes flesh and dwells among us.[11] People may well receive a word of hope, grace, and hospitality whether they

---

[11] John 1:14.

are nonreligious, Hindu, Muslim, Buddhist, Jewish, Christian, or of any spirituality different from the caregiver. Likewise, the caregiver may receive grace and new insight from interactions with the care-receiver, regardless of particular spiritual experience or theological perspective.

Whether or not caregivers make explicit Christian references, they aim to be channels of grace by being present with the patient or family and discerning the appropriate use of language. A caregiver might choose not to speak with her or his preferred language for addressing spirituality, recognizing that nonverbal communication of good news is also a profoundly spiritual language. The presence and nonverbal communication of the chaplain can incarnate messages of grace, unconditional acceptance, hope, forgiveness, and so on.

In some cases, an expression of comfort may be communicated by the minutes a chaplain spends holding the hand of a person in her or his care. In many ways, the language of touch, used appropriately, can convey more about comfort and support than any words can. While touch can also be healing among people of the same religious tradition, when it comes to interfaith spiritual caregiving, such nonverbal, tactile language can be an especially significant bridge.[12] While it is crucial to continually develop greater awareness of and sensitivity to spiritual and religious diversity, one's learning will always be incomplete. For this reason, the nonverbal language of presence and care is significant in carrying the fundamental messages of unconditional acceptance and hope.

Expressing personal convictions

The chaplain may articulate personal convictions, but not in such a way as to impose beliefs. Most likely, the caregiver will express convictions—perhaps in the manner of a brief testimonial statement—in response to comments or questions raised by the patient regarding the beliefs of the caregiver, or in response to statements of belief made by the care-receiver that either promote or hinder the healing process. Again, the situation may require translation on the part of the chaplain who seeks to communicate personal convictions. For example, a patient had just had a cancerous tumor removed. His wife said to the chaplain in the patient's presence, "Everything happens for a reason. Do you believe that?" Aware of a potential for the patient to feel that his wife was unduly spiritualizing his experience, the chaplain responded by saying, "I trust that the possibilities of love and healing are present also in the face of illness and pain." When faced with the opportunity to state personal convictions, the caregiver has the responsibility to do so in a way

---

[12] A note of caution is in order: Chaplains must always determine carefully under what circumstances physical contact with patients and others is desirable and appropriate. Indeed, not only must they be aware of cross-cultural factors involved but also of cross-gender dynamics. Further, chaplains must realize that some care-receivers (for example, abuse survivors) may not welcome touch at all.

that contributes to the care-receiver's healing process while maintaining personal and spiritual integrity.

Comforting, encouraging, guiding, reconciling

In other essays in this book, our colleagues provide many illustrations of caregiving practices aimed at comforting, encouraging, guiding, and reconciling in the light of Christian faith. They demonstrate specific instances of the caregiver's competence in employing the language of therapeutic communication, whether or not the care-receiver experiences the specific interaction as pastoral.[13]

A caregiver's primary concern is to communicate unconditional acceptance and utmost respect. While such language may not ring explicitly of faith or spirituality, it communicates a concern for the whole person, that is, the understanding that she or he is part of a larger context that includes vocation, culture, and communities of care. Therefore, a collaborative conversation about any aspect of the person's well-being, such as the frustrations and hopes about one's compromised physical condition, cannot help but address the person's well-being as a whole, and therefore the spiritual well-being, even if the language of faith or religion is not explicitly present. Occasionally, the spiritual caregiving relationship may play a significant role in the healing of painful religious memories. In some cases, chaplains may help patients achieve some degree of reconciliation with their faith or church tradition. This seems to have happened for Sunny, who expressed a desire to reconnect with a Christian faith community. Further, in the presence of the chaplain and one sister, Sunny expressed her intentions to do what she could to foster reconciliation with her sisters. The chaplain's presence may have provided a kind of accountability that could support and encourage such intentions.

Guidelines for the practice of language care

The following guidelines pertain to the caregiver's ability to serve as a catalyst for fruitful interfaith communication.[14] Both the personality and the moral character of the chaplain are very important, together with certain professional practices and competencies. The most effective caregivers enjoy a high level of self-awareness, including a realistic view of their gifts and vulnerabilities. They have the ability to maintain personal, theological, and spiritual integrity while responding to the experience and needs of care-receivers and to care-receivers' preferred ways of expressing spirituality and

---

[13] For our understanding of the distinction between pastoral and spiritual care, see the book's introduction. Although we recognize the spiritual care made available to Sunny as pastoral care, we would not distinguish the interaction with Steve as pastoral care.

[14] The topic of guidelines for interfaith communication calls for a more comprehensive treatment. We have engaged in a research project focusing on interfaith spiritual caregiving that we are carrying out in collaboration with other colleagues as an international and ecumenical endeavor.

religious convictions. Such caregivers are clear about their vision of human wholeness and the good life. They are capable of ministering with spirituality that is definable in terms of conjunctive faith.[15] Their moral character presents key virtues and attitudes that are indispensable for encountering strangers as neighbors and in caring for and learning from them. Further, effective spiritual caregivers who minister in interfaith situations develop certain care and communication skills. The main competencies they use stem from having become spiritually and theologically "multilingual." Finally, these caregivers regularly engage in necessary practices such as self-care and theological reflection on their ministry.

The person of the caregiver

Self-awareness. Self-awareness is one of the greatest assets in intercultural communication, because it involves recognizing and honoring one's own spirituality and faith journey as well as one's strengths and growing edges. James L. Griffith and Melissa Elliott Griffith suggest the importance of also knowing one's shortcomings when they write, "We try always to stand alongside others, to see and learn from their vantage points, but this, too, is through our own vision, with its special acuities and blind spots."[16] Because self-awareness is the starting place for intercultural communication, it is crucial that we heighten awareness of our assumptions, perspectives, and values, as well as our ideological biases and prejudices.

Being mindful of one's own linguistic-conceptual framework is essential, because such awareness allows a caregiver to be sensitive to the linguistic-conceptual framework of the care-receiver and to listen and hear hospitably. But as David W. Augsburger has demonstrated, having a clear understanding of our values and commitments must be combined with a capacity for welcoming, entering into, and appreciating other worldviews without undervaluing their legitimacy. He states, "Cultural values held as central commitments can free us and provide a flexible resilience. Cultural views maintained as external boundaries isolate and encapsulate us."[17]

Consistent philosophy. In addition to self-awareness, maintaining clarity and consistency about views on human wholeness, truth, the good life, and excellence in professional practice is another key to fostering interfaith and intercultural communication. Ministry based on an ethic of care and respect is fundamental to the proper use of religious languages in spiritual care. As we discussed in the previous chapter, such an ethic calls for a balance between

---

[15] The term *conjunctive faith* comes from James W. Fowler and denotes a desirable level of faith development, as briefly described below. See Fowler's *Stages of Faith: The Psychology of Human Development and the Quest for Meaning* (San Francisco: Harper & Row, 1981), 184–98.

[16] James L. Griffith and Melissa Elliott Griffith, *Encountering the Sacred in Psychotherapy: How to Talk with People about Their Spiritual Lives.* (New York: Guilford Press, 2002), 6.

[17] David W. Augsburger, *Pastoral Counseling across Cultures.* (Philadelphia: Westminster Press, 1986), 18.

maintaining personal and spiritual integrity and responsively attending to the care-receiver's experience, needs, and preferred ways of expressing their spirituality and religious convictions.

Care-receivers and caregivers will not always agree on what constitutes wholeness and the good life. Spiritual caregivers themselves will differ on these matters. In any event, chaplains will not unreflectively endorse any philosophy they encounter in the hospital; rather, they will minister from their own vision of reality, wholeness, and the good life by asking appropriate questions and helping care-receivers clarify alternatives and make wise choices. It is therefore helpful for the caregiver to be aware of the intercultural and interfaith challenge to be faced in each interaction and to anticipate within reason the difficulties to be encountered. Practicing a balanced (that is, neither superficial nor too emphatic), explicit recognition of this challenge in advance will help transform the potential difficulty into an occasion for building rapport with the care-receiver.

Conjunctive faith and ministry style. Caring deeply and effectively in the face of cultural differences and religious diversity requires important, transformative learning. We must learn to assume that the culture and faith of any care-receiver has worth equal to ours; indeed, we must be open to celebrating difference and diversity as a gift. Such learning in turn is possible to the extent that we can deal creatively with ambiguity and paradox and to the degree that we are able to hold multiple interpretations of reality in view. James Fowler identifies personal spirituality and ministry marked by such qualities as conjunctive faith. Marks of conjunctive faith, according to Fowler, include:

- Awareness of the need to face and hold together several polar tensions in our life (for example, integrating the feminine and masculine, conscious and unconscious, constructive and destructive sides of ourselves, etc.).
- A felt sense that truth is multiform and complex. Therefore, one must approach its richness, multidimensionality, and ambiguity, from several angles of vision simultaneously.
- A post-critical receptivity and readiness to participate in the reality expressed in symbols, myths, and rituals. Beyond demythologizing and critical analysis, conjunctive faith welcomes a "second naiveté."
- A genuine, disciplined openness to the truths of communities and traditions other than our own (not to be equated with relativism). Such openness stems from the experience of faithful commitment to our own tradition and the recognition that truth requires dialectic interplay of perspectives.[18]

---

[18] James W. Fowler, *Becoming Adult, Becoming Christian: Adult Development and Christian Faith* (San Francisco: Jossey-Bass, 2000), 51–54.

Chaplains must sustain interfaith spiritual caregiving, then, by the kind of spirituality that Fowler characterizes as follows: "Although it exhibits a committed belief in the truth claims of a particular tradition, [this spirituality] insists on the humility that knows that the grasp on ultimate truth that any of our traditions can offer needs continual correction and challenge. This is to overcome the blind spots (blind *sides*) as well as the tendencies towards idolatry (the over-identifications of our symbolizations of transcending truth with the reality of truth) to which all of our traditions are prone."[19]

Moral character: attitudes and virtues. Closely connected with the quality of conjunctive faith is the content of the moral character of effective interfaith spiritual caregivers. What follows is, again, a partial list of inter-related attitudes and virtues (that is, embodied values) that help define the heart of such caregivers. These caregivers experience and demonstrate:

- A capacity to wonder, including nonintrusive curiosity, mingled with awe and respect, in the face of the other, or stranger, with different culture and faith.
- Sensitivity and receptivity connected with the suspension of judgment, while tolerating uncertainty and ambiguity.
- The courage to risk and to be surprised and the freedom to become vulnerable and open to transformative learning and growth.
- The disposition to recognize, accept, and honor those perceived to be different.
- The gift of hospitality grounded in compassion, humility, and generosity.
- The creative energy to transform the inherent violence of separation, prejudice, and alienation into a reconciled way of being with (empathy) and being for (sympathy) the other, or stranger, as neighbor and partner in care and healing.

Competencies and practices

Specific professional competencies. Along with this caregiving character and ethic, several professional competencies and practices of the caregiver are worth noting. These include becoming spiritually and theologically "multi-lingual," discerning the use of fitting religious and spiritual language for the sake of care, becoming a reflective practitioner, and developing competence in reflecting theologically on ministry experience (practical theologizing), and practicing self-care.

"Becoming spiritually and theologically multilingual" refers to the care-giver's ability to identify and communicate love, care, grace, and hope in a variety of ways (including through nonreligious spiritual languages). Just as the fluency in several languages (Spanish, English, and Japanese, for example) enhances one's communication abilities, so does familiarity with the variety

---

[19] Ibid., 52–53.

of spiritual and religious languages.[20] As we mentioned above, the ministering person has the responsibility to bridge the communication gap; the caregiver does not expect the care-receiver to accept the same degree of responsibility for facilitating the interfaith communication event. Essential to the practice of spiritual caregiving is a respect for persons that acknowledges and values unconditionally their humanity, honoring the ways they are similar to and different from oneself and others.

Our main concern as caregivers is that, regardless of our own spiritual or religious context, we interact with care-receivers in ways that affirm and nurture humanization and hope. Whether we counsel or visit with patients, families, or staff members who are part of the same religious tradition we are, or with those whose tradition or lifestyle differs from our own, we seek to use language that communicates acceptance and trust that resources are available for the healing process. These resources are present first in a person's own life and context. We may also wish to bring resources of our own to patients and families, in addition to those that the caregiving team and the hospital as such can make available. The capacity to bear hope and good news in the hospital setting is by no means limited to one standard language.

Along with being multilingual, equally significant for caregivers is the ability to discern when and how to use what language. For example, during her first visit with Sunny, Leah Dawn offered to pray aloud with her. Whereas many others who had volunteered that they were Christians but did not attend church invited the caregiver's praying, Sunny declined. Sunny's response required the chaplain to continue listening closely to Sunny in order to participate in the particular ways that would communicate support to Sunny. Making empty promises or giving band-aid solutions is sometimes tempting when the pathways of interfaith communication are rough. In these instances, the incarnational presence of the chaplain, communicating acceptance, support, and care may be much more powerful and authentic than statements such as, "God will be with you." Pat answers may arise out of good intentions, but they also stem from caregivers' urgencies and sense of helplessness. Sincere well-wishes that acknowledge the difficulty of the situation are always more helpful.

As noted above, developing competence in the discernment of fitting religious language for the sake of care (that is, from the care-receiver's perspective), often involves translation on the part of the chaplain. One example of such translation is the ability to recognize and speak of the presence of the holy, or of grace, according to the preferred language of the care-receivers, whether or not they speak in Christian terms. The chaplain must be able to

---

[20] A helpful resource for understanding religious diversity, the uniqueness of faith traditions, and appropriate therapeutic approaches is P. Scott Richards and Allen E. Bergin, eds., *Handbook of Psychotherapy and Religious Diversity* (Washington, DC: American Psychological Association, 2000).

determine if there is sufficient equivalency of meaning and value (theologically and existentially) in the preferred language, and to what extent such convergence matters in the therapeutic communication process. Therefore, the psycho-linguistic and other skills involved in becoming spiritually and theologically multilingual, practicing discernment as language care, and applying translation are key to the therapeutic communication process in spiritual caregiving.

Reflecting on practice and articulating a practical theology.[21] In the process of growing professionally as ministering persons, and particularly as they seek to practice language care for effective interfaith caregiving, chaplains must reflect critically and constructively on their ministry experience. They must carefully ponder those experiences in light of what it means to be a competent spiritual caregiver in a given setting, a responsibility that includes the integration of theological, psychological, and ethical understandings. At the same time, their understanding of this role and the subsequent improvement of their theology of spiritual caregiving must inform the ways they go about putting ministry into practice on a daily basis. Chaplains may articulate their reflections as they write, speak with other spiritual caregivers, and converse with friends, mentors, and supervisors from their own religious community or with friends and others from different religious or nonreligious contexts. In sum, a reflective practitioner daily remains aware of the ways theory affects practice and vice versa.

Chaplains may thus construct pastoral and practical theology as they use appropriate language to describe, analyze, interpret, evaluate, and report on their spiritual caregiving ministry. In turn, they may also reflect their usually implicit pastoral and practical theology, not only in visits with patients, families, and staff, but also in meditations and sermons, workshop presentations, lectures, and in other forms of speech; all of these settings require respect for the diversity of religious and spiritual contexts of the listeners. Chaplains can thus make a special contribution to the necessary work of theoretical and theory-practice integration. By continually reflecting on the ways experience informs theology and vice versa, the caregiver grows in competence in interfaith communication.

Self-care. Finally, another essential practice is self-care, especially in the forms of adequate attention to emotional and relational needs and to spiritual nourishment.[22] If caregivers are clear about their own questions and needs, their boundaries and limitations, as well as their particular areas of strength and expertise, they will be less likely to violate the spiritual integrity and boundaries of patients, families, or coworkers. When a chaplain is the only person employed in the department of spiritual care, he or she faces the danger

---

[21] For our understanding of the term *practical theology* and its relation to pastoral theology, see chapter 16.

[22] See Myra Raab's essay, "Principles and Practices of Self-Care," chapter 8.

of becoming isolated. For this reason, self-care for such chaplains includes relating professionally with other chaplains in consistent and intentional ways. One may become a member of a national or international association or a smaller local or regional group. Opportunities to meet regularly with colleagues provide settings for accountability and support for the ministry of spiritual caregiving. Maintaining an optimal level of personal health and professional competence, supported by consistent, holistic self-care, in turn enhances the ability of chaplains to engage fruitfully in interfaith communication.

Conclusion

We have argued that by practicing the art of language care, chaplains can become facilitators of interfaith communication, understood as a special form of intercultural communication. Underlying our discussion is a twofold anthropological and theological conviction that sustains our endeavors; we state it succinctly in the following paragraphs.

The first part of our conviction claims that simply because we are humans, we are essentially spiritual beings with the potential and the need to love, to know, and to create. As human beings, we simultaneously face the conditions of finitude, moral failure, and woundedness. In naming these limitations, we recognize three distinguishable, interrelated conditions of human need that often call for some kind of caregiving ministry. First, human beings encounter limitations and precariousness, that is, contingency and fragility that are products of our creatureliness or natural finitude (for example, a serious infection that overwhelms our physical defenses, or suffering resulting from an inadvertent medical mistake). Second, human beings are prone to sinfulness or fallenness, connoting direct moral responsibility (for example, injury or disease directly caused by irresponsible behavior). Third, human beings endure woundedness and brokenness, often resulting from immoral or sinful behavior on the part of others (for example, victimization because of abuse or carelessness on the part of medical staff), oppressive social systems, their own religious structures, and so on. Because of the complexity of human existence and behavior, we rarely encounter these categories in pure form.

Situations that make caregiving necessary always involve a fundamental longing for healing, wholeness, and transformation, regardless of the particularities of culture, religion, or other identifiers and potential boundaries. We claim that the gracious Spirit (God) somehow participates in the joys and the struggles of being human within the cosmos and throughout history. We further claim that the Spirit somehow makes available resources to attend to those situations calling for the specialized care of hospital chaplaincy ministry, regardless of the religious or theological claims of any faith tradition, including nonreligious traditions.

The second part of our twofold conviction maintains that the effective and theologically sound practice of spiritual caregiving always necessitates personal, theological, and spiritual integrity, the commitment to an ethic of care and respect, and the competencies and abilities to practice caregiving as a specialized communication process oriented to healing and transformation. Further, interfaith communication is not just a special case of needing to deal with significant ideological differences between caregiver and care-receiver but is actually inherent in some way in all caregiving interactions. Consequently, awareness of and competence in interfaith communication is, in principle, a requirement for all situations facing spiritual caregivers. Nevertheless, the circumstances in which interfaith communication stands out as a major factor defining the spiritual caregiving event call for special attention. Thus we have highlighted certain understandings, virtues, attitudes, and skills necessary for the practice of spiritual caregiving focused primarily as a form of interfaith communication. On the one hand, we have affirmed the essential place of language care in spiritual caregiving as a case for professional and ministerial competence. On the other hand, in light of our theological convictions, we make the claim that, ultimately, the source of all healing and life-giving transformation is not the excellence of our ministry but the Spirit of grace and wisdom with whom we are partners.

About Pandora Press

Pandora Press is a small, independently owned press dedicated to making available modestly priced books that deal with Anabaptist, Mennonite, and Believers Church topics, both historical and theological. We welcome comments from our readers.

Visit our full-service online Bookstore:
www.pandorapress.com

Gerke van Hiele with Marion Bruggen, Ina ter Kuile and Frans Misset, *Encountering the Eternal One: A Guide for Mennonite Churches* (Kitchener: Pandora Press, 2006) Softcover, 120 pages. ISBN 1-894710-75-4

Richard MacMaster, *Mennonite and Brethren in Christ Churches of New York City* (Kitchener: Pandora Press, 2006) Softcover, 366 pages. ISBN 1-894710-70-3

Peter Riedemann, *Love is like Fire: The Confession of an Anabaptist Prisoner* (Kitchener: Pandora Press, 2006) Softcover, 84 pages. ISBN 1-894710-72-X

Andreas Ehrenpreis and Claus Felbinger, *Brotherly Community: The Highest Command of Love* (Kitchener: Pandora Press, 2006) Softcover, 146 pages. ISBN 1-894710-74-6

Jakob Hutter, *Brotherly Faithfulness: Epistles from a Time of Persecution* (Kitchener: Pandora Press, 2006) Softcover, 250 pages. ISBN 1-894710-73-8

Robert John Russell, *Cosmology, Evolution, and Resurrection Hope* (Kitchener: Pandora Press, 2006) Softcover, 118 pages. ISBN 1-894710-67-3

Nathan E. Yoder and Carol A. Scheppard, eds., *Exiles in the Empire: Believers Church Perspectives on Politics* (Kitchener: Pandora Press, 2006) Softcover, 266 pages. Scriptural and topical indexes. ISBN 1-894710-68-1

Helmut Isaak, *Menno Simons and the New Jerusalem* (Kitchener: Pandora Press, 2006) Softcover, 158 pages. Bibliography. ISBN 1-894710-69-X

Leah Dawn Bueckert and Daniel Schipani, eds. *Spiritual Caregiving in the Hospital. Windows to Chaplaincy Ministry* (Kitchener: Pandora Press, 2006) Softcover, 230 pages. ISBN 1-894710-65-7

Lawrence M. Yoder, *The Muria Story. A History of the Chinese Mennonite Churches in Indonesia* (Kitchener: Pandora Press, 2006). Softcover, 386 pages. ISBN 1-894710-60-6

Ralph Lebold, *Strange and Wonderful Paths. The Memoirs of Ralph Lebold.* (Kitchener: Pandora Press, 2006). Softcover, 236 pages. Bibliography, index. ISBN 1-894710-66-5

Karl Koop, ed. *Confessions of Faith in the Anabaptist Tradition, 1527-1660* (Kitchener: Pandora Press, 2006). Softcover, 366 pages. Scripture index. ISBN 1-894710-62-2

Alle Hoekema and Hanspeter Jecker, eds. *Testing Faith and Tradition. A Global Mennonite History: Europe* (Kitchener: Pandora Press, 2006; co-published with Good Books). Softcover, 324 pages. Indexes. ISBN 1-56148-550-0

John A. Lapp and C. Arnold Snyder, gen.eds., *Anabaptist Songs in African Hearts. A Global Mennonite History: Africa* (Kitchener: Pandora Press, 2006; co-published with Good Books) Softcover, 292 pages. Indexes. ISBN 1-56148-549-7

Harry Loewen, *Between Worlds. Reflections of a Soviet-born Canadian Mennonite* (Kitchener: Pandora Press, 2006). Softcover, 358 pages. Bibliography. ISBN 1-894710-63-0

H. H. Drake Williams III, ed., *Caspar Schwenckfeld. Eight Writings on Christian Beliefs* (Kitchener: Pandora Press, 2006). Softcover, 200 pages. Index. ISBN 1-894710-64-9

Maureen Epp and Carol Ann Weaver, eds., *Sound in the Land: Essays on Mennonites and Music* (Kitchener: Pandora Press, 2006). Softcover, 220 pages. Bibliography. ISBN 1-894710-59-2

Geoffrey Dipple, *"Just as in the Time of the Apostles": Uses of History in the Radical Reformation* (Kitchener: Pandora Press, 2005). Softcover, 324 pages. Bibliography and index. ISBN 1-894710-58-4.

Harry Huebner, *Echoes of the Word: Theological Ethics as Rhetorical Practice* Anabaptist and Mennonite Studies Series (Kitchener: Pandora Press, 2005). Softcover, 274 pages. Bibliography and index. ISBN 1-894710-56-8 ISSN 1494-4081

John F. Haught, *Purpose, Evolution and the Mystery of Life*, Proceedings of the Fourth Annual Goshen Conference on Religion and Science, ed. Carl S. Helrich (Kitchener" Pandora Press, 2005). Softcover, 130 pages. Index. ISBN 1-894710-55-X

Gerald W. Schlabach, gen. ed., *Called Together to be Peacemakers: Report of the International Dialogue between the Catholic Church and Mennonite World Conference 1998-2003* (Kitchener: Pandora Press, 2005). Softcover, 77 pages. ISBN 1-894710-57-6 ISSN 1711-9480

Rodney James Sawatsky, *History and Ideology: American Mennonite Identity Definition through History* (Kitchener: Pandora Press, 2005). Softcover, 216 pages. Bibliography and index. ISBN 1-894710-53-3 ISSN 1494-4081

Harvey Neufeldt, Ruth Derksen Siemens and Robert Martens, eds., *First Nations and First Settlers in the Fraser Valley (1890-1960)* (Kitchener: Pandora Press, 2005). Softcover, 287 pages.Bibliography and index. ISBN 1-894710-54-1

David Waltner-Toews, *The Complete Tante Tina: Mennonite Blues and Recipes* (Kitchener: Pandora Press, 2004) Softcover, 129 pages. ISBN 1-894710-52-5

John Howard Yoder, *Anabaptism and Reformation in Switzerland: An Historical and Theological Analysis of the Dialogues Between Anabaptists and Reformers* (Kitchener: Pandora Press, 2004) Softcover, 509 pages. Bibliography and indexes. ISBN 1-894710-44-4 ISSN 1494-4081

Antje Jackelén, *The Dialogue Between Religion and Science: Challenges and Future Directions* (Kitchener: Pandora Press, 2004) Softcover, 143 pages. Index. ISBN 1-894710-45-2

Ivan J. Kauffman, ed., *Just Policing: Mennonite-Catholic Theological Colloquium 2001-2002* (Kitchener: Pandora Press, 2004). Softcover, 127 pages. ISBN 1-894710-48-7.

Gerald W. Schlabach, ed., *On Baptism: Mennonite-Catholic Theological Colloquium 2001-2002* (Kitchener: Pandora Press, 2004). Softcover, 147 pages. ISBN 1-894710-47-9 ISSN 1711-9480.

Harvey L. Dyck, John R. Staples and John B. Toews, comp., trans. and ed. *Nestor Makhno and the Eichenfeld Massacre:* (Kitchener: Pandora Press, 2004). Softcover, 115pages. ISBN 1-894710-46-0.

Jeffrey Wayne Taylor, *The Formation of the Primitive Baptist Movement* (Kitchener: Pandora Press, 2004). Softcover, 225 pages. Bibliography and index. ISBN 1-894710-42-8 ISSN 1480-7432.

James C. Juhnke and Carol M. Hunter, *The Missing Peace: The Search for Nonviolent Alternatives in United States History,* 2nd ed. (Kitchener: Pandora Press, 2004) Softcover, 339 pp. Index. ISBN 1-894710-46-3

Louise Hawkley and James C. Juhnke, eds., *Nonviolent America: History through the Eyes of Peace* (North Newton: Bethel College, 2004, co-published with Pandora Press) Softcover, 269 pages. Index. ISBN 1-889239-02-X

Karl Koop, *Anabaptist-Mennonite Confessions of Faith: the Development of a Tradition* (Kitchener: Pandora Press, 2004) Softcover, 178 pages. Index. ISBN 1-894710-32-0

Lucille Marr, *The Transforming Power of a Century: Mennonite Central Committee and its Evolution in Ontario* (Kitchener: Pandora Press, 2003). Softcover, 390 pages. Bibliography and index, ISBN 1-894710-41-x.

Erica Janzen, *Six Sugar Beets, Five Bitter Years* (Kitchener: Pandora Press, 2003). Softcover, 186 pages. ISBN 1-894710-37-1.

T. D. Regehr, *Faith Life and Witness in the Northwest, 1903–2003: Centenninal History of the Northwest Mennonite Conference* (Kitchener: Pandora Press, 2003). Softcover, 524 pages. Index, ISBN 1-894710-39-8.

George F. R. Ellis, *A Universe of Ethics Morality and Hope: Proceedings from the Second Annual Goshen Conference on Religion and Science* (Kitchener: Pandora Press, 2003) Softcover, 148 pages. ISBN 1-894710-36-3

Donald Martin, *Old Order Mennonites of Ontario: Gelassenheit, Discipleship, Brotherhood* (Kitchener: Pandora Press, 2003). Softcover, 381 pages. Index. ISBN 1-894710-33-9

Mary A. Schiedel, *Pioneers in Ministry: Women Pastors in Ontario Mennonite Churches, 1973-2003* (Kitchener: Pandora Press, 2003) Softcover, 204 pages. ISBN 1-894710-35-5

Harry Loewen, ed., *Shepherds, Servants and Prophets* (Kitchener: Pandora Press, 2003) Softcover, 446 pages. ISBN 1-894710-35-5

Robert A. Riall, trans., Galen A. Peters, ed., *The Earliest Hymns of the* Ausbund: *Some Beautiful Christian Songs Composed and Sung in the Prison at Passau, Published 1564* (Kitchener: Pandora Press, 2003) Softcover, 468 pages. Bibliography and index. ISBN 1-894710-34-7.

John A. Harder, *From Kleefeld With Love* (Kitchener: Pandora Press, 2003) Softcover, 198 pages. ISBN 1-894710-28-2

John F. Peters, *The Plain People: A Glimpse at Life Among the Old Order Mennonites of Ontario* (Kitchener: Pandora Press, 2003) Softcover, 54 pages. ISBN 1-894710-26-6

Robert S. Kreider, *My Early Years: An Autobiography* (Kitchener: Pandora Press, 2002) Softcover, 600 pages. Index ISBN 1-894710-23-1

Helen Martens, *Hutterite Songs* (Kitchener: Pandora Press, 2002) Softcover, xxii, 328 pages. ISBN 1-894710-24-X

C. Arnold Snyder and Galen A. Peters, eds., *Reading the Anabaptist Bible: Reflections for Every Day of the Year* (Kitchener: Pandora Press, 2002) Softcover, 415 pages. ISBN 1-894710-25-8

C. Arnold Snyder, ed., *Commoners and Community: Essays in Honour of Werner O. Packull* (Kitchener: Pandora Press, 2002) Softcover, 324 pages. ISBN 1-894710-27-4

James O. Lehman, *Mennonite Tent Revivals: Howard Hammer and Myron Augsburger, 1952-1962* (Kitchener: Pandora Press, 2002) Softcover, xxiv, 318 pages. ISBN 1-894710-22-3

Lawrence Klippenstein and Jacob Dick, *Mennonite Alternative Service in Russia* (Kitchener: Pandora Press, 2002) Softcover, viii, 163 pages. ISBN 1-894710-21-5

Nancey Murphy, *Religion and Science* (Kitchener: Pandora Press, 2002) Softcover, 126 pages. ISBN 1-894710-20-7

Biblical Concordance of the Swiss Brethren, 1540. Trans. Gilbert Fast and Galen Peters; bib. intro. Joe Springer; ed. C. Arnold Snyder (Kitchener: Pandora Press, 2001) Softcover, lv, 227pages. ISBN 1-894710-16-9

Orland Gingerich, *The Amish of Canada* (Kitchener: Pandora Press, 2001) Softcover, 244 pages. Index. ISBN 1-894710-19-3

M. Darrol Bryant, *Religion in a New Key* (Kitchener: Pandora Press, 2001) Softcover, 136 pages. Bib. refs. ISBN 1-894710- 18-5

Trans. Walter Klaassen, Frank Friesen, Werner O. Packull, ed. C. Arnold Snyder, *Sources of South German/Austrian Anabaptism* (Kitchener: Pandora Press, 2001; co-published with Herald Press.) Softcover, 430 pages. Indexes. ISBN 1-894710-15-0

Pedro A. Sandín Fremaint y Pablo A. Jimémez, *Palabras Duras: Homilías* (Kitchener: Pandora Press, 2001). Softcover, 121 pages. ISBN 1-894710-17-7

Ruth Elizabeth Mooney, *Manual Para Crear Materiales de Educación Cristiana* (Kitchener: Pandora Press, 2001). Softcover, 206 pages. ISBN 1-894710-12-6

Esther and Malcolm Wenger, poetry by Ann Wenger, *Healing the Wounds* (Kitchener: Pandora Press, 2001). Softcover, 210 pages. ISBN 1-894710-09-6.

Otto H. Selles and Geraldine Selles-Ysselstein, *New Songs* (Kitchener: Pandora Press, 2001). Poetry and relief prints, 90 pages. ISBN 1-894719-14-2

Pedro A. Sandín Fremaint, *Cuentos y Encuentros: Hacia una Educación Transformadora* (Kitchener: Pandora Press, 2001). Softcover 163 pages. ISBN 1-894710-08-8.

A. James Reimer, *Mennonites and Classical Theology: Dogmatic Foundations for Christian Ethics* (Kitchener: Pandora Press, 2001) Softcover, 650 pages. ISBN 0-9685543-7-7

Walter Klaassen, *Anabaptism: Neither Catholic nor Protestant*, 3rd ed (Kitchener: Pandora Press, 2001) Softcover, 122 pages. ISBN 1-894710-01-0

Dale Schrag & James Juhnke, eds., *Anabaptist Visions for the new Millennium: A search for identity* (Kitchener: Pandora Press, 2000) Softcover, 242 pages. ISBN 1-894710-00-2

Harry Loewen, ed., *Road to Freedom: Mennonites Escape the Land of Suffering* (Kitchener: Pandora Press, 2000) Hardcover, large format, 302pages. ISBN 0-9685543-5-0

Alan Kreider and Stuart Murray, eds., *Coming Home: Stories of Anabaptists in Britain and Ireland* (Kitchener: Pandora Press, 2000) Softcover, 220pages. ISBN 0-9685543-6-9

Edna Schroeder Thiessen and Angela Showalter, *A Life Displaced: A Mennonite Woman's Flight from War-Torn Poland* (Kitchener: Pandora Press, 2000) Softcover, xii, 218 pages. ISBN 0-9685543-2-6

Stuart Murray, *Biblical Interpretation in the Anabaptist Tradition*, Studies in the Believers Tradition (Kitchener: Pandora Press, 2000) Softcover, 310pages. ISBN 0-9685543-3-4 ISSN 1480-7432.

Loren L. Johns, ed. *Apocalypticism and Millennialism* (Kitchener: Pandora Press, 2000) Softcover, 419 pages. Indexes. ISBN 0-9683462-9-4 ISSN 1480-7432

Later Writings by Pilgram Marpeck and his Circle. Volume 1. Trans. Walter Klaassen, Werner Packull, and John Rempel (Kitchener: Pandora Press, 1999) Softcover, 157 pages. ISBN 0-9683462-6-X

John Driver, *Radical Faith. An Alternative History of the Christian Church*, ed. Carrie Snyder. Kitchener: Pandora Press, 1999) Softcover, 334 pages. ISBN 0-9683462-8-6

C. Arnold Snyder, *From Anabaptist Seed*. (Kitchener: Pandora Press, 1999) Softcover, 53 pages. ISBN 0-9685543-0-X
   Also available in Spanish translation: *De Semilla Anabautista*, from Pandora Press only.

John D. Thiesen, *Mennonite and Nazi? Attitudes Among Mennonite Colonists in Latin America, 1933-1945* (Kitchener: Pandora Press, 1999) Softcover, 330 pages. Bibliography, index. ISBN 0-9683462-5-1

Lifting the Veil, ed. Leonard Friesen; trans. Walter Klaassen (Kitchener: Pandora Press, 1998). Softcover, 128 pages. ISBN 0-9683462-1-9

Leonard Gross, *The Golden Years of the Hutterites*, rev. ed. (Kitchener: Pandora Press, 1998). Softcover, 280 pages. Index. ISBN 0-9683462-3-5

William H. Brackney, ed., *The Believers Church: A Voluntary Church*, (Kitchener: Pandora Press, 1998). Softcover, viii, 237 pages. Index. ISBN 0-9683462-0-0 ISSN 1480-7432.

An Annotated Hutterite Bibliography, compiled by Maria H. Krisztinkovich, ed. by Peter C. Erb (Kitchener: Pandora Press, 1998). (Ca. 2,700 entries) 312 pages. Softcover, electronic, or both. ISBN (paper) 0-9698762-8-9/(disk) 0-9698762-9-7

Jacobus ten Doornkaat Koolman, *Dirk Philips. Friend and Colleague of Menno Simons*, trans. W. E. Keeney, ed. C. A. Snyder (Kitchener: Pandora Press, 1998). Softcover, xviii, 236 pages. Index. ISBN: 0-9698762-3-8

Sarah Dyck, ed./tr., *The Silence Echoes: Memoirs of Trauma & Tears* (Kitchener: Pandora Press, 1997). Softcover, xii, 236 pages. ISBN: 0-9698762-7-0

Wes Harrison, *Andreas Ehrenpreis and Hutterite Faith and Practice* (Kitchener: Pandora Press, 1997). Softcover, xxiv, 274 pages. Index. ISBN 0-9698762-6-2

C. Arnold Snyder, *Anabaptist History and Theology: Revised Student Edition* (Kitchener: Pandora Press, 1997). Softcover, xiv, 466 pages. Index, bibliography. ISBN 0-9698762-5-4

Nancey Murphy, *Reconciling Theology and Science: A Radical Reformation Perspective* (Kitchener, Ont.: Pandora Press, 1997). Softcover, x, 103 pages. Index. ISBN 0-9698762-4-6

The Limits of Perfection: A Conversation with J. Lawrence Burkholder 2nd ed., with a new epilogue by J. Lawrence Burkholder, Rodney Sawatsky and Scott Holland, eds. (Kitchener: Pandora Press, 1996). Softcover, x, 154 pages. ISBN 0-9698762-2-X

C. Arnold Snyder, *Anabaptist History and Theology: An Introduction* (Kitchener: Pandora Press, 1995). Softcover, x, 434 pages. Index,bibliography. ISBN 0-9698762-0-3

Pandora Press
33 Kent Avenue Kitchener, ON N2G 3R2

Tel.: (519) 578-2381 / Fax: (519) 578-1826
E-mail: info@pandorapress.com
Web site: www.pandorapress.com